C000067308

RED AMERICA

RED AMERICA

GREEK COMMUNISTS IN THE UNITED STATES, 1920–1950

KOSTIS KARPOZILOS

Translated by Panagiotis Kechagias

berghahn
NEW YORK · OXFORD
www.berghahnbooks.com

First published in 2023 by
Berghahn Books
www.berghahnbooks.com

© 2023 Kostis Karpozilos

Originally published in Greek as
Κόκκινη Αμερική: Έλληνες μετανάστες και το όραμα ενός Νέου Κόσμου 1900–1950.
Original Greek-language edition © 2017 Crete University Press.
Translation done by Panagiotis Kechagias.

All rights reserved. Except for the quotation of short passages
for the purposes of criticism and review, no part of this book
may be reproduced in any form or by any means, electronic or
mechanical, including photocopying, recording, or any information
storage and retrieval system now known or to be invented,
without written permission of the publisher.

Library of Congress Cataloging-in-Publication Data

Names: Karpozilos, Kostis, author. | Kechagias, Panagiōtēs, 1978– translator.
Title: Red America : Greek Communists in the United States, 1920-1950 / Kostis
    Karpozilos; [translated by Panagiotis Kechagias].
Other titles: Kókkinī Amerikī. English | Greek Communists in the United States,
    1920–1950
Description: New York : Berghahn Books, 2023. | "This book was originally
    published in Greek in 2017." | Includes bibliographical references and index.
Identifiers: LCCN 2022045356 (print) | LCCN 2022045357 (ebook) |
    ISBN 9781800738553 (hardback) | ISBN 9781800738560 (ebook)
Subjects: LCSH: Greeks—United States—Politics and government—20th century. |
    Immigrants—Political activity—United States—History—20th century. |
    Communism—United States—History—20th century. | Greeks—United
    States—20th century. | Communists—Greece—20th century. | Greek
    Americans—United States—Politics and government—20th century.
Classification: LCC E184.G7 K35613 2023 (print) | LCC E184.G7 (ebook) |
    DDC 973/.04893—dc23/eng/20221108
LC record available at https://lccn.loc.gov/2022045356
LC ebook record available at https://lccn.loc.gov/2022045357]

British Library Cataloguing in Publication Data

A catalogue record for this book is available from the British Library.

ISBN 978-1-80073-855-3 hardback
ISBN 978-1-80073-856-0 ebook

https://doi.org/10.3167/9781800738553

CONTENTS

Acknowledgments

This book has a long history. I defended my PhD thesis on Greek American radicalism at the University of Crete, back in 2010. The years that followed were the worst of the Eurozone crisis and conditions in the Greek academic setting offered few opportunities for research and employment. As many others of my generation, I left Greece. I am indebted to the Stavros Niarchos Foundation and Columbia University that offered me, in 2012, a postdoctoral fellowship and to the Stanley C. Seeger Center for Hellenic Studies at Princeton University that allowed me to extend my postdoctoral research until 2015. I am deeply grateful to Mark Mazower and Dimitris Gontikas for these unique opportunities that allowed me to expand my historiographical horizons and work on a manuscript that led to a book, in Greek, published by Crete University Press in 2017.

Since then, I occasionally thought about translating and adapting it to English, but, as often happens, new projects stood in the way. I am extremely grateful to Angelos Dalachanis, a friend and colleague, for his encouragement to submit a proposal to Berghahn Books. I am obliged to Marion Berghahn for endorsing this project and to editorial associate Sulaiman Ahmad for his assistance and guidance. My appreciation extends to production editor Keara Hagerty and Eliah Bures for his valuable remarks and copyediting of the manuscript.

Chloe Howe-Haralambous had translated, years ago, the introduction, and I am still thankful to her. Panagiotis Kechagias was an ideal translator and working with him was a pleasure. I want to thank him not only for his interest and excellent job but also for his flexibility and dedication to the project. Sotiris Paraschas and Nikos Theodoropoulos helped me in finalizing details and preparing the manuscript for submission.

ABBREVIATIONS

ACPFB: American Committee for the Protection of Foreign Born

AFL: American Federation of Labor

AHEPA: American Hellenic Educational Progressive Association

ALP: American Labor Party

ARGD: American Relief for Greek Democracy

CARE: Cooperative for American Remittances to Europe

CIO: Committee of Industrial Organization/Congress of Industrial Organizations

CPUSA: Communist Party of the United States of America

DEEG: Dēmokratikē Enōsē Ellinōn Gallias (Democratic Association of Greeks in France)

EA: Ethnikē Allēlengyi (National Solidarity)

EAM: Ethniko Apelephtherōtiko Metōpo (National Liberation Front)

ELAS: Ellēnikos Laikos Apelephtherōtikos Stratos (Greek People's Liberation Army)

EON: Ethnikē Organōsis Neoleas (National Youth Organization)

EPON: Eniaia Panelladikē Organōsē Neōn (United Panhellenic Organization of Youth)

FLD: Foreign Language Division

FNB: Foreign Nationalities Branch

GAPA: Greek American Progressive Association

HUAC: House Un-American Activities Committee

IWW: Industrial Workers of the World

KKE: Kommounistiko Komma Elladas (Communist Party of Greece)

NIRA: National Industrial Recovery Act

NRA: National Recovery Administration
ONA: Overseas News Agency
OSS: Office of Strategic Services
OWI: Office of War Information
SLP: Socialist Labor Party of America
SWOC: Steel Workers Organizing Committee
UFMA: United Fur Manufacturers Association

INTRODUCTION

The Wretched: Between "The New Colossus" and "The Internationale"

This book's protagonists are marginal characters: Greek immigrants whose experiences in the United States were intertwined with the socialist and especially the communist movement. Focusing on their history from the beginning of the twentieth century to the Cold War, my aim is to see how the foreigner, the immigrant, the hyphenated American turned to the Left in search of an escape from the constraints of their present. This quest for a radical alternative did not take the form merely of entry into an existing social and political universe. They remade that world. *Red America* argues that the thoughts, desires, and activism of immigrants were themselves crucial in shaping the labor, socialist, and communist movements in the United States.

In my view there is a thread that links transatlantic immigration and political radicalism. Both immigration and revolutionary ideas seemed to raise the prospect of salvation from a dreary present, beckoning those willing and daring enough to claim it. The United States stood for new beginnings, free from totalitarian oppression, sectarian persecution, class discrimination, and the grueling and constant battle for survival that marked rural poverty in central, eastern, and southern Europe. "Give me your tired, your poor, your huddled masses yearning to breathe free," Emma Lazarus's verses called out to European societies from the base of the Statue of Liberty. Between 1892 and 1924, nearly twenty million people heeded that call and reached Ellis Island. Mobility demonstrated the magnetic force of the American summons. The seemingly limitless expanse of American land, the absence of sovereign lords, the guarantee of religious freedom, and especially the promise of individual prosperity captivated the imagination of millions, who projected onto the United States the limitless potential of the future. There, everything was possible; the United States was an emblem of the future. It was, after all, the New World.

The prospect of a "new world" formed the ideological world for nineteenth- and twentieth-century revolutionaries. Regardless of their internal differences and ideological divergences, socialists, communists, anarchists, and others shared a foundational tenet: all believed they stood at the threshold of a new historical epoch of social equality and political freedom. The new world—this new social order—was the common vision of those who aspired to end, in Marx's phrase, the "prehistory" of man: the age of war, exploitation, and class inequality. The United States held a singular place in this imaginary, for American history was marching inexorably toward crises and confrontations. From strikes to world wars, mounting conflicts would bring world capitalism ever closer to the breaking point, presenting an exhilarating opportunity to usher in a new social order. It may seem strange today, but many of the revolutionaries of the nineteenth and early twentieth centuries were convinced that their own new world would emerge in the place where anything could—the New World of the United States of America.

A single, surprising resemblance encapsulates the interweaving of histories of migration and revolutionary movements. Compare the American translation of "The Internationale" and Emma Lazarus's sonnet, "The New Colossus," written in 1883 and etched into the base of the Statue of Liberty in 1903. Earlier, I referred to a few verses to illustrate the invitation the United States extended to "those who long to breathe free." In the following verse, the invitation becomes more specific: "Give me your wretched refuse." The New World stood poised to receive the "wretched" downtrodden of the Old, offering to them the certainty that the future could be theirs. In 1902, a Chicago-based socialist publishing house circulated a collection of workers' and revolutionary songs from Western Europe. "We American Socialists are only beginning to sing," the publisher explained.[1] Its aim was to adapt European verses to American conditions. There, between "The Red Flag" and the "Marseillaise," the American version of "The Internationale" made its first appearance. Charles H. Kerr, the volume's publisher and editor, chose to base his translation on the French prototype, disregarding the existing British version (even though he followed "our English comrades" in numerous cases). In the first verse, "The Internationale" calls on the workers of the world to rise up, conjuring the eternal realm of equality and freedom as their prize. Kerr chose his words carefully: "Arise ye wretched of the Earth."[2]

"The wretched," the silent victims of the past, feature in both poems as historical subjects uniquely endowed with the vital power to transform not only the terms of their own lives but the entire social universe that surrounds them. In other words, what the United States held in common with the ideas of social equality was the invitation it extended to the "wretched" and its faith in them as the saplings of a new social order—a future to be reaped from the boundless possibilities expressed by the New World as opposed to the stultifying constraints of the Old. This, then, is the starting point of *Red America*: the threads—real or imagined—that bound the vision of a new socialist world to the social, political, and economic realities the United States had to offer the "wretched."

Becoming a Radical: Ethnicity and Class

Migrants of all nations formed the backbone of much of the American Left from the nineteenth to the first half of the twentieth century.[3] Print culture was crucial to migrant workers' radicalism. The era saw a proliferation of communist and socialist books, pamphlets, newspapers, and journals written and distributed by immigrant organizations affiliated with political bodies of the American Left. The duration of the phenomenon is worth stressing: from 1918 to 1956, successive newspapers (*Ē Phonē tou Ergatou* [Voice of the worker], 1918–24; *Empros* [Forward], 1924–39; *Eleutheria* [Freedom], 1939–41; *Ellēnoamerikanikon Vēma* [Greek American tribune], 1941–56) expressed, in Greek, the intellectual, social, and political mission of the Left. Of course, this was not solely a Greek phenomenon. It is only by understanding their shared experience of migration that we can begin to appreciate the ways in which radical ideas were recast within each community.

For immigrants who reached the United States from Greece or from the Ottoman Empire, socialist or union activism was a novel universe. In this sense, they differed, for instance, from Jewish immigrants, who frequently hailed from eastern European socialist heartlands, or from Italian workers of the industrialized North, who imported an established tradition of collective organization and bargaining. The case of Greek migrant radicalism thus presents politicization on the Left as a distinct version of radical Americanization, as migrants turned to the Left in their efforts to interpret their position in a novel landscape of industrial labor, the exploitation of labor power, and the social marginalization of the worker. That is not to claim that the rupture with the Old World was absolute. Despite the radicals' assertions of a definitive break between their past and the future, events in Greece continued to move them, and their turn to the Left in the United States often reflected their attitudes toward the world they had left behind. Developments in Greece helped shape the Greek American Left. These migrant revolutionaries thus offer a representative instance of the uneven and contradictory nature of radicalization, where identifying with the global constituency of the oppressed was, paradoxically, one manifestation of an itinerant national identity.

Not all Greek immigrants were active in the communist movement. Indeed, the majority had no contact with it at all, seeking instead to structure their subsistence, social life, and political concerns around various national bodies and Greek American institutions, including the Orthodox Church. Even in such instances, however, the influence of the Left in its varying degrees offers insights into the histories of migrants' relations to their own Greek and American identities. Dominant narratives concerning the ideological allegiances of Greek migrants typically hinge on the zealous anti-communism and disdain for the "un-American" that took hold of Greek American communities in post-WWII America. While such narratives do, to a great extent, hold true, what they elide, and what the present study seeks to retrieve, are the ways in which Greek American anti-communism was shaped in opposition to a previous militant tradition: the Greek American communist movement.

The study of the Greek American Left allows us to explore the broader conflicts and transformations that informed the Greek presence in the United States. My focus on issues of migrant wage labor and class conflict attempts to foreground the contradictions between employers and workers that frequently lay at the heart of migrant communities but which the primacy of ethnic loyalty helped obscure or render invisible. Workers' resistance, bred in Greek restaurants, in furriers' workshops run by merchants from Ottoman Kastoria, in small-scale industries built on the cheap labor of "compatriots," has much to reveal about the rhythms, conditions, and cultures that formed the uncharted landscape of migrant entrepreneurship. Similarly, close study of the development of strong trade unions in the Great Depression unearths the national networks embedded within large industrial units, the complex relations between ethnic and class identity, and the impact the crisis itself had on the perceptions and cultures of first- and second-generation immigrants. In brief, my wish is not to propose the social history of the migrant presence in the United States as the history of the Left. What I do mean to suggest is that the history of the Left has much to contribute to the social history of immigration.

An important tension conditions this relationship. The multiethnic composition of the American working class brought radicals of all stripes to grapple with a fundamental problem: how could the ethnic and linguistic heterogeneity of the workforce be reconciled with notions of the unity of wage labor? The American Left's response rested on the certainty that the immigrants' awakening into class consciousness would be the crucial enabler for their integration into the most ethnically diverse nation of modern history. To this end, parties of the Left permitted and, in fact, encouraged the formation of migrant organizations that could address workers' communities in their own language, with the strategic aim of awakening and radicalizing their audience. The American Left's proposition was one of labor Americanization: the migrant worker was called upon to recognize his or her material interests and to join fellow workers in the American present, irrespective of ethnic differences. In other words, Americanization amounted to a shift from nation to class as the primary site of identity. But this process itself required the worker to be addressed in a familiar language—one that moved him. This was the strategic function of migrant radical organizations and publications.

Indeed, for many, radicalization into the communist movement or into trade unions (the two were not always synonymous) was an experience of Americanization to the degree that it involved daily contact with people of different origins bound by a common vision; recasting America's ethos of multicultural assimilation, people from all over the world subscribed to the same publications, attended meetings in English, and shared a preoccupation with American politics and social life. However, while radicals remained firm in their belief that such commitments would overshadow and, eventually, nullify migrants' attachments to their origins, research reveals a far more complex reality: even as their radicalization was indeed a process of Americanization, migrants never relinquished those bonds, continuing to communicate with those they had left behind and to remain invested in political developments at home. As such, the case of the Greek American Left exposes the limitations of teleological narratives of integration and homogenization. What it reveals most is the dynamic relation between the migrants themselves and their American reality. We sometimes treat the United States as a well-defined grid where migrants needed only find their place. This book offers an alternative viewpoint: it was the migrants themselves who perpetually transformed the American social and political landscape.

When I began this research ten years ago, my primary aim was to reckon with dominant representations of the Greek migrant experience in the United States. Chief among these is the narrative of entrepreneurial success—a linear and unhindered progression of social development unfolding within insular, conservative circles. My aim then was to propose an alternative narrative of Greek American history and to recover the thread of a story that had been lost. Connecting fragments of a forgotten past, I hoped to weave a single, coherent narrative. The search for information in archival collections scattered across the US, Greece, and elsewhere brought me to focus on disparate sources and to learn the art of discovering what most people believed never to have existed. In short, my research followed one of the basic principles of social history: the attempt to give voice to those who had left but a few traces of their presence in time.

This was the context that determined the writing of my dissertation in the Department of History and Archaeology at the University of Crete (2010). Almost immediately following its completion, I was offered a unique opportunity to adapt my dry academic text into a screenplay. *Taxisyneidēsia* (a specifically Greek American adaptation of the phrase "working-class consciousness") is an hour-long documentary on the untold story of Greek American radicalism.[4] It was first screened in 2013, at the fifteenth Documentary Film Festival of Thessaloniki. As usual, chance and circumstance acquired a power far greater than authorial intentions. I could not have known it when I began my research, but the deepening of the economic crisis and the new age of mass population movements both contributed definitively to the success of *Taxisyneidēsia*, which was screened in dozens of film theaters, cultural centers, and lecture halls in Greece, the United States, the UK, France, Germany, and elsewhere. Along with other contributors to the documentary, I often had the good fortune of participating in discussions with the audience at the end of the screenings. The relationship between interwar and contemporary economic crises was a constant theme, difficult to overlook. In one scene from the Great Depression, an elderly New Yorker rummages through the garbage in search of food; the image bore similarities to the struggle for survival facing contemporary Greeks for the first time in many years, and it inspired questions about how the study of the past might aid us in the present.

The reaction is reasonable, of course, but it also attests to our tendency to narrow the horizon of our imaginations by way of a reflexive turn to the past. Our resort to the past for guidance—the instrumental mining of the past for "lessons" to be gleaned for the future—highlights a certain collective sense of disorientation, even desperation. The harsh truth is that the past rarely has much to offer by way of example or guidance; it discloses no blueprint of the next stages of historical development. What it can provide is insight into the ways in which contemporary realities have been conditioned by the cycle of hope and disappointment that framed the course of the twentieth century. Historical research can nuance our understanding of what those expectations were, the ways in which societies envisioned their future at specific historic conjunctures, the role of a vanguard of thinkers and activists in mapping it, and the ways in which their visions helped transform political imaginaries. In other words, the unforeseeable ways in which the expectations or certainties of the past were thwarted suggests that what the past has to teach us is precisely the *unpredictability* of historical development.

American history offers an exemplary case study in the instability of notions of historical certainty. At the height of the political transformations that marked 1917, the interwar crisis of 1929, and the end of the Second World War, the Left—and not only the American Left—saw the collapse of capitalism as imminent; they predicted that these transformations would accelerate the passage of history and produce a definitive rupture with the capitalist system. American communists' efforts to reconcile that certainty with (what turned out to be) the relative stability of existing economic and political systems offers insights into the power as well as the limitations of the twentieth century political imaginary of the Left. It was this series of contradictions that brought me to revisit my research on migrant radicalism in the United States and to produce this book.

Chapter 1 ("Radicals of Two Worlds") traces the workings of the socialist diaspora in the United States. Beginning with the massive strikes on the eve of World War I, it discusses the dynamism of the socialist movement and the militant trades unions that proliferated among immigrant workers. Publications appeared with titles like *Organōsis* [Organization] and *Ē Phonē tou Ergatou* [Voice of the worker], translations of socialist texts spiked; the threads that connected Greek immigrants with socialist organizations in Greece all serve to highlight the diasporic and transnational flow of socialist ideas. The central moment of the chapter refers to the expectation of imminent revolutionary change in the United States in the wake of World War I and the European revolutions: migrants emerged as the potential subjects of great social change.

Chapter 2 ("Americanizing Communism") carries the story forward, concentrating on the 1920s, a decade marked by the ebb of revolutionary prospects and the efforts of the communist movement to adapt to the novel realities of capitalist stabilization. Specifically, it analyzes the attempts of the migrant Left to interpret the thwarted expectations of the previous decades through the prism of *taxisyneidēsia* (working-class consciousness). The term attests to the Americanization of the radical experience. These processes are intertwined with the reimagining of political activism in a period of economic prosperity. The chapter analyzes the transformations in radical thought, as the American Dream became a more realistic, more potent ideological force.

The following two chapters explore the period of the Great Depression, the American 1930s. Chapter 3 ("Crisis and Revolution") highlights the corrosive effects of the 1929 market crash and emphasizes its impact on the social and economic peace on both sides of the Atlantic. The chapter examines the revival of revolutionary aspirations amid the crisis, the collapse of proto-welfarist structures of communal support, and the emergence of new solidarities. My central concern here is the link between two crises. The catastrophe wrought by economic chaos tested hegemonic certainties about politics and identity—these were years when immigrant identities changed dramatically and fueled new forms of political action. This change was felt in the workplace of course, but much more broadly too. The experience of capitalist modernity was deeply shaken and reworked during these years, in fields ranging from consumption to popular culture. Chapter 3 analyzes the activities of the Greek American Left against that backdrop, exploring its efforts to rebuild the labor movement amid novel social and political divisions within immigrant communities.

Chapter 4 ("Turmoil and Compromise") sheds light on the transnational dimension of political and social divisions in the United States, focusing on their relationship to emerging fascist and anti-fascist movements in Europe, and especially in Greece. The chapter examines the attempts by the regime of Ioannis Metaxas to propagandize within the United States and the anti-fascist activities of the Greek American Left in response. Migrants in America took on a key role in coordinating the main centers of the Greek diasporic and migrant presence (Britain, Egypt, France, the USA) and forming a front against the Metaxas regime. These developments, nominally concentrated on a distant homeland, in fact took place in conversation with social and political tensions within the United States amid the reorientation of the New Deal after 1935. The transformations in immigrant communities thus highlight a meeting of Greek and American histories.

This encounter is further stressed in chapter 5 ("Planning the Future") and chapter 6 ("Cold War Nation"), which make up the last part of the book. These two chapters examine the activities of the Greek American committees formed to support national liberation movements in Europe and then to design the postwar world through a hoped-for convergence between the New Deal and the socialist planned economy. American and European experiences were fused, together informing the bid to imagine a better future. The study of that forgotten expectation highlights the role played by Greek Americans in Greece's 1940s, the impact of the December 1944 events in the United States, and the role of immigrant communities as dual ambassadors of Americanism in Europe and of European anti-fascism in America. The transformation of this role in the Cold War period is the subject of the final chapter of this book. The new global role of the United States along with postwar upward social mobility shifted the political orientation of immigrant communities and enabled the emergence of a new transnational framework for Greek American identity in which the Left was still central but in a very different guise: this was an identity premised on the ideas and practices of anti-communism.

The Power of the Unpredictable

The belief that the United States would sit at the epicenter of an overwhelming and electrifying transition toward a new—and, naturally for the Left, a better and planned—social order might seem to us a naive fantasy, perhaps even a dangerous one. Today, notwithstanding our own global economic crisis and the preponderance of critiques of neoliberalism and economic inequality, we are far from the emergence of a radical political project capable of mobilizing people with anything like the passion, perseverance, and dedication common to nineteenth and twentieth century radicals. What is most notably absent is the *certainty*—a basic building block for these revolutionary movements of the past—that capitalist crisis will lead to a new social order. Such confidence is absent today not only on a theoretical level, but on an experiential one as well; that is, we lack the invigorating sense of participation within a global movement possessed of a clearly worked out strategic roadmap to engineer radical social change. This absence in our lived experiences and in our imaginations enforces strict limits on the political imaginary of the twenty-first century. In envisioning the future, we flit between apocalyptic scenarios and resignation in the face of the grinding continuation of a familiar present.

It is difficult, then, to remember and to reconstruct a period in which radicals took the "wretched" of the earth to constitute a real revolutionary subject. The experience of the nineteenth and twentieth century American Left highlights the primacy of immigrants, African Americans, and others among the oppressed in the theory and practice of revolutionaries. This primacy did not, of course, always ensure an unproblematic relationship between the Left and the marginalized. But the fact remains that the Left formed a political and a social landscape in which the demand for equality was often transformed from rhetorical proclamation into everyday practice. In the trenches of the Spanish Civil War, the multiethnic Abraham Lincoln Brigade provided American history's first ever example of white soldiers serving under the command of an African American officer. Such episodes should not erase our awareness of the tensions and prejudices among nominal comrades, but they do remind us that the Left has historically been an internationalist undertaking based on the belief that social change was primarily the concern of all those who had a material interest in its success.

Today, the outlook of the Western Left has changed. It often stresses sensitivity and compassion but rarely assigns a leading role in delivering political change to the modern oppressed, such as refugees, migrants, and youths of migrant origin inhabiting the margins of capitalist metropoles. This change is, surely, the result of a grand shift in Western radical movements to match the conditions of political stability and economic prosperity that the post-WWII social contract secured. The moment of crisis and breakdown did not last. That developing capitalist stability was, this book argues, the insurmountable limit with which the American Left could not successfully reckon. The 1950s marked the decline of old radical organizations and the absorption of militant interwar unions into more mainstream industrial politics. In the end, American capitalism emerged triumphant from its successive crises, thwarting the expectations of all those who had been certain of its inevitable collapse. The triumphant trajectory of American grandeur reconstructed in retrospect relied to a great degree on the postwar world's ability to erase the memories of the interwar crisis, and so to forget the many who had sought through agitation and protest to resolve the crisis in socialist directions, an effort that ultimately failed.

Against that backdrop, this book could be read as the history of a failure. But to map the hopes, expectations, disappointments, and disillusionments of past revolutionary projects is also to insist on the unpredictability of history. That uncertainty is with us still, and it gives us reason to hope as well as to fear.

Notes

1. Kerr, *Socialist Songs*, 1.
2. Kerr, *Socialist Songs*, 3.
3. The bibliography is extensive, while the relatively recent transnational turn in historiography has generated a renewed interest in political and social radicalism among exilic, diasporic and immigrant groups. I finished writing this book in 2015 (the Greek edition came out two years later) and my outlook was influenced by works that addressed different migrant communities and diverse expressions of ethnic radicalism. For instance, Guglielmo, *Living the Revolution*; Bencivenni, *Italian Immigrant Radical Culture*; Hoffman and Srebrnik (eds), *A Vanished Ideology*; Michels, *A Fire in Their Hearts*. In the years that have passed, I have obviously reconsidered aspects of my work. I resisted though the temptation of updating the bibliography (and been drawn to an overall rewriting of the original manuscript) for obvious reasons. The enemy of the good, is—in all languages— the perfect.
4. *Taxisyneidēsia: Ē agnōstē istoria tou ellēnoamerikanikou rizospastismou.* The documentary was bilingual. The English version was titled: *Greek American Radicals: The Untold Story* (director: Kostas Vakkas, script: Kostis Karpozilos, production: Non-profit organization "Apostolis Berdebes," 2013).

CHAPTER 1

Radicals of Two Worlds

Workers of the World

There is plenty of rage in the article of Anastasios Papas, a young Greek immigrant, published in the *International Socialist Review* in August 1914: "Woe to the hands that shed this costly blood! Over the bodies of these martyrs do I prophesy that this foul deed will someday be avenged! . . . O, Capitalism, Capitalism, thou marble-hearted fiend! You have starved us, outraged our mothers, wives and sisters; driven us to desperation and we shall pay you back. Until every parasite has been put to work, let no wage slave rest!"[1] He had every reason to feel that way. On 20 April 1914, the Colorado National Guard had violently suppressed a militant strike in the coal mines of the Colorado Mine and Fuel Company. When the armed national guardsmen retreated from Ludlow, one of the strikers' main camps, they left behind a scene of devastation. Smoke was billowing from the strikers' torched tents and shanties while distraught people were searching for their relatives among the wreckage. Their search ended in tragedy. Eleven children and two women had suffocated to death when they took refuge in a basement. Their names were added to a long list of casualties; more than seventy people had lost their lives in fights during the strike in the Colorado coal mines.

Among the victims of the "Ludlow Massacre," as it came to be called, was a previously unknown immigrant from Crete.[2] Louis Tikas (born Elias Spantidakes) had been a leading figure among the hundreds of Greek immigrants who were employed in the surrounding mines and had joined forces with immigrants from various parts of the world in launching the strike. On the day that the sporadic skirmishes between the national guard and the strikers led to the brutal suppression of the strike, Tikas had tried to avert the escalation of hostilities. In the general confusion, a patrol arrested and summarily executed him. At the time, such incidents were not unheard of;

the violent suppression of any form of protest went part and parcel with rapid industrialization, strip-mining for raw materials, and the expansion of the railroad network. Industrial violence was not the exception—it was the norm.

Even so, the unprovoked attack by the National Guard led to a bloodshed that could not go unnoticed. The contrast between the immigrant workers, dressed in rags and living in makeshift camps, and the limitless wealth of John Rockefeller, owner of the Colorado Mine and Fuel Company, brought to the forefront the intrinsic inequality that defined and enabled the meteoric rise of US capitalism. In this context, developments in Colorado seemed to encapsulate the rising tension between corporate interests and a new protagonist in the country's working-class history: the foreign-born immigrant workers. The strike in the Colorado Mine and Fuel Company was the latest episode in a wave of labor activism that spanned the whole country, from the East Coast to the West. In 1912 and 1913, industrial cities and remote camps that had been known for their vast concentration of immigrant workers were now becoming visible loci of labor unrest and unionizing activities.

For socialists, the events in Colorado demonstrated not only the heavy price of industrial development, but also the transformative power of capitalism in creating class consciousness among the thousands of workers who arrived every day in the United States. In 1911, a state committee estimated that about 60 percent of workers in the US industrial sector were first- or second-generation immigrants; recently arrived immigrants made up 90 percent of miners. In the vast steel mills of the United States Steel Corporation, 11,694 out of 14,395 workers hailed from southeastern Europe; 77 percent of 14,000 workers in the Ford Motor Company were registered as "foreign born."[3] Among them there were hundreds or thousands of Greeks. From the beginning of the 1890s up to 1924, the year signaling the end of mass immigration, US authorities had registered some five hundred thousand Greek citizens and persons "belonging to the Greek race"—this was how Greeks hailing from the Ottoman Empire were typically registered.[4] Their motives were manifold, as numerous as the personal histories that each carried. However, they all had one thing in common: the quest for work. Greek immigrants—typically young male agricultural workers—were visible in industrial cities, mines, and railroad construction works offering cheap unskilled labor.

There is nothing atypical about unskilled laborers who moved from place to place, learned the particulars of different modes of production, were eager to earn a wage without being very demanding, and who participated in a mass transformation of the composition of the working-class without paying much attention to the language of organized labor. Most contemporary commentators would note, in passing, that political radicalism, unionism, and collective demands were not to be found among the mass of Greek unskilled labor. "Socialism finds no followers among the people of this race in the United States," was the reassuring verdict of sociologist Henry Pratt Fairchild, who wrote a pioneering dissertation on Greek immigration.[5]

Colorado disproved such convictions. This explains why the *International Socialist Review*, the preeminent journal of the Socialist Party's left wing, sought out a Greek to comment on these recent events. Anastasios Papas, a young immigrant who was active in the socialist circles of Minnesota, had nothing to report on the actual events. His indignation over the news coming from Colorado went hand in hand with the conviction that the brutal realities of immigrant work would surely result in the transformation of immigrants, who "never saw a mine, factory, railroad or other modern industry before coming to America," into a "class." "Capitalism is their tutor," Papas wrote, echoing the topoi of Marxist rhetoric. Life in the coal mines was unwittingly creating the "gravediggers" of the capitalist system.[6]

Such statements, abstract as they may be, not only reveal the teleological and schematic perception of class consciousness but are also inscribed in an ongoing debate within the socialist movement concerning the ability of immigrants to adapt and alter capitalist realities. When Anastasios Papas emphasized the militancy of his fellow Greeks, he was partaking in an ideological clash that was at the intersection of internationalism, working-class interests, and the quest for the revolutionary subject of the twentieth century. The phenomenal rise of transatlantic immigration had resulted in two antithetical readings that both spoke in the name of socialism.

Karl Kautsky, for instance, perceived the evolution of the "modern proletarian," who was torn from his agrarian background and was becoming a "citizen of the world," as a threat to workers with a higher standard of living, "who will be hindered in their class-struggle by the influx of those with a lower standard and less power of resistance."[7] Immigrant labor was cheap, expendable, and endlessly renewable: these were the traits that fueled the animosity of the established labor unions toward the newcomers. In the United States, the American Federation of Labor (AFL) saw immigration as a capitalist ploy aiming to reduce wages by creating a surplus army of willing and unskilled laborers. This outlook found many adherents in the ranks of the Socialist Party of America. Socialists fighting for rigorous restrictions on transatlantic immigration argued that the level of capitalist development in various parts of the world determined the ability of newcomers to participate in the working-class movement. Therefore, those from eastern Europe or Asia were seen as intrinsically unfit to adapt to the novel and demanding realities of class competition. "The majority of the American socialists," concluded Morris Hillquit, "side with the trade unions in their demand for the exclusion of workingmen of such races and nations as have as yet not be[en] drawn into the sphere of modern production and who are incapable of assimilation with the workingmen of their adoption, and of joining the organization and struggles of their class."[8] On these grounds, the American delegates in the International Socialist Congresses of 1906 and 1908 spoke in favor of measures limiting transatlantic immigration.[9]

The boundaries between a socialism of this kind and racial theories were often fuzzy. The influence of scientific racism on Anglo-Saxon socialism resulted in an amalgam of viewpoints, at whose core lay the different levels of capitalist development across the world. Historical determinism dictated that capitalist development was a necessary prelude for the transition to the "higher" economic and political system of socialism. According to this way of thinking, societies that were still at the base of the capitalist pyramid belonged to the past and proved unfit to keep abreast with contemporary developments. Therefore, immigrant workers from "underdeveloped" regions of the world were seen as being a priori devoid of agency, as mere puppets in the hands of capitalists. What is more, they represented a threat to the advances of socialist politics, as they hindered the unity and success of the American working class.

In November 1916, a Greek carpenter who lived in the United States sent a letter to Jack London to complain that one of his stories was racially biased. The two men had met the previous year, and Spiro Orfans clearly believed that the sympathy they shared toward socialist ideals was enough for them to engage in open dialogue. "As you know, I happen to be one of those brown-eyed, skin-pigmented sub-mortals," he stated in his letter, in order to draw attention to the problem of generalizing the inferiority of those coming from the eastern Mediterranean. London responded with a jeremiad on the superiority of the "pure breed." He argued that Greeks had "mongrelized themselves by breeding with the slush of conquered races," and therefore they now expressed—as the poor immigrant had—their ingratitude toward the superior races of the civilized world.[10] The discourse of class analysis could become a powerful tool of discrimination and segregation, while socialism was a privilege of the few.

On the other hand, radical trends inside and outside both the international and American socialist movements saw in immigrants a rising force in the formation of the contemporary revolutionary subject. Focusing on the "wander[ing]" worker, Vladimir Lenin depicted immigration as a progressive force that emancipated the agrarian laborer from the ethnic and racial prejudices of his past. In this line of thought, the movement of people across borders and their integration into capitalist production were producing the archetypical proletarian of the future.[11] The idealizing of the immigrant worker reflected the radical conviction that young immigrants, men and women, irrespective of their level of familiarity with the conditions of industrial labor, were fulfilling the Marxist description of those who had nothing to lose but their chains. Where the critics of transatlantic immigration saw the sinister plans of capital, their adversaries detected the self-destructive function of the dominant economic system. One can detect an intriguing contradiction here: in the socialist mind and heart, capitalism would either be portrayed as an invincible and powerful agent that carefully orchestrated historical developments, or as a weak structure that was fighting for its survival but could not escape its inevitable doom and imminent collapse.

In the American setting, immigrants—identified with the promethean industrial worker—were suggested as people who had known oppression in the past, had come to the United States seeking a new life, and, through the harsh conditions of labor and social marginalization, were waking up to their historical mission of eliminating the system of wage labor. The immigrant was juxtaposed to the "American worker" who had lost the revolutionary spirit and was subject to the false ideology of class cooperation. "The immigrant," wrote Margaret Sanger in the first issue of *The Woman Rebel* in March 1914, "is the one who had the courage to leave behind the familiar past for the unknown future . . . and brings with him a spirit of defiance that generations of Americans have lost forever."[12]

At that point, Sanger was romantically involved with a Greek immigrant. The case of Ioannis Rompapas (1874–1961) offers a unique glimpse into the fluid and shifting intellectual environment of New York's radical circles. Rompapas had emigrated in 1910 and, having the means to do so, he launched an export-import company with associates in Greece and the Ottoman Empire.[13] Mystery and intrigue abound in the life and times of Rompapas. When, in March 1913, an anarchist assassinated King George I of Greece in Thessaloniki, there were rumors claiming that Rompapas was involved. These allegations were unfounded, but they were attributed to the fact that in 1912 Rompapas had launched the publishing house Rabelais Press and was quickly becoming a well-known figure in New York's radical ecosystem. In just a few short years, the virtually unknown immigrant was lecturing in the Ferrer Center and was counted as one of the city's "futurists."[14] Mable Dodge Luhan describes a self-confident speaker who defended in her salon the possibility of social emancipation through "true love," before going on to express his own—unrequited—attraction to her.[15]

Individuals like Rompapas fascinated New York radical intellectuals. When in 1914 he published in English a 194-page manifesto, *The Book of My Life*, Hutchins Hapgood praised it, saying "it breathes nobility and temperamental strength and courage."[16] This was a very generous approach to what in fact was a delirious confession of Rompapas's feelings for Margaret Sanger, the editor of *Rebel Woman*, who in the summer of 1914 was waxing eloquent about the rejuvenating effect of immigrants in American society. Rompapas and Sanger enjoyed a brief but stormy affair that can be seen as symbolic of the transformations taking place within the US radical movement: Sanger left her husband, a moderate socialist, and their three children in order to have an affair with the mysterious Greek. Their affair had tangible results. Sanger published a massively successful book with Rabelais Press, introducing to the United States the European debate on methods of contraception.[17] Around that time, Rompapas funded the journal *Social War* and a *Revolutionary Almanac*, an anarchist calendar, both endeavors connected to the notorious expatriates Edward Mylius and Hippolyte Havel.[18]

It is not known whether it was Sanger's legal battles, the Rabelais Press's ambitious publications, or his other endeavors (or, more probably, a combination of all three) that led Rompapas to go bankrupt in 1915. The many things we do not know about him are certainly more than the handful that we do. However, the meteoric rise and sudden disappearance of Ioannis Rompapas provide a glimpse into the scene of New York radicalism, where people of uncertain background, fortune hunters, the unemployed, workers, and intellectuals appeared to reinvigorate the world of the American Left.

Workers of the World, Unite!

Between 1912 and 1914, an unprecedented wave of protests resulted into protracted clashes and labor strikes. In Lowell and Lawrence, Massachusetts, in Grays Harbor and Seattle, Washington, in Ludlow, Colorado, in the great copper mines of Michigan, and in Patterson, New Jersey, thousands of immigrant workers went on strike, organized themselves into multiethnic committees, marched side by side with fiery orators, and endorsed the radical practices of militant labor unions such as the Industrial Workers of the World (IWW). This was an unprecedented turn of events. The people at the forefront of the labor movement were the same ones who had often been described in the pages of the socialist press as incapable of grasping the value and logic of collective organizing. Factories and industrial sites that had witnessed the violent struggle between immigrant communities over workplaces and wages were being turned into spaces of experimentation around practices of multiethnic solidarity under the rallying cry "Workers of the world, unite!" Ethnic mobilization was becoming a powerful tool of class solidarity and labor militancy. The lyrics of a popular song reflect this dimension: "In the good old picket line / In the good old picket line / The workers are from every place / From nearly every clime / The Greeks and Poles are out so strong / And the Germans all the time / But we want to see more Irish / In the Good old picket line.[19]

What was the trigger that turned yesterday's unskilled immigrant workers into resolute strikers? The low standard of living was one of the main factors. Lowell, Massachusetts, was one of the main industrial centers of New England, boasting many textile mills and factories. The work was backbreaking and living conditions squalid. Workers put in fifty-eight hours of work per week, and there were increased rates of work-related injuries and respiratory diseases, high rates of child mortality, and crowded conditions in slums.[20] Within the world of labor existed a clear-cut dichotomy between skilled and unskilled workers; this division was along ethnic lines. The median yearly income of "locals," which included the descendants of older immigrants, was 573 dollars, while "immigrants" (mainly Greeks, Italians, and Syrians) earned on average 384.[21] In 1912, Italian workers decided to strike against a reduction in work hours, which would result in a reduction of their already meager wages. The success of the strike depended on the participation of the other immigrant communities. The makeshift Greek Orthodox churches hosted great gatherings in which the strikers addressed their coworkers with the help of interpreters. As a result, thousands of Greeks decided to join.[22]

In this two-year period of labor unrest possibly the most impressive thing of all was the domino effect as the rallying cry to "organize" and the demand for an immediate betterment of work conditions sounded from far-flung and remote townships, from different industrial sectors with different work conditions. No centrally organized plan or defining event can be discerned here, such as, for example, a financial crash. The causes of unrest can be traced to the accumulated resentments fueled by the systematic exploitation of human labor to the point of utter physical exhaustion. In this context, an accident, a mistake in the weighing of a day's production, or a pay cut could function as a fuse that set fire to a tinderbox of accumulated tensions.

"An aging worker hurt his leg and was moaning day and night. We beseeched the company three times to take the old man to the hospital, but they did nothing. We called a meeting and decided to quit before someone else was hurt even worse—and that's what we did, all forty of us," a Greek miner in Utah wrote, recounting the chain of events that led to a militant strike in March 1912.[23] When the group of workers decided to quit, they probably had not been familiar with the slogan of the IWW's union organizers, "An injury to one is an injury to all," but they were following its spirit.

Radical publications and groups played an important role in transforming these incidents into a visible social movement. Eager correspondents and militant labor organizers had their ear to the ground about the outbreak of immigrant protests. They were quick to reach the epicenter of the protest, and then made sure the news was disseminated. The pages of the *International Socialist Review* were full of vivid descriptions concerning the ways that the immigrant workers organized, prompting its readers to form solidarity committees. It was through these networks that industrial unrest reached the major city centers. In one famous incident, radical intellectuals and unionists in New York City went to the train station to welcome dozens of children from textile workers' communities in New England. It was an inspired move, since it relieved the strikers' families from the costs and concerns of caring for the children, and it also provided the movement with a powerful symbol: the children's protest march in the streets of New York, which highlighted the sweeping entrance of young immigrants to the forefront of American society.

Meanwhile, socialist immigrant groups were spreading the message of workers' emancipation to their respective ethnic audiences. "What wonder! The hall was full. 300 attended."[24] The secretary of the San Francisco chapter of the Union of the Working Classes of Greece (an Athens-based socialist group) could not contain his enthusiasm. On 31 March 1912, hundreds of immigrants answered the call of the city's Greek socialists to attend a discussion concerning the developments in the Pacific Northwest. There, in Greys Harbor, Greeks and Finns who were working unseen in the endless forests and the great timber mills had joined forces in a militant strike against the powerful owners of the mills, who employed armed militias. After a few weeks, order was restored. Hundreds of striking workers and IWW agitators boarded the trains and left the region for good. The "Greek strike of the Industrial Workers of the World" had failed, but its echo resounded far and wide, moving the hearts of many more.[25]

Until that point, the activities of the San Francisco Greek socialists had been limited to conversing in the café Anorthōsis (Recovery), reading the Greek socialist newspapers, and sending money to the Union of the Working Classes of Greece in Athens. Their eyes were turned to the world they had left behind. Now, following the strike, things changed. For the first time, the speakers did not hail from the narrow pool of the city's Greek socialists. The hundreds of people that made up the night's audience had the opportunity to hear Austin Lewis and Caroline Nelson urging Greek workers to join the city's labor unions. Optimism was quite common among the socialists of the period, and the San Francisco correspondent for the Greek socialist review *Ereuna* (Inquiry) was no exception. He saw the strikes multiply, he took note of the poverty in the streets of San Francisco, and he witnessed the rising interest of immigrants who up to that point had been indifferent to socialist ideas. He ended his letter thus: "A revolution is imminent one of these days."[26]

That day did not come. The 1912–14 strike wave ended under the impact of suppression and the devastating Great War. Nonetheless, it was a revolutionary event; it had transformed the invisible world of immigrant labor into a visible factor of social change. In March 1912, the dozens of immigrant children who appeared before a Congressional committee on the recent strikes in the New England textile mills put a face on the statistics concerning the day-to-day life of workers. Urged by the head of the committee to "speak up," fifteen-year-old Charles Casiersky, fourteen-year-old Victoria Wennaryzk, and sixteen-year-old Rosary Contarino answered the committee members' questions by describing incidents of child labor and the identification of family life with life in the factories. The young immigrants' depositions were at times sarcastic ("I think not," was how John Boldelar, a fourteen-year-old Lithuanian, responded to a question about whether they had carpeting in their house). They could also be disarming: the fourteen-year-old Camella Teoli, in a toneless voice, recounted how an accident involving a loom machine shattered part of her skull, how she was hospitalized for seven months, and how she had to go back to work in order to support her family.[27]

In these stories, radicals and revolutionaries—inside and outside the Socialist Party—detected the inexorable march of history toward revolution. "Trust-Capitalism creates a new proletariat," Louis Fraina, of Italian descent, wrote from New York City, predicting that the rise of unskilled labor in the steel mines would "sound the call for the Social Revolution."[28] In New York City, anarchist groups tried to bring class conflict to the heart of American life. The bombings they carried out, dedicated to the memory of the dead in Ludlow, culminated in the destruction of an entire building in Greenwich Village when a faulty bomb went off, killing three conspirators in the process.[29] The IWW's momentum intensified the belief that the New World was on the brink of social war. The IWW rhetoric and practice was an amalgam of direct action and working-class self-initiative aiming to cripple the capitalist economy in order to pave the way for an "Industrial Republic" governed by elected representatives from the labor unions. The dynamism, independence, and resourcefulness of the IWW appealed to many in the Left and the labor movement. Others were not fascinated at all. "They preach anarchy, not unionism," stated the president of the AFL at the moment when the Italian workers in Lowell confirmed him, since they marched chanting the slogan "No gods, no masters."[30]

Tsars, Slaves, and American Flags

The IWW's influence on the 1912–14 strike wave reflected their readiness to provide interpretations and practices that made sense to the immigrant workers. Emphasis on solidarity, the clear-cut dichotomy between capital and labor, and the targeting of foremen and labor recruiters resonated with the accumulated dissatisfaction and anger caused by the daily experiences of harsh labor. Moreover, the IWW organizers appeared to be determined. They encouraged the destruction of the means of production; they clashed with scabs; they challenged the monopoly of violence exerted by local authorities and company-led gangs. In the aftermath of the "Ludlow Massacre," a company representative emphasized that Greek strikers were "veterans of the Balkan Wars" and therefore capable of handling guns and engaging in battle. In his eyes, their attitude was shaped by radical unions, which "led [them] to believe that the mines really belong to them and that the organization behind them is so powerful that they cannot be punished for any violence they commit."[31]

Those who criticized the strikers' violent activities usually overlooked how proportional they were to the realities of immigrant labor. In the case of the Colorado mines thousands lived isolated in scattered locations, slept in shanties, and faced brutal conditions due to the nature of their work, the physical environment, and the lack of basic necessities. Work-related accidents were frequent and often resulted in fatalities. The absence of any form of state authority transformed the armed foremen and company gangs into indisputable masters of a daily life saturated with tensions, complaints, and invisible conflicts. The topography of exploitation was enhanced by the fact that local shops and shanties were owned by the company. As a consequence, a significant part of the workers' wages went right back to their employer. In this unique case of entrapment, in which the line between a worker and a serf was often blurred, any form of complain or protest was transformed into a revolutionary act of reclaiming individual and collective liberties.

This relation, between protest and revolt, proved to be a puzzle for radicals of all stripes. Putting forward their self-fulfilling prophesies concerning the awakening of immigrants as the new revolutionary subject, they failed to notice that strikers did not necessarily extend their militancy to the pursuit of a future free from capitalist exploitation. "The Big Fight has just begun" the *International Socialist Review* assured its readers, introducing "the greatest victory in American labor history" following the strike in the textile mills of New England.[32] In the lexicon of the movement the "great battle" referred to the decisive clash between labor and capital that would result in socialism. The issue carried an impressive series of photographs from the nine-week strike, coordinated by a committee in which twenty immigrant communities were represented. The cover photograph illustrated the militancy of the conflict. The National Guard's bayonets were turned toward the strikers. They, in turn, were brandishing two huge American flags. This was not the only time. The American flag appeared frequently in the hands of strikers and protesters before the Great War broke out. It is a telling detail: immigrant workers emphasized their commitment to the republican ideals of the United States and their wish for social and political equality. The vocabulary and symbols of labor protests underlined their expectations for a life in the New World that would be radically different than the one they left behind.

"Where are we, in the free country of Amerika [*sic*] or in a country dominated by a despotic form of government as under the subernity [*sic*] of the Sultan?" was the rhetorical question posed by Greek miners in Utah.[33] Their outcry targeted a popular practice that they perceived as a violation of the social promise carried by the United States. The padrones were immigrant middlemen who were recruited by companies in order to provide workers from the ranks of their countrymen. This practice evolved into a pattern that expanded from the industrial sites of the American West to small villages in the southeast Mediterranean. The prospective immigrant signed a contract, before his departure, that secured a job placement and at the same time obliged him to pay a lump sum and monthly installments to the padrone for various expenses. As Gunther Peck has shown, the padrones system permitted the companies to outsource the hiring process to individuals who had access to a willing but still untapped workforce.[34] Leon Skliris was one of those, a notorious padrone who was extremely powerful and made a profit from contracts and the operation of numerous shops in small workers' communities in the American West.[35] In September 1912, the Greek miners of the Utah Copper Company turned against him, and with the help of the radical miners' union a strike resulted in the end of Skliris's reign.[36]

Leaving other issues aside (especially the legislation against the padrone system), the vocabulary of the labor protests was consistent with the representation of the United States as the free country par excellence, in stark contrast to the shackles and restrictions of the Old World. Therefore, immigrant workers called the padrones "tsars"—or as in the eyes of Greeks in Utah the padrone was a "Sultan"—and the mounted policemen "Cossacks." These references to an autocratic past emphasized the demand for political and social equality in the present. "I do not believe that Lawrence is on the map of this country at all; it would be all right for China or Russia" a twenty-nine-year-old Jewish immigrant said, denouncing a police assault on a workers' gathering.[37] From this perspective, the immigrant strikes expressed frustration with the false promise of the New World, but at the same time their protest echoed a demand for restoring this exact same promise. For some, this was indeed linked with revolutionary plans for a radical transformation; but for most it was limited to the establishment of new, favorable terms, which would improve their everyday life and augment their income. For instance, the Greek workers who had led the strike against the Greek padrone were in essence invoking their right to the unrestricted and unmediated sale of their labor. This was far from the aims of radical labor unions that envisioned the immediate abolition of the capitalist system.

The end of labor unrest came with the United States' entry into World War I. The social question was suppressed by nationalism. Those who opposed the war were imprisoned and persecuted. Radical unions and groups, such as the IWW, never fully recovered. Nonetheless, the immigrant strikes succeeded in improving living conditions, in abolishing practices such as the padrone system, and in creating a legacy of collective organization. Years after the Ludlow events, a Greek lawyer from Colorado noted that local Greek miners remained in the ranks of the labor union and participated in strikes.[38] For some immigrants, the experience of taking part in a strike became a defining moment that changed their lives and led to an active involvement in radical politics. This had an impact on the American socialist movement: the 1912–14 strikes, along with international developments, exacerbated the ideological differences and the rifts between moderates and revolutionaries. The latter had been bolstered by a new dynamic factor—the diverse world of the immigrant Left. The strikes had demanded that immigrant labor become visible and that immigrants be presented as political subjects who could raise their own claims in the language they understood best. And they succeeded, in part, in those demands. The American Left up to that point had observed and evaluated immigrant labor according to its own priorities—either demonizing or idealizing the immigrant worker. Now, immigrants were fighting to make their voice heard inside a movement that was promising full political and social equality for all.

Radical Diaspora

"The final battle between the Working Class and the Plutocracy will be waged in America," predicted in 1912 Spyridon Metaxas, a Greek immigrant living in Savannah, Georgia.[39] Metaxas was sending news from the United States to Greek socialist journals and newspapers. His writings reveal a fascination with America's rapid capitalist development and with that particular belief in historical determinism that perceived the United States as the ideal place for the final and decisive battle. Metaxas, a self-educated worker, was in essence following in the footsteps of the German social-democratic intellectual Werner Sombart, who in 1905 had expressed socialist admiration for what was taking place in the United States: "The time that Marx could foresee only in his imagination when he wrote Capital has already arrived in the United States."[40] This admiration was intertwined with a denunciation of the flagrant inequalities between the power wielded by modern tycoons and the destitution of millions of industrial workers.

The misery of urban centers, the work-related accidents in mines and railroads, wage inequality, child labor, and the sense of expendability that hounded itinerant workers constituted for socialists an axiomatic proof of the need for radical change.[41]

When Metaxas was sending his correspondence to Greece, the socialist movement had reached its peak: the strikes and revelations about labor realities brought the social question to the forefront of public discourse. Eugene Debs gathered nearly a million votes in the presidential elections, the Socialist Party grew to unprecedented numbers, and in small towns and agrarian communities socialists were elected to power. Metaxas was certainly fascinated with all this activity. Born on the island of Kefalonia, he had emigrated to the United States in 1908, aged thirty-two, and had settled down in Savannah, Georgia. Very soon he gathered a circle of likeminded Greek immigrants around him.[42] This was not the only such case. In the pages of the socialist review *Ereuna*, letter-writers "from America" were expressing their fervent wish to contribute in any way possible to "the downfall of the wretched plutocratic slavery," and they reported the establishment of "chapters" of the Union of the Working Classes of Greece across the United States.[43] In October 1913, in the midst of the Balkan Wars, the newfound Socialist Party of Greece published a list of donations; more than fifty came from Greek immigrants in the United States who had signed with *viopalaistēs* (wage worker).[44]

They were thousands of miles away from the Greek socialist movement. Regardless, their gaze, their thought, and their activities were all turned in that direction. Launching local chapters in the United States, reading *Ereuna*, sending letter, translating texts, and donating funds were practices aimed to preserve and straighten their links to the imaginary headquarters of the movement.[45] Immigrant socialists in the United States were reproducing a long-lived diasporic tradition that had shaped Greek socialism. Starting from the nineteenth century, the world of Greek socialism had relied on groups and intellectuals who were operating outside the nation's borders. In Western Europe, Egypt, and the Russian Empire, students, intellectuals, and workers were creating diasporic groups that were focused on the question of a national and social revival; their focus was primarily, if not exclusively, on Greece. In this context, immigrants in the United States added another piece to the transnational network of Greek socialism that expanded to communities across the globe in order to foster a sense of common belonging through the circulation of publications, translations, and ideas.

The Greek socialist activities in the United States allowed an intellectual connection to the ethnic center and did not follow a centralized plan. In essence, they followed the common immigrant practice of reproducing, in new and unknown circumstances, a familiar social and intellectual topography. The signs outside the small immigrant shops bearing names of villages and islands from the Old World present perhaps the most visible indication of the newcomers' efforts to connect their new everyday life with their memories and images of the reality they had left behind. In a similar way, socialists aimed to create an alternative political geography that overcame distance with their fervent efforts to support the imaginary community of Greek socialism. This choice also reflected the dominant immigrant strategy of perceiving the American present as a temporary condition before the triumphant return to the country they left behind. The immigrants' intense interest in Greek events had many expressions: the establishment of patriotic associations, repatriation in order to fight in the Balkan Wars, or the reproduction of Old World political conflicts in the American continent. Seen in this light, the Greek socialists' attachment to their own intellectual and emotional center, the various Greek socialist groups, can be easily interpreted. After all, socialists were themselves immigrants.

At the same time, though, they belonged to an international movement that proclaimed the need to transcend national differences in favor of common class interests. Immigrant socialism was facing a constant challenge: it was addressing compatriot workers and asking them to join the rest of the workers, irrespective of nationality. Addressing "the worker," this abstract and almost mythical figure of the socialist vocabulary at the time, one of *Ereuna*'s regular lyric-writers from the Unites States adapted the call of the "Internationale": "Workers of every race and every land / Become one body to crush the common enemy."[46] These verses by a self-taught worker from New York City capture the nature of diasporic socialism. Its aim was to provide an interpretation that would link the abolition of intensive exploitation and vast inequality with the prospect of workers' emancipation Such a transition, though, presupposed the collective organization, both economic and political, of those who produced the wealth. And these subjects, the workers, lived and worked in the United States of America.

Organōsis: Socialism as Education

The emerging world of immigrant socialism entered the American socialist movement in the form of Language Federations that operated as autonomous structures of immigrants who shared a common (actual or imaginary) ethnic and linguistic past. Their history is interwoven with the flexible structure of the socialist movement in the early twentieth century and is related to a rich theoretical discussion on the relation between the common interests of the working class and the undeniable fact of its heterogeneity. Following the end of World War I, one third of the Socialist Party members belonged to the ten biggest immigrant groups and Language Federations that operated within its ranks.[47] Their gradual incorporation (1911: Italian, Scandinavian, Slavic; 1912: Hungarian, Bohemian; 1913: German, Jewish, Polish, Slovak; 1915: Russian, Ukrainian, and Lithuanian) reflected the self-confidence and importance of immigrant socialist groups that had developed their own social and cultural world, as expressed in publications, working-class clubs, and communication networks. In the decentralized structure of the Socialist Party, the Language Federations developed into enclaves of diverse traditions and ideological references that often related to legacies and traditions of the Old World. The result was a triumph of diversity: a Chicago reader at the turn of the twentieth century could choose among four English-language publications (from the messianic *Christian Socialist* to the militant *International Socialist Review*) and eight foreign-language newspapers (including the Italian *Parola Proletaria*, the Polish *Dziennik Ludowy*, the Scandinavian *Social-Demokraten*, and the Slovak *Proletarec*) that addressed the city's immigrant communities.

We should not imagine these publications as mere translation agencies of American socialist thought. Quite the contrary, they expressed the diverse worlds of immigrant radicalism, while translating—and most importantly transmitting—ideas, references, and practices to the American socialist setting. The Language Federations—or any other form of organizational link to American socialist parties—represented an integration process for diasporic groups that were up to that point primarily concerned with developments in Europe. This process was far from a linear one; however, it highlights the gradual realization that life in the United States was not a parenthesis. In this context, the desire of immigrant socialist groups to become organic elements of the American socialist parties was intertwined with the immigrant strikes of the period and the demand for social and political equality. It was indeed a process, as James Barrett has illustrated, of an alternative and radical Americanization.[48] It was a process of transcending ethnic boundaries. Socialist ideas, especially for those immigrants who came into contact with them for the first time in the United States, offered a radical vision of Americanization: a social and political universe where they were equal among different people sharing a common ideal that in turn made all differences between them obsolete.

The first Greek-language socialist newspaper in the United States was *Organōsis* (Organization), a four-page monthly newspaper that began publication sometime between the end of 1916 and the beginning of 1917 in Cincinnati, Ohio. It went through many transitions, changing its place of publication and periodicity, and finished its run in 1924 in New York City. *Organōsis* was bound with the fate of the Greek Federation of the Socialist Labor Party of America and with the life of a certain Petros Tsistinas.

Tsistinas had been born in 1882 in Ottoman Kastoria, in a Greek Orthodox family. He first came into contact with socialism in Serbia, where he had emigrated before making the transatlantic trip to the United States in 1907. In 1910 he was living in Cincinnati among thousands of immigrants like him. Tsistinas was sharing an apartment with three other Greeks—one of whom was his brother. All of them had arrived in Cincinnati around the same time and were working as *piatades* (dishwashers) in one of the city's biggest hotels, a popular choice for those who did not want to work in factories or for the railroad.[49]

Tsistinas was a correspondent for socialist publications in Greece. His letters reveal that at the same time he was in contact with Balkan socialist groups that were active in Ohio. "I recently read a Serbian pamphlet on socialism that has been translated from Russian," Tsistinas wrote introducing socialists in Athens to a treatise on the international struggle of the working class.[50] This episode's geographic indicators reveal much about the unpredictable dimensions of the interplay between human mobility and political radicalism. An immigrant from Cincinnati sent to Athens a Greek adaptation of a Russian socialist text that had been translated into Serbian in the United States. The equation becomes even more complex when one takes into account that Kastoria, Tsistinas's hometown, had just transitioned from the Ottoman Empire to the Greek State (and therefore Tsistinas would become a nominal citizen of Greece), while he was soon to apply to become a naturalized citizen of the United States.

There is an additional layer here. Tsistinas's exposure to the multiethnic Ottoman Empire, and to the world of Balkan socialism, defined his choices in the American socialist movement. Cincinnati was the home of *Radnicka Borba*, a local socialist newspaper, connected to the Socialist Labor Party of America (SLP). Following its example, Tsistinas joined the Socialist Labor Party in a choice that defined the rest of his life. From 28 September 1912, when he purchased a few prepaid cards for new members (among them was one of his roommates), until 4 June 1955, when he added two new subscribers, his name was rarely absent from the regular columns of the *Weekly People*, the SLP newspaper.[51] In 1916, Tsistinas proudly informed his Athenian comrades that he had formed a Greek socialist group in Cincinnati that was affiliated with the Socialist Labor Party.[52] A year later, *Organōsis* came out.

Organōsis had minimal influence but was instrumental in the creation of a solid sense of belonging to Greek socialists in the United States. Clustered around industrial towns in the Midwest (Youngstown, McKeesport, Cincinnati, Zeigler, Chicago, and Detroit), its three hundred subscribers followed the SLP's carefully ordered and doctrinaire system of thought.[53] In their insular world, numbers did not really matter. "Organization is the important factor, not the numbers themselves," D. S. Kotsonis assured his audience, using the militaristic vocabulary of socialist rhetoric that compared social competition with the art of war, insisting that the members of the party had to be "disciplined soldiers, well supplied, and always at [their] station."[54] In this battlefield of ideas, the SLP members were equipped with the works of Daniel De Leon, the party's founder. Lengthy excerpts, as well as long-winded party decisions, took up two of the four pages of *Organōsis*, while the Greek members translated and disseminated the works of De Leon.[55] These cheap pamphlets offered an alternative interpretation of the workers' experience in the United States by emphasizing the inevitable awakening of the workers and the arrival of the "industrial socialist confederation," which was not yet feasible given the conditions at the time.

The world of the Greek SLPers was messianic and missionary in outlook. In a rare autobiographical sketch, Tsistinas described his childhood at the side of the bishop of Kastoria, and how socialism came to replace Christianity in his personal belief system.[56] There is no question that his frenzied activity in securing subscriptions and donations betray a tireless propagandist who was preaching while moving from one industrial town to the next. The fact that *Organōsis* translated and published Eugène Sue's *The Silver Cross* (a novel that had attracted Daniel De Leon's interest) underlines the impact that messianic rhetoric had on Greek immigrants who joined the party. Their self-confidence, stemming from diligent readings of texts by De Leon, and their insistence on daily propaganda through the printed word is reminiscent of the term "evangelical materialism" that Jonathan Rose used to describe self-educated British coal miners.[57] In the SLP world, the harsh realities of immigrant labor were presented as a necessary price that workers had pay in order to arrive, inevitably, at the point of their emancipation. Faith in the inexorable march of historical evolution stripped *Organōsis* of any emotional or personal content and turned its pages into a space for abstract theorizing that proved the superiority of socialism, without leaving room even for the experiences of its own readers.

Ē Phonē tou Ergatou: Waiting for the Revolution

"The strong and truly liberating winds blowing from Russia," wrote Georgios Livas from Chicago, helped "the movement to grow in leaps and bounds."[58] In his long letter, Livas informed socialists in Athens that a Greek socialist newspaper had just been published in New York. *Ē Phonē tou Ergatou* (Voice of the worker), launched in the summer of 1918, was the official organ of the Greek Federation of the Socialist Party of America. Georgios Livas had every reason to be glad. As the secretary of a Greek socialist club in Chicago, he had seen, within a few weeks, its membership skyrocket to 180. The difference from the small groups he had hitherto participated in was immense. Without a doubt, the Russian Revolution had played a role. But it was not just the echo of Russian events. The cataclysmic developments in Russia were strengthening the internationalist tendencies within the American socialist movement (for instance the newspaper *Revolutionary Age* was subtitled "A Chronicle and an Interpretation of Events in Europe") and giving prominence to immigrant socialist groups.[59]

In these new circumstances, the immigrants were proclaimed the ambassadors of the revolutionary call to the United States. One illuminating incident is the meeting of twenty leading figures of the Left, in the winter of 1916, in Brooklyn. Among them were the Russian political refugees Leon Trotsky, Nikolai Bukharin, and Alexandra Kollontai, Sen Katayama (the founder of the Japanese Socialist Group in the United States and later the Communist Party of Japan's delegate in the Comintern), Ludwig Lore, Louis Fraina, and Louis Boudin, an American intellectual of Russian descent. These last three would go on to establish, in May 1917, *Class Struggle*, a review "dedicated to international socialism," which mined the European revolutionary networks for declarations from the uprisings in 1919, anti-imperialist calls to the army advancing in Ukraine, and news from all over the world.[60] The October Revolution had definitely fascinated the American Left.

And not only that. The Revolution had an impact on the shape of the American Left. Perry Anderson has written about a global "transfer of loyalties" that defined the breakup of the dominant socialist parties.[61] The United States was no exception. From the end of 1917, the tensions inside the Socialist Party pointed to an imminent split as the dynamic left wing of the party sought, with increasing urgency, to align with the Bolshevik paradigm. "While the SLP spent all of its time *talking* about socialism, the CP seemed to be actively pursuing it," was how Steve Nelson, a Croat immigrant, explained his decision to join the communists.[62] In this shifting reality, the Language Federations played a leading role as they echoed the fervent European revolutionary realities and, in the case of the Russian Federation, the successful model of the Russian Revolution. The Greek Socialist Union (the group that evolved into the Greek Federation of the Socialist Party) was formed in November 1917 as a result of the unprecedented turmoil inside the socialist movement, which was sparked by conflicting news coming out of Russia. As *Ē Phonē tou Ergatou* noted, regardless of whether the Bolsheviks consolidated their power, one thing was certain: "You poor wretches [meaning the bourgeoisie] whether it happens or not . . . your reign in Russia is over."[63]

This certainty went hand in hand with the newspaper's rhetoric on the rising tide of the working class. *Ē Phonē tou Ergatou* introduced itself as the newspaper of the workers: "Workers write in it, workers read it, with workers' money it keeps going. . . . *Ē Phonē tou Ergatou* is a workers' newspaper, aimed at workers, promoting workers' interests."[64] This was not an especially original proposition. What was certainly new, though, was how the newspaper defined Greek workers in the United States. The literal words were "of Greek descent residents of America." Here we can discern a paradigm shift. Previously, socialists would refer to "Greek immigrants." *Ē Phonē tou Ergatou* initiated a reorientation of radicals' ethnicity toward the common interests of the American working class. This compliance followed the social transformations at the end of the Great War, most importantly the consolidation of immigrants' presence in the United States and the new ways that ethnicity was intertwined with everyday life.

The content in the first issues of *Ē Phonē tou Ergatou* reflects the priority given to education, since the reader could find columns explaining "what is socialism," learn the basics about the "war of the classes," and read socialist news from all over the world in order to agree with the editor's main position: "socialism is coming." The propagandist nature of *Ē Phonē tou Ergatou*, something not at all unheard of in the socialist press, shows that the New York "Bolsheviks" saw class consciousness as something that would manifest itself if only they exposed the laws governing the capitalist system and the workers' historical mission. The educational dimension of the newspaper can be easily discerned in the English-language advertisement of *Ē Phonē tou Ergatou*: "The first attempt of the Greek Socialists in America to teach Socialism and Revolution to the Greek workers. . . . Help us to locate them."[65]

On a more practical level, emphasis on the working-class identity of the newspaper was a way of overcompensating for the fact that the founding figures behind its publication were intellectuals. More specifically, they were journalists employed by *Atlantis*, the city's Greek royalist daily newspaper. Initially, this did not seem to be a problem. The *Atlantis* leadership was quite tolerant toward the "Bolsheviks," as they were labeled by an eager journalist who informed his editor in chief of the socialist activities of his colleagues.[66] This relaxed stance was possibly a transatlantic reflection of the recent (and up to a point paradoxical) cooperation between socialists and royalists in Greece against the Great War, or it merely reveals an underestimation of the seriousness of the new publishing project. For socialists, this was a blessing; they could publicize their activities in the pages of *Atlantis*, and most importantly they could enjoy privileged access to the newspaper's extremely important printing facilities with Greek movable type.[67] The information on the early days of *Ē Phonē tou Ergatou* is scarce, but it is evident that the Greek Socialist Union acquired considerable traction. This allowed socialists to rent a three-story building at 793 Second Avenue and expand their network to different parts of the United States, from the East Coast to the West.

Great Expectations, Lost Illusions

The shifting realities of the American Socialist Party defined the course of the Greek Socialist Union. Between 1919 and 1920, the Socialist Party suffered successive splits with the main question being the stance vis-à-vis the emerging Communist International. In this process, the party's Language Federations (especially the ones relating to eastern and southern Europe) were completely at odds with Anglo-Saxon members who were initially wary of the Bolsheviks, and eventually hostile to them. In the small world of American communism, immigrants represented the majority. Sixteen Language Federations made up the organizational network of the Communist Party. In 1919, one in four members was of Russian descent, while three out of four members belonged to immigrant organizations from central and eastern Europe. Following the foundation of the Workers Party, just 5 percent of members identified themselves as natives and 50 percent did not know how to speak English.[68] In November 1919, during a meeting with Greek communists, when the exhausted speaker had finished reading the latest party decision, he asked how many of the attendees understood English. Only five out of twenty people present raised their hand.[69]

The Greek Socialist Union sided with the Language Federations that belonged to the party's left wing. In November 1920, the union denounced the Socialist Party, as the latter had decided to reject the twenty-one conditions set forth by the Communist International. Certainly, the Socialist Party of America had more important problems to deal with than the departure of a few hundred Greeks. But for those who left, it was a defining moment. In December 1920, delegates from the various chapters of the Greek Socialist Union met in New York to decide on their next steps. Their first action was to send a brief letter to the "Soviet Republic" in Moscow in which they declared their agreement on the program of the Third International and their decision to fight until the abolition of capitalism and the establishment of a global communist society."[70]

From that point onward, the Greek socialists participated in the founding processes of the fledgling communist movement. Undoubtedly, a fascination with the emerging Soviet power along with a belief in an imminent global upheaval was an important factor. But there was also something else. The communist movement created a new sense of equality for immigrants, in stark contrast with the peripheral role they had in the Socialist Party. Georgios Livas from Chicago was trying to explain this to his comrades in Greece by emphasizing his disappointment with the "phony[,] . . . indecent, selfish . . . conduct of the American socialists."[71] In the communist movement, things were different. In 1921, the year when he announced his break with the socialists, Livas founded, along with two American comrades, a bookshop in Milwaukee, which stocked radical titles and "books on science, philosophy, and sex, in many languages."[72] Theodore Draper's remark bears repeating: many immigrants realized their American dream of equality in the left wing of the US socialist movement.[73] There they met people with similar experiences and backgrounds, something that played a major part in their decision to join the communists.

It was a strange period. Great expectations were met with meager organizational numbers and hairsplitting differences. The wearying debates running to many pages and the strongly opposed arguments of the Communist Labor Party, the United Communist Party, the Proletarian Party, and the Communist Party of America, all founded between 1919 and 1921, bear witness to the tensions, to the point of psychological exhaustion, which went hand in hand with the anticipation of the revolutionary moment. The impact on the day-to-day activities of the party was often tragicomic. At some point, a Greek reader sent a letter to the *Communist*, the journal of the Communist Party of America, complaining that it carried misguided information on socialist affairs in Greece. The editors published the letter, discreetly noting that it should be addressed to a different journal by the same name belonging to the Communist Labor Party of America—the anxious comrade had mixed them up.[74] There were many incidents like this one, which justified the indignation of a member of the Socialist Party, who stormed out of a meeting of one of the new communist groups, shouting: "I did not leave a party of crooks to join a party of lunatics!"[75]

The frenetic quest for the correct revolutionary line related to the conviction that this was the prerequisite in order to discern the moment of the great social awakening. Communists in the United States were following the Bolshevik example, where numbers were a secondary matter. What was important was to have a revolutionary purpose and to seize the revolutionary moment. By estimating that the global capitalist system was on the brink of collapse, the Socialist Party's left wing and the fledgling communist organizations believed that they had shouldered a supreme historical responsibility. This responsibility was compounded further by the dominant position of US capitalism in the global sphere, and the many questions that surrounded its transition from a wartime economy to the new conditions.

When workers in the industrial city of Seattle announced a general strike in February 1919, the city came to resemble a "photo of the Parisian Commune," and these expectations came quite close to becoming reality.[76] The

strikers in Seattle seemed to reconnect with the prewar militant labor traditions, and their demands echoed the slogans of the October Revolution. The
unrest spread, but the National Guard was sent in to suppress the nascent
movement. However, from a radical standpoint, even this negative development was a prelude to an imminent revolution. "The ultimate decision as
to whether Capitalism or Socialism shall control the world will be rendered
in the United States," wrote Louis Fraina, a career revolutionary and self-
educated intellectual, upon hearing the news from Seattle.[77] In September
of that same year, the American correspondent for the Comintern magazine described the United States as an "erupting volcano."[78] Despite these
colorful—and hopeful—descriptions, the 1919 strikes failed to bring about
imminent revolutionary events. The great Seattle strike remained an isolated
incident, and its conclusion signaled the end of the era of industrial violence
that had nurtured, since the beginning of the decade, revolutionary expectations. The communist movement now had to adapt to the new realities that
were being shaped by the enhanced global status of the United States after
World War I, as well as to the period of financial prosperity that followed
the first (and, as it proved, brief) depression of the postwar transition.

Even though the 1919 unrest did not create the conditions for a revolution that the communists were hoping for, it did worry the US government.
The response was a coordinated campaign, known as the Palmer Raids,
against the newfound communist movement and militant labor unions.
On the second anniversary of the October Revolution, in 1919, the police
raided Russian workers' clubs in twelve cities and arrested hundreds of
immigrants. The result was the deportation of close to five hundred people
(among them the leading figure of immigrant anarchism, Emma Goldman)
to the Soviet Union.[79] The antiradical campaign in 1919–20 was based on
the demonization of immigrants, who were seen as introducers of radical
ideas and practices into the United States. This resulted in the deportation of
arrested immigrants and had an impact on the cohesion of immigrant socialist groups. The police raid on the headquarters of the Greek Socialist Union
in New York City, and the deportation, early in 1921, of its secretary,
Kostas Papadogiannis (who later opened a leftist publishing house in Athens), led to a brief interruption in the publishing schedule of Ē Phonē tou
Ergatou. What's more, the attention of the authorities activated conservative sentiments in immigrant communities. Until 1920, the daily immigrant
newspapers saw Greek socialism in the United States as something acceptable, but their stance changed after the Palmer Raids: the "Bolsheviks" were
a threat and the period of tolerance ended right there and then.

The decline in revolutionary fervor and the internal ideological crisis had
an impact on the communist movement. By 1921, American communism
concerned only a small number of dedicated members. After the expulsion

of hundreds of Russian immigrants to the Soviet Union, the Palmer Raids, and the detrimental, successive splits, the Workers (Communist) Party membership had fallen to around ten thousand. The fanatically compiled monthly records revealed some circumstantial fluctuation, such as members who had caught up or had fallen behind on their monthly dues, but it did not alter the big picture. The Greek Federation remained stable somewhere in the middle of the rank of immigrant communism: during 1923 and 1924 its members numbered between two and three hundred, while *Ē Phonē tou Ergatou* had a stable subscription base of about a thousand readers.[80] Contrary to *Organōsis*, which was still circulated mainly in the Midwest, *Ē Phonē tou Ergatou* was circulated from the East Coast all the way out to the West Coast. Based on this, the Greek Federation of the Workers (Communist) Party had managed to cement its influence. Their real problem was the realization that the revolution was not imminent after all.

Iakovos Kazavis's book *O Sosialismos erchetai* (Socialism is coming), published in New York in 1924, is a perfect example of the vacillation between expectancy and disillusionment. The author, who had come from the remote Greek island of Nisyros, belonged to the circle of radical intellectuals who had founded the Greek Socialist Union in 1919. The first essay in the book declared that social transformation was more than certain: "It is an indisputable fact that socialism is coming, crowned with a victor's laurels." A few pages later, the author's tone becomes somber. Addressing the Greek workers in the United States, he notes that "the majority of the working class today, of the Greek working class," are not conscious of their position in society, and this is why they get furious at the socialists, who argued that wage labor is "slavery," and compared workers with "slaves" before emancipation. In one of the essays, the march of history is likened to "the flow of the Niagara," while in the next "the path is rough, uphill, full of obstacles." This way of thinking played a major part in the formation of the immigrant Left, since it bestowed upon its members the sense of a mission and the pride of belonging to the vanguard of historical evolution.

At the same time, though, it reflected an awareness of their limitations and the indisputable fact that the vast majority of their potential audience was indifferent to their call. In 1923, the editors of *Ē Phonē tou Ergatou* decided to rename their newspaper. The reasoning was simple: "The Greek workers either do not admit, or they do not know, that they are workers." As a consequence, "in order to approach them and tell them [that they are workers], we must not scare them away with the title of the newspaper."[81] Throughout the 1920s communists were constantly concerned with the insufficient class consciousness of their compatriots. This resulted in a multi-faceted working-class educational project. For the time being, though, in mid-1923, the readers of *Ē Phonē tou Ergatou* had the opportunity to propose a new title for the newspaper with the aim of luring those who did not identify as workers. Many suggestions were published in successive issues of the paper, which offer a unique view into the full spectrum of ideological, social, and textual references of the immigrant Left's audience.

Some of the proposals followed the beaten path of immigrant press titles: *Ellēnikē Enōsis* (Greek union), *Neos Ellēnismos* (New Greekness), but also *Ellin Kommounistēs* (Greek communist). Another group of readers, probably belonging to the first generation of socialist immigrants, relied on an outdated political vocabulary combining rational order: *Orthoviotikē Koinonia* (Orthobiotic society), *Epikouros* (Epicure). The revolutionary movement's messianic character fascinated a much larger section of the readership. Their suggestions reveal once more the persistence of traditional patterns, such as *Anagennēsis* (Rennaissance), *Anaplasis* (Reformation), *Nea Idea* (New idea), *Nea Plasis* (New creation), *Anakainisis* (Renewal), *Anastasis* (Resurrection), *Anthrōpotēs* (Humanity), *Afypnisis* (Awakening). Others repeated older titles from the Greek nineteenth-century radical press, for example *Neon Fōs* (New light). Finally, still others referred to the ultimate goals of radical social transformation: *Aiōn Afypniseōs* (Century of awakening), *Enōsis tou Kosmou* (Union of the world), *Nea Zōē* (New life), *Nea Koinōnia* (New society), *Neo Lavaro* (New banner), *Neo Systēma* (New system). When this goal was defined by a single example, then there was only one model—the October Revolution: *Diethnēs Epanastasis* (International revolution), *Kommounistēs* (Communist), *I Bolshevikia* (The Bolshevik), *Syneidētē Palē* (Conscious struggle), *Astro tou Voria* (Northern star), *Erythra Froura* (Red guard), *Kokkini Simaia* (Red flag), *Kokkinos* (The red), *Kokkinos Astēr* (Red star), *Neos Proletarios* (New proletarian), *Thriamvos tis Epanastaseōs* (Triumph of the revolution).

There is something naive and at the same time moving in this process. And not merely because of the readers' desperate identification with their preferred newspaper, but also because of their faith that the right title would unleash the full potential of emancipation for the "proletariat of America." The final choice was a safe one. The editors of *Ē Phonē tou Ergatou* announced the newspaper's new title in the summer of 1923: "The title is vivid and rolls off the tongue, and is also well known among Greeks, because it has been appropriated by a bourgeois newspaper in Athens. It is also the first word of the [Greek translation of the] 'Internationale.' It is an exceedingly symbolic title, without causing suspicion or arousing the reader's prejudice: *Empros* [Forward]."[82]

Notes

1. Anastasios Papas, "Greek Workers in America," *The International Socialist Review*, August 1914, 112–13.
2. Concerning the Ludlow Strike, see Papanikolas, *Buried Unsung*.
3. Lipset and Marks, *It Didn't Happen Here*, 127; Dubofsky, *Industrialism and the American Worker*, 10; Myer, *The Five Dollar Day*, 10, 77.
4. Kitroeff, "Ē Yperatlantikē Metanasteusē," 128. Immigrants registered as "belonging to the Greek race" increased after 1907–08 in correlation with the expansion of mandatory army service in the Ottoman Empire. See Papadopoulos, *Ē metanasteusē apo tin Othomanikē Autokratoria stēn Amerikē*, 36–46.
5. Fairchild, *Greek Immigration to the United States*, 209. See also Georgakas, "Greek-American Radicalism," 207–32.
6. Papas, "Greek Workers in America," 112. Papas was in contact with Greek socialism. See for instance his letter to the Athens-based socialist review *Ereuna*, 27 November 1911, 1.
7. Kautsky, *The Class Struggle*, 205.
8. Morris Hillquit, "Immigration in the United States," *International Socialist Review*, August 1907, 74–75.
9. Miller, *Race, Ethnicity, and Gender*, 209–11.
10. Reesman, *Jack London's Racial Lives*, 344.
11. Lenin, "Capitalism and Workers' Immigration," 454–57.
12. Margaret Sanger, "Why the Woman Rebel," *The Woman Rebel*, March 1914, 4.
13. *The New York Times*, 20 March 1913, 3; Burgess, *Greeks in America*, 71. Rompapas was registered as an exporter of linen and an importer of agricultural goods, cooperating with merchants in Athens and Salonika.
14. *New York Tribune*, 3 January 1915, 6.
15. Luhan, *Movers and Shakers*, 61, 65–66.
16. Rompapas, *The Book of My Life*; for the advertisement of the book, see "Post-Impressionism in Philosophy," *The New Review*, May 1914, 320.
17. Sanger, *What Every Mother Should Know*. Regarding her affair with Rompapas and the publication of Sanger's book, see also Baker, *Margaret Sanger*, 64–73.
18. Longa, *Anarchist Periodicals in English*, 228–29; Havel, *The Revolutionary Almanac*.
19. Kornbluh, *Rebel Voices*, 179–80.
20. The Commonwealth of Massachusetts, *Forty-Third Annual Report*, 39–40.
21. The Commonwealth of Massachusetts, *Forty-Third Annual Report*, 29.
22. "Lowell. 10,000 Greeks Willing to Join IWW," *Christian Science Monitor*, 11 March 1912, 1.
23. Cononelos, *In Search of Gold Paved Streets*, 157.
24. *Ereuna*, 3 June 1912, 3.
25. Dreyfus, "The IWW and the Limits of Inter-Ethnic Organizing," 450–70.
26. *Ereuna*, 3 June 1912, 3.
27. United States Congress, *The Strike at Lawrence, Mass.*
28. Louis Fraina, "The Call of the Steel Worker," *International Socialist Review*, August 1913, 84.
29. Jones, *More Powerful than Dynamite*, 164.
30. United States Congress, *The Strike at Lawrence, Mass.*, 86.
31. Cononelos, *In Search of Gold Paved Streets*, 208.
32. Leslie H. Marcy and Frederick Sumner Boyd, "One Big Union Wins," *The International Socialist Review*, April 1912, 613–30.
33. Cononelos, *In Search of Gold Paved Streets*, 259.
34. Peck, *Reinventing Free Labor*, 78–81.
35. For a biographical note and a description of Skliris's activities, see Peck, *Reinventing Free Labor*, 31–40.
36. For the strike, see Peck, *Reinventing Free Labor*, 31–40, 204–23; Papanikolas, "The Great Bingham Strike of 1912," 121–33.

37. United States Congress, *The Strike at Lawrence, Mass.*, 116.
38. Diplomatic and Historical Archives of the Hellenic Ministry of Foreign Affairs (YDIA/ MFA), 1921/B/45(2), B, 7–8.
39. *Ereuna*, 6 May 1912, 2.
40. Sombart, *Why Is There No Socialism in the United States?*, 6.
41. Kraditor, *The Radical Persuasion*, 213–14.
42. *Ereuna*, 10 February 1912, 3.
43. *Ereuna*, April 1910, 51; 25 November 1911, 3; 3 April 1911, 3; 4 November 1912, 3.
44. Leaflet of the Greek Socialist Party – Union of the Working Classes of Greece in English, October 1913. Nikolaos Giannios Papers, Hellenic Literary and Historical Archive Society (ELIA).
45. *Ereuna*, 27 May 1912, 3.
46. *Ereuna*, 3 June 1912, 2.
47. Shannon, *The Socialist Party of America*, 44–45.
48. Barrett, "Americanization from the Bottom Up," 996–1020.
49. 1910 United States Federal Census [on-line database, last access: September 13, 2022].
50. *Ereuna*, 9 December 1912, 3.
51. *The Weekly People*, 28 September 1912, 6; 4 June 1955, 6.
52. Letter by Peter Tsistinas to Nikolaos Giannios, March 1916, Nikolaos Giannios Papers, Hellenic Literary and Historical Archive Society (ELIA).
53. See for example *Organōsis*, 1 January 1924, 1.
54. *Organōsis,* September 1922, 1.
55. For the works of Daniel De Leon that were translated into Greek and published by *Organōsis*, see the relevant section of the bibliography. The Greek SLP members also translated and published a pamphlet by Clyde Croubaugh and Eugène Sue's novel *O Argyrous Stauros*.
56. *Organōsis*, 15 November 1923, 2.
57. Rose, *The Intellectual Life of the British Working Classes*, 300.
58. Letter by Georgios Livas to Nikolaos Giannios, 28 February 1919, Nikolaos Giannios Papers, ELIA.
59. "To our dead comrades," *Revolutionary Age*, 25 January 1919, 1.
60. Bell, *Marxian Socialism*, 108.
61. Anderson, "Communist Party History," 152–53.
62. Nelson, *Steve Nelson*, 19.
63. *Ē Phonē tou Ergatou*, July 1918, 3.
64. *Ē Phonē tou Ergatou*, July 1918, 1.
65. "The Voice of the Worker, organ of the Greek Socialist Union of America," *The Intercollegiate Socialist*, April–May 1919, 55.
66. Vasilios Zoustis to Solon Vlastos, 22 May 1918, *Atlantis*, National Daily Greek Newspaper Records, Box 58.1, Labor Relations, Historical Society of Pennsylvania (HSP).
67. Greek Socialist Association to Solon Vlastos, 2 May 1918, *Atlantis*, National Daily Greek Newspaper Records, Box 58.1, Labor Relations, HSP.
68. "Report of the Central Executive Committee to the Second National Convention (1922)," Russian State Archives of Socio-Political History (RGASPI), f. 515, op. 1, d. 141; Draper, *The Roots of American Communism*, 190, 392.
69. "Greek Branch," *The Communist*, 29 November 1919, 7.
70. Greek Socialist Union to Soviet Republic, 5 December 1920, RGASPI, f. 515, op. 1, d. 37, l. 8. Published also in *Ē Phonē tou Ergatou*, 18 December 1920, 1–4.
71. Georgios Livas to Nikolaos Giannios, 1 February 1921, Nikolaos Giannios Papers, ELIA.
72. An advertisement for the bookshop, *The Church Times*, September 1920, 7.
73. Draper, *The Roots of American Communism*, 34.
74. P., "A Protest Protested," *The Communist*, April 1921, 12–13.
75. Draper, *The Roots of American Communism*, 180.
76. Bell, *Marxian Socialism in the United States*, 117.
77. Louis Fraina, "Problems of American Socialism," *Class Struggle*, February 1919, 26.

78. Y., "America: The Foundation of a Communist Party," *The Communist International*, September 1919, 84.
79. For the deportations, see Post, *The Deportation Delirium of Nineteen-Twenty;* For the Palmer Raids, see Kovel, *Red Hunting in the Promised Land*, 14–22.
80. "Membership Series by Language Federation for the Workers Party of America (1923)," RGASPI, f. 515, op. 1, d. 206, l. 10; Membership Series by Language Federation for the Workers Party of America (1924), RGASPI, f. 515, op. 1, d. 341, l. 22; *Ē Phonē tou Ergatou*, 9 June 1923, 4. See also "Report of the Federation Secretaries (September 1922)," according to which the newspaper's circulation was between two and three thousand copies: RGASPI, f 515, op. 1, d. 67, l. 35–36.
81. *Ē Phōnē tou Ergatou*, 26 May 1923, 2.
82. *Ē Phōnē tou Ergatou*, 9 June 1923, 4.

CHAPTER 2

AMERICANIZING COMMUNISM

"Be American!"

"It is not meant for a joke, but it is a very earnest proposal that we should at least start a movement within our party for the recognition of the government of the United States of America."[1] Under normal circumstances, such a heretical proposition would have resulted in the immediate expulsion of its proponent. However, John Pepper (born Jozseph Pogany) was in no such danger. The "short, stocky, swarthy, bespectacled" Hungarian revolutionary had arrived in the United States claiming to be a representative of the Communist International.[2] In May 1923, urging his comrades to recognize the government of the United States of America, the experienced communist was promoting a radical vision of Americanization: immigrants ought to direct their struggles to the American social and political setting. This proposal entailed an organizational restructuring of the communist movement. John Pepper condemned the "Babel" produced by the numerous Language Federations and proposed a simple solution: "Be American!"

From that point on and until the mid-1930s, Pepper's admonition permeated the world of American communism as it evolved from the Workers Party of America to the Workers (Communist) Party, and finally, in 1929, to the Communist Party of the United States of America (CPUSA). The demand for Americanization was combined with the overall effort to "Bolshevize" the party according to the directives of the Communist International. The cornerstone of this process was the imposition of a new organizational structure around the policies of democratic centralism; in tension with this structure, however, was the existence of the Language Federations, which reflected the polycentric tradition of the socialist movement. Therefore, they were seen as a problem. The Fourth Convention of the Workers Party, in 1925, issued resolutions that, in party language, are usually called "historic": the delegates adopted democratic centralism, added the designation "communist" to the party's name, and abolished the Language Federations that up to then made up a significant portion of the communist ecosystem in the US. The rationale was quite simple: the sixteen Language Federations reproduced the ethnic diversity (and fragmentation) of the American working class and kept the immigrants' attention centered in Old World developments, thus hampering their social and political integration into the United States. If in the years of the Socialist's Party left wing the diverse and polyglot Language Federations were perceived as fascinating expressions of European revolutionary movements, gradually they were seen as an obstacle, as "remnants of 'leftist' sectarianism" and as indications of "insufficient enthusiasm" for "the working class's financial and political demands in the United States."[3]

In order to justify the dissolution of the Language Federations, the communists emphasized the shifting landscape of immigration after the end of World War I. In 1921 and 1924, Congress had imposed quotas on immigration, signaling an end to the era of mass immigration. The new system transformed the immigrant presence in the United States. Immigrant communities could not count on fresh arrivals for their renewal, those who stayed in the country were becoming permanent residents, and the undesirability of returning to war-ravaged Europe and the birth of a second generation cancelled the prospect of repatriation. As in every transformation, these developments were not instantaneous; however, the communist movement had no room for middling solutions. "The historic reasons for the present form of Party organization have been, in large measure, outlived," was how the introduction to the party's Fourth Convention framed the attack on Language Federations.[4] The party's vocabulary, despite assertions to the contrary, reproduced the dominant understanding of Americanization as a linear and progressive evolution from backwardness to modernity.

In this context, the American communist movement developed its own melting-pot theory: industrial labor was a transformative process that led to the fading of the immigrant past in favor of a new synthesis. There was little difference between Israel Zangwill's "the great Melting Pot where all the races of Europe are melting and re-forming" and Vladimir Ilyich Lenin's image of "a millstone which grinds down ethnic traits," an image Lenin used to describe the "the glorious historical process" that would bring about the collapse of ethnic difference in the "huge factories and mines of America."[5] Immigrants ought to align themselves with the present and leave the Old World behind. In the words of the Greek American newspaper *Ē Phonē tou Ergatou*, "the workers in Greece should deal with the Greek capitalist themselves; we should put all our strength into the creation of an American labor movement. Every foreign worker, . . . from the first moment he steps on American soil, should be aligned with the social and economic conditions of the country in which he struggles for a living."[6]

Following the 1925 convention, the Language Federations were replaced by a byzantine bureaucratic system. The Central Committee of the new-found Workers (Communist) Party supervised, through a subcommittee, the "Language Bureaus," which were responsible for the publication of newspapers and party literature, the organization of cultural and educational activities, and the guidance of working-class associations with an ethnic background (e.g., the Greek Workers Educational Association in Detroit). The main difference with the past was a limit on autonomy (as in the case of the transfer of assets from the old Language Federations to the new Central Committee) and the imposition of a surveillance system that, for instance, monitored immigrant newspapers and calculated the percentage of news that had been reprinted from the *Daily Worker*, while criticizing ethnic content (such as advertisements) as "petit-bourgeois."[7] The new structure echoed the principles of democratic centralism and aimed to ensure that immigrants would transfer to English-language party cells, not according to their ethnicity but their place of employment or habitation. "Every Party member—irrespective of what language he speaks—must thru his activity show that he is a member of the Communist Party here in America," argued one writer, echoing a common refrain.[8]

In practice, this shift proved extremely difficult. The coordination and reorganization of membership led to a copious bureaucratic effort with detailed relocation lists that produced pitiful results. For many, the dissolution of their Language Federation was the excuse for abandoning the party altogether; others were not thrilled with the new organizational directives and disappeared for some time. The cleanup revealed the crisis of the communist movement as party membership plummeted in the months following the Fourth Convention: from 14,037 in September to 7,213 in October 1925.[9] It was not just a matter of numbers. The policy of Americanization was based on the idea that the old customs would evaporate and the realities of the present would produce a unified working class in which ethnic origins would be of minor importance. The only problem—by no means minor—was the paradoxical way, to the communist way of thinking, that immigrants themselves recast their own ethnic past in the American present. Their interest in, and emotional attachment to, the working-class movement in their country of origin went hand in hand with the shaping of an immigrant radical activism in the United States. This was inconceivable to the party leadership, leading to a constant tension with the Language Bureaus, which—despite their commitment to the party line—were never fully aligned with the prerequisites of party Americanization. In the words of the party, "our fractions are following the bourgeois organizations too much in keeping the workers occupied with problems of the home country only."[10]

Diasporic Communism

Greek American communists continued to be keenly interested in Greek developments and conceived of themselves as a point of reference for the multifaceted world of the Greek communist diaspora, as they were privileged to have a newspaper and a publishing house. *Empros* dedicated a whole page in every issue (from the mid-1920s the newspaper was published weekly) to correspondence from "Greek Proletarians Around the World." Letter writers, along with the newspaper's columnists writing under a pseudonym, described in dramatic terms the experiences of exploitation and praised the rare hopeful moments of working-class enlightenment by workers who up to that point had been indifferent to the ideas of class struggle. Even though *Empros*'s repetitive writing does not offer many surprises, the geographic dispersion of its readership provides a panorama of the Greek and Greek-speaking diaspora: immigrants from Asia Minor in Marseilles and Paris, Cypriot workers in London, intellectuals in Egypt, immigrants in Australia and Latin America, and Greek Bolsheviks in the Soviet Republics made up a reliable network of correspondents and readers. Of the 3,500 copies of each issue of *Empros*, 500 were circulated outside the USA, providing a detailed map of the Greek communist diaspora.[11]

This network became even more important in 1925, when an authoritarian regime outlawed the Communist Party of Greece. At that point, *Empros* was the most important Greek-language communist newspaper, and Greek American communists undertook a campaign to send material support to political prisoners who were exiled in the Aegean islands.[12] This allowed, for example, the exiles of Icaria, in 1926, to complement their ideological training with publications from the Ergatiko Vivliopōleio (Greek Workers Bookshop) that had been founded in Chicago.[13] These links led the Greek state to take note, for the first time, of the "vigorous" activities "of Greek communists in America." The Ministry of Foreign Affairs contacted the American embassy in Athens, requesting that measures be taken to "impose a publication ban on the Greek-language newspaper *Empros* in America, many copies of which are circulating in Greece." The embassy responded that this was impossible (for obvious reasons) and this led the Greek authorities to an equally doomed plan: they sent an expelled communist to the United States in order to combat the influence of the "Reds."[14]

The revived interest in Greek affairs was intensified when an internal crisis broke out in the Communist Party of Greece. Greek American communists acknowledged that "developments in our movement back in Greece have a commensurate impact on the Greek proletariat in America and especially on the class-conscious Greek workers."[15] According to the American communist movement, the class-conscious workers ought to act with "their gaze turned to the USA."[16] *Empros*'s coverage of developments in Greece (either of society in general or specifically communist affairs), the fervent solidarity drives for Greek political prisoners, and the overall orientation of the Greek Workers Educational Associations caused consternation in the party's higher echelons. On the other hand, the party's Greek Bureau argued that it knew best what captured the immigrants' attention. For example, at the end of 1927, the newspaper's editors decided against running a Comintern proclamation that would take up many pages, arguing that "it would hurt circulation."[17]

Such initiatives were at odds with the principles of democratic centralism and led to a conflict between Greek American communists and the Central Committee of the Workers (Communist) Party. The crisis had begun in May 1926 when the Greek Bureau had requested to transfer its headquarters from Chicago to New York City, maintaining that this would lead to a daily *Empros,* as the Greek American newspaper would step in and fill the gap left by the ban of *Rizospastēs*, the daily newspaper of the Communist Party of Greece. The request was rejected by the Central Committee, leading to conflict over a number of minor and major issues. Comparing the circulation of *Empros* with the *Daily Worker*, the Greek American communists were actually implying that they were more effective in reaching the "masses."[18] In this way, they were challenging the decision of the party to establish its headquarters in Chicago as proof of its Americanization (contrary to the cosmopolitan New York). Addressing Charles Ruthenberg, the party's secretary, Louis Chriss, a member of the Greek Bureau, sternly decried his proposals as "blackmail," warned him that "we can too use similar methods to settle matters," and concluded: "You never thought that the issues of the Greek Bureau and *Empros* were worth even half an hour of your valuable time."[19] The crisis was eventually defused, but incidents such as this contributed to a conviction among the party leadership that Greeks were "hard to control."[20] They were not the only ones. By the end of the 1920s, the demand for Americanization had sparked similar tensions in the Jewish, Armenian, Lithuanian, German, and powerful Finnish Bureaus.[21]

The result was the imposition of the will of the party. Under the auspices of democratic centralism, and with the encouragement of the Comintern, the autonomy of Language Bureaus was curtailed, and expressions of dissatisfaction were treated as expressions of anti-party sentiment. The Central Committee of the Workers (Communist) Party was not sympathetic to the requests of the Language Bureaus, and this was evident in the conscious effort to minimize immigrant presence in its composition. The foreign born constituted the vast majority of the membership, but they were not accordingly represented in the hierarchy of the party. Harvey Klehr's biographical analysis of the Central Committee's members highlights an "unnatural increase in the percentage of nonimmigrants" between 1922 and 1925.[22] This development coincided with the emergence of a new generation of revolutionary cadres with an immigrant background who had been radicalized in the United States. Observing strife within the Hungarian Bureau, John Pepper identified the divergent trends among the "veterans" and the "1919ers"—those who had joined the communist movement after the split in the Socialist Party.[23] The latter were younger, spoke better English, and were in full agreement with the politics of Bolshevization.

A similar internal crisis led to the renewal of the members of the Greek Bureau. The details are not that interesting, but what is striking is the constant turnover of members through successive resignations and reappearances, as well as the meteoric rise of new cadres who were totally unknown up to that point. At the heart of this organizational frenzy lay the question of Americanization. The younger generation was more attuned to the party's official line, causing the reaction of the bureau's older members. The decision to organize a public event against the Greek Liberal Party government, which was allied with the Greek American royalists, led to a decisive intervention by the party leadership. Accusing the Greek Bureau of nationalism, it ordered the expulsion of leading members such as Karolos Solounias (Charles Solon), who had argued in favor of keeping in touch with Greek developments and believed that the main issue was the orchestrated efforts by the Greek state (and the Greek Orthodox Church) to control immigrant communities in the United States.[24] The expulsion of Solounias was the first step in a total reorganization of the Greek Bureau; when, in 1933, the *Party Organizer* published its resolutions, there were no members left from the 1920s.[25]

Party Life

"Seven years old and stronger by the day." The cartoon on the front page of *Empros*, on 4 September 1926, celebrated the seventh anniversary of the American communist movement. It depicted a muscular kid working out with weights, stepping on a book bearing the title *Marxism*, and gazing at a small portrait of Lenin hanging on the wall.[26] This image reflected a shift. The fervent belief, back in 1919, in the imminence of a social revolution had given way to a patient and systematic effort through which the Communist Party would gain strength and prepare for the moment when the conditions would be ripe for action. Moreover, the seven-year-old kid's sturdy figure reflected how the communist movement perceived itself: as the youth of the world that carried a promise for the future to come. Finally, apart from the obvious motivational function of Lenin's portrait, the book at the kid's feet demonstrated the central role that revolutionary education played in the communist worldview.

The Greek American communists were feeling more powerful by the day. In 1926 they had been actively involved in a successful fur workers' strike in New York City, something that had bolstered their self-confidence. In 1927, the Greek Bureau reported significant gains: it owned two linotype machines; *Empros* was a daily newspaper; its circulation had surpassed 4,000 copies; the publications by the Greek Workers Bookshop had print runs ranging from 2,000 to 3,000 copies; and leaflets by the Greek Bureau were circulated on a number of issues, ranging from the legislation on the "foreign-born" to developments in Greece.[27] *Empros* was at the epicenter of this activity. The five hundred "guardians of *Empros*" provided a stable subscription base that secured its daily schedule, while the newspaper was circulated in more places than ever. The geography of Greek American communism expanded from cities with increased immigrant presence (New York, Chicago, and San Francisco), to Midwest industrial cities (Detroit and Pittsburgh), to working-class towns (Canton, Akron, Youngstown, Toledo, McKeesport, Cleveland, Wheeling), and to traditional strongholds of Greek immigration (such as Denver and Newark).

The local Greek Workers Educational Associations were the main expressions of Greek American communist cultural activities. Operating in rented halls or small buildings, the associations functioned along the lines of numerous educational or recreational immigrant clubs. They organized lectures, English-language lessons, excursions, theater performances, and dances. What set them apart was the systematic emphasis on the working-class dimension, as evinced in the Workers' Mandolin Orchestras, the Workers' Soccer Clubs, or the Workers' Theater Groups that advertised their activities in the pages of *Empros*. It was a close-knit social and cultural world, with Red weddings, babies named after Lenin, and restaurants like O Bolsevikos (The Bolshevik) in Denver. The daily gatherings at the Greek Workers Educational Association highlight a distinct working-class culture that provided its participants with a sense of security, with the feeling that they belonged to a collective with a strong sense of identity and deep social ties. When a member of the Greek Bureau had to be hospitalized in a sanatorium, the readers of *Empros* raised a thousand dollars on his behalf.[28]

Theater was the most popular expression of this distinct working-class identity. The "Red Stage" movement functioned as a metaphor for the capacity of the working class to rise and take a leading role in the narrative of social evolution. With minimal financial investment, plays were staged—based on Greek social novels marked as "fit to be staged"—that criticized bourgeois and petit bourgeois mores and attracted crowds that far exceeded the Workers Educational Associations' regular followers.[29] Theater also became the vehicle for the rise of a younger generation of Greek American radical intellectuals. Contrary to party cadres, who were self-educated, they often had some kind of formal education and were involved in the translation of theatrical plays or in the writing of Greek American proletarian short plays. Not many things are known about them, since the communist ethos of celebrating communal working-class effort led to the concealment of any biographical details or attributes that would set intellectuals apart from the rest. Theano Papazoglou-Margari is one exception. Born in Istanbul in 1906, she emigrated to the United States after the end of the Greco-Turkish War in 1922. By the mid-1920s she was already a member of the communist movement. She married Babis Margaris, who published translations in *Empros*, and became a leading figure of the workers' theater of that period. She is mentioned frequently but vaguely. She is described as "active," "organizing," and "tireless," which were the usual virtues that every party member should exhibit.[30]

Life in the party reflected how communists envisioned the future. Joining the communist movement demanded a high degree of selflessness; the frequent meetings and fundraising drives, public events, conferences, demonstrations, and celebrations made up a revolutionary calendar filled to the brim with the activities of the party, the labor union, the Workers' Educational Association, the Workers International Relief, the *Daily Worker*, and *Empros*. Burnout was not uncommon and there were many who left the party, in effect turning their involvement into a brief interlude of political experimentation.[31] Being a "Red" meant to wage battle on multiple fronts at once, and often, as Aileen Kraditor notes, those who joined the Left were outcasts and misfits.[32] As the communist movement became more and more rigid, members originating from the socialist world abandoned the world of radical politics. By the mid-1920s, the founding editors of *Ē Phonē tou Ergatou* had made a discreet exit, disagreeing with the transition from the Greek Socialist Union's tolerant ideological eclecticism to the monolithic Bolshevik Party.

For the newcomers and for those who remained active, constant activity went hand in hand with organizing, planning, and assessing, in a quest for the ideal synthesis between a "Russian revolutionary sweep," in the words of Joseph Stalin, and "American efficiency."[33] This was especially true for the members of the Greek Bureau. Their modest lifestyle (party wages ranged between ten and thirty dollars per week, which was what a worker would expect to make) was combined with absolute devotion to the cause and frequent relocations from one place to another according to the party's priorities, while ordinary members had to ask for permission to travel back to Greece.[34] The ideal communist embodied reliability, practicality, organizational competence, and persistence. The communist movement created its own trailblazers. Theodoros Tiriris, for example, was awarded the International Labor Defense medal for adding seventy-nine subscribers to the *Labor Defender* subscription list—even Stakhanovites, it seemed, needed an occasional acknowledgment of their work.[35]

"Taxisyneidēsia": Greek American Class Consciousness

Joining the communist movement gave one a unique sense of purpose. The emphasis placed on the significance of the working class in historical development, the Marxist interpretation of social phenomena, as well as an intrinsic belief that history moved toward a predefined end offered communists a feeling of superiority. In his introduction to a long-winded treatise with the ambitious title *Ta Eglēmata tou Politismou* (The crimes of civilization), Georgios Katsiolis emphasized how his work was a response to those who questioned whether a self-educated worker like himself could wrestle with such a complex project. Katsiolis had been active in the IWW and remained a devoted communist up to his expulsion in the late 1920s.[36] His treatise offers a panorama of American history from the eighteenth century until the forthcoming socialist revolution based on diverse sources, including Herodotus, Emma Goldman, the Old Testament, and Upton Sinclair. The chaotic amalgamation of anecdotes, quotes, and empirical observations had a single goal: to explain the "Capitalist System." Without this "diagnosis," the hoi polloi appear as victims. "The deceit of the masses continues unabated, but among Greeks it is truly terrifying."[37]

Katsiolis's selection of sources demonstrates his experiences in the precommunist world, when theoretical references were not confined to what eventually became a codified Marxism-Leninism. Today, it's extremely difficult to follow him, but on the other hand the author is a self-educated working-class radical who read a lot, relied on books that contained references to other foundational texts, and believed that scientific knowledge provided answers to all questions, regardless of their complexity. In this worldview, the protagonist of history is the class-conscious worker, the class-conscious producer of wealth. The word Katsiolis used—*taxisyneidētos* (class-conscious worker)—is an interesting one. It appeared for the first time in the vocabulary of Greek American communists in the mid-1920s and is a translation of the English term "class conscious" formed by taxē (class) and syneidētos (conscious). In Greece, it was never used; this was a Greek American term that reflected the immigrant adaptation of a Marxist lexicon that referred to questions of class struggle. The *taxisyneidētos* was a Promethean figure: he fought against capitalist exploitation in the present and belonged to those whose "minds started working and . . . eyes started seeing the radiant light of truth."[38]

This apocalyptic understanding of consciousness was a major part of the communist mindset as it constructed its opposite—the many, the majority of wage laborers, who were not interested in the ideas of class struggle. They were the "naïve," the "hypnotized," the "lethargic" or "sleeping" workers who could not see the obvious truth, which would serve their material interests. The extremely popular duality between "asleep" and "awake" (and, by extension, being "in the dark" or "seeing the light") revealed the Manichaean nature of communist thought. "Great is the capitalism and worthy of praise, how it manages to keep the worker blind," a member of the SLP exclaimed, after he went into a café where the workers were playing cards, indifferent to the ideas that would explain their plight.[39] This dualistic interpretation had no room for doubts about whether the workers' indifference or outright hostility to revolutionary convictions could be their own, entirely conscious choice. In their view, the worker was a field of battle between the bourgeoisie and his own working class and in this context often he was portrayed as lacking the capacity to make the right choice.

For Greek American radicals in the early twentieth century the explanation of immigrant indifference to class struggle was related to the precapitalist world that immigrants had left behind and to ignorance of the laws of capitalist production. However, in the 1920s, this argument could not stand. The end of mass immigration had signaled the end of the replenishment of the working class from abroad, while immigrants had already gone through years of exposure to harsh industrial and menial labor. In this context, a new interpretation came to dominate communist thought: the worker was bound by "emotions" that inhibited the evolution of class consciousness. When, in 1927, *Empros* appealed to its readers, emphasis was put on reason. "We do not appeal to emotions. . . . *Empros* underlines the simple truth that cannot be denied: the working class cannot disappear, because the disappearance of workers would signal the disappearance of humans from the face of the earth."[40] The constant juxtaposition of emotions and consciousness produced a rhetorical opposition between poison and the antidote that would lead to the great awakening. In an autobiographical statement, Emmanuel Fotinakis described his course in familiar terms. He was influenced by bourgeois newspapers that were "poisoning his mind" until he started reading treatises on social and historical issues that led him to join the Communist Party.[41]

The "antidote" or "remedy" to capitalism was workers' education. This entailed the interpretation of class exploitation, knowledge of the laws of social evolution, and a recognition of the historical mission of the working class. The importance that communists attributed to the educational process reflected older traditions of the socialist movement coupled with the influence of Lenin's writings on how class consciousness came "from the outside" and not merely as an outcome of material conditions. The *Empros* editor was obviously versed in these theoretical foundations when he insisted on "distinctive workers' education" as the ideal way to develop working-class consciousness.[42] "Organization and workers' education" was the slogan of the Workers Educational Association in Pittsburgh; in the pages of *Empros* strikes were called "the school of class struggle," party meetings "the school of communism," the Greek Workers Bookshop was named "the organizer and educator of the working class."[43] The Greek translation of the Workers Party statute began with the phrase "the meetings of the Workers Associations constitute an important school," while the structure of the statute itself—containing paradigmatic dialogues and a detailed guide on how to host a meeting—resembled a school textbook.[44] The Red Unions belonged to the Trade Union Educational League, while Workers Educational Associations were meeting points of those who had "subscribed to the ideas of class struggle."[45] The reader of *Ē Phonē tou Ergatou* who wrote "worker, this newspaper reveals to you the reason why you're wearing pants with holes in them" encompassed a long revolutionary tradition that linked emancipation with the significance of the printed word.[46]

The slogan on the back cover of books published by the Greek Workers Bookshop encapsulates the confluence between the revolutionary perception of historical time and the role of workers' education: "Read Today—Govern Tomorrow." The list of "books fit for workers" included "Marxist literature" translated from English, analysis on current political trends, and works by Greek authors. The books were priced for a working-class audience: for 35 cents one could get Lenin's *State and Revolution* (the first Greek translation was published in New York in 1920), for 25 cents one of the five thousand copies of the *Critique of the Gotha Program*, and for 15 cents the proletarian play *Gia to Psōmi kai tēn Leuteria* (For bread and liberty), written by a Greek working-class intellectual. The frequent publication of new titles (for example, six of them appeared in 1924 alone), the uniform design (the books were numbered, they had green covers, and the same image graced the back covers), as well as print runs that were generally between one and five thousand copies exhibit professionalism and care for maintaining the interest of the reading public.

The communist educational project was at the same time "emancipatory and rigid, open and intolerant."[47] Greek American communists came into contact with classic works of world literature as well as the main philosophical schools of thought; they attended meetings on the theory of evolution and the colonial history of Latin America; and they participated in a multifaceted system of knowledge, whose central tenet was the prospect of social emancipation. At the same time, this system was exclusionary, since it followed the regulatory framework of the interwar communist movement as it evolved through its internal conflicts. For example, by 1930, the works of Trotsky had been removed from the lists of the Greek Workers Bookshop. However, apart from individual examples, the communist system of knowledge operated under a rigid understanding of historical development.

The equation between the laws of social and biological evolution (along the parallel between Darwin and Marx) was a favorite topic of the Greek Workers Educational Associations, since it provided a deterministic interpretation that inevitably led to revolution. The proletarian bestseller of the 1920s was the Greek translation (by Christos Chrysovergis) of William Montgomery Brown's *Communism and Christianism: Analyzed and Contrasted from the Marxian and Darwinian Points of View.*[48] It featured an impressive cover: a rising sun was combined with the hammer and sickle and the slogan (in Greek) "Banish Gods from Skies and Capitalists from Earth." As Peter Kivisto has noted, emphasis on the natural sciences (and especially on Darwin's theory of evolution) "added credibility and significance" to the intrinsic belief that capitalist contradictions would lead to new stage in historical development.[49] The psychological dimension was of paramount importance. For Greek American communists—individuals who often were marginalized by their respective communities—the formalistic and unambiguous "proletarian education" functioned as a sanctuary that bolstered their self-confidence. The many were ignorant, whereas they possessed the hermeneutical keys to the inner workings of history.

Ignorance was often equated with religion. Greek American communists attacked "religious and patriotic sentiments" not only because they hindered class consciousness but also because they intensified the immigrants' ties with the Old World.[50] On the other hand, they reproduced a deterministic worldview that emulated elements of the Orthodox tradition: the battle between the forces of good and evil, the quest for justice, and the role of the revelatory moment in one's biography. The references to the "scientific gospel of Marx and Engels" reveal the impact and resilience of a religious mindset that substituted Orthodox gospels with materialistic ones. The Greek American communists carried with them the world that had shaped their intellectual and emotional background. This was the Old World of orthodox traditions and close-knit communities around the Church. The self-referential and cohesive communist microcosm functioned as a substitute for religious sentiment. This parallel did not escape contemporary commentators. In a lengthy report to the Greek Bureau, Louis Chriss noted alarming levels of anti-intellectualism within the party ranks and the concurrent "fetishistic celebration of the 100 percent ignorant proletarian" that led to new members' "religious" passage into the party.[51] The movement that had aimed to do away with religious influence was building its own system of contemplation and ritual, with its own belief in dogma—and this was not exclusive to Greek American communism or to communism in the United States of America.

Nor was this the sole contradiction. Despite claims to a "distinct" working-class culture, the Greek American communist world was not as separate as it thought it was. Those who attended the great dance organized by *Empros* in October 1926 enjoyed a concert by a mandolin orchestra, readings of revolutionary poetry, and a performance of the international workers' hymn, but they also witnessed a traditional theatrical monologue from Crete, Charleston music, and "dancing until dawn."[52] Aside from reminding us that communists knew how to party, such events demonstrate that there was a dialogue going on between the ethnically defined working-class culture and an emergent American popular culture that was accessible to immigrants. Seen in this light, the communists were not as different as they themselves probably thought from the vast majority of immigrants who encountered novel venues of Americanization. Purchasing a radio or a gramophone, watching a Hollywood movie or a boxing match, did not automatically make one "an American." However, these activities are significant because they reveal a dynamic interplay that transcended the narrow limits of ethnic communities in the early twentieth century.

By the late 1920s, the advertisement section of *Empros* differed significantly from the small entries that had appeared a decade earlier in *Ē Phonē tou Ergatou*. If back then they had concerned forthcoming publications and medical supplements of dubious efficacy, they were now echoing the vocabulary of mass consumption: cigarettes, radios, and off-the-rack garments. These were American products targeting immigrant demographics, and so their ad copy had been translated into Greek. The influential and liberal *Ethnikos Kēryx* (National herald) included advertisements about electricity providers and phone services, sales in auto dealerships, classifieds from credit institutions, pictures of mannequins from "modern" clothing stores, and illustrated pages about the usefulness of home appliances.

The Greek American communists did not acknowledge the rise of consumerism. The reason was simple: if they admitted that immigrants were benefiting from the general sense of affluence then they would have to recognize the limits of their perception of the worker as a synonym of the "wretched of the earth." Social inequality was still prevalent, but the era of intensive exploitation and the expendability of human life seemed to belong to the past. The rise in workers' wages, pay hikes linked with productivity, and bank loans permitted thousands to participate, for the first time under such terms, in the reborn American Dream. A house of one's own, even if it was mortgaged, seemed to many people like the final escape from the hardships of the past. These transformations mostly affected the immigrant working class, who had linked the prospect of a final settlement in the USA with the betterment of their living standards. The prosperous turn of the economy seemed to suggest that the era of nomadic work, of insecurity, and of exploitation to the point of exhaustion was finally over. The rail network was complete and new mining methods led thousands of workers to settle in major cities along the West Coast, putting an end to a long period of hard and hazardous work. However, these transformations challenged the central tenets of communist thought concerning the incompatibility between the interests of capital and labor. Despite recognizing postwar capitalist stabilization, the communist movement insisted that conditions for the majority of the working class were worsening. *Empros* kept using the same old stereotypes of the hard life of the working class, ignoring any improvement in work conditions or the opportunities created by financial prosperity.

This was at odds with workers' own experiences. As we shall see in the next chapter, the increase of small ethnic businesses after World War I was an undeniable reality in the Greek American communities. The attempt of the communists to confirm the prophesies about constantly worsening living standards in the United States led them to theoretical leaps that treated the world of small business and the world of wage labor as equivalent. In the language of the Greek Bureau, the owners of small businesses belonged to the "proletarianized petite bourgeoise." However, the prospect of an escape from the working class stirred even the hearts of those who spoke on its behalf. The New York branch of the Workers Party's Greek Federation organized a lecture on whether "communists are allowed to own a business or think about opening one."[53] *Ē Phonē tou Ergatou* carried advertisements proving that some members had already answered in the affirmative: "When you pass by Newark, visit the café of c[omrade] Irakleous Nikolaou, The Garden of Eden" or "Comrades in New York and Environs, if you want virgin olive oil, olives, cheese, and salted foods, as well as every Greek product, come find them in c[omrade] Nikogiannis's shop."[54] The interplay between class and ethnicity produced unpredictable results. Sometimes they challenged the communists' perceptions, sometimes they confirmed them emphatically.

Organizing the Unorganizable

On 17 November 1925, Jay Lovestone, head of the Organizational Section of the Workers (Communist) Party Central Committee, was apprising a certain "John" of the following brilliant plan: the party would charter a ship that would carry a delegation of American workers to Leningrad in order to partake in the international convention of "Red" labor unions.[55] This move would reflect the recent successes of the communist movement in "organizing unorganized workers." To name a recent example, Lovestone referred to "one thousand Greek workers in New York City" who were taking part in a strike in the fur industry. His enthusiasm was entirely justified. For years, the American labor movement had been in retreat; in 1925 the number of workers who had gone on strike was one tenth of what it had been in 1919. In the foundries, in transportation, and in the steel industry, the number of strikes barely exceeded 60, whereas in 1919 they had numbered 850.[56] The assault by employer associations on the right to organize, antiradical legislation, and the rise of employer paternalism, which identified a company's prosperity with the prosperity of its workers, led to a crisis of radical and nonradical labor unions alike.[57] Greek American communists were not particularly visible in the labor movement. The readers of *Empros* and the members of Workers Educational Associations would report on the harsh realities of wage labor, but this was rarely translated into concrete action. The Greek Bureau did not have much to report aside from some organizing efforts among "food workers" across the country.[58]

With this in mind, we can only imagine the excitement on the morning of 27 October 1925 when a strike broke out in the Greek fur workshops that were scattered in the narrow alleys of Manhattan's Lower West Side. Greeks had been active in the fur industry since the early twentieth century. Immigrants from the fur-producing city of Kastoria (part of the Ottoman empire, and after 1913 part of Greece) brought with them their expertise, and by 1915 twenty-five Greek-owned workshops were active in New York City. After World War I, the growing demand for fur coats and fur linings in cuffs and collars led to the sector's overall expansion. Greek workshops multiplied from 144 in 1925 to 250 in 1929: 250. Opening a workshop did not require significant investment, whereas gains could be substantial due to low wages, the intensive nature of the work, and a demand that was constantly on the rise. The Greek fur workshops were small enterprises (operating out of small one- and two-room apartments) and their growth was based on cheap labor provided by fellow Greek workers.[59] The vast majority of Greek workshops were owned by immigrants from Kastoria. Among the approximately one thousand employees, there were two visible groups: immigrants who hailed from Kastoria, and immigrants who hailed from Istanbul and Asia Minor. The boundary between owners and workers was often fuzzy, since many transitioned from one category to the other depending on the circumstances, while in most small workshops the employer was working alongside their employees.

Greek workers had nothing to do with the International Fur Workers Union nor, most importantly, with the militant, powerful Fur Workers Joint Board in New York. Dominated by Jewish labor, the latter in 1912 had succeeded in imposing a closed-shop system; in order to be hired, a worker had to carry a union card in his or her pocket. A shining example of the American labor movement, the Joint Board represented the diversity of Jewish radicalism and brought together radicals of every stripe, including anarchists, socialists, and communists. The growth of the Greek fur workshops posed a threat to its power. This became evident in 1920 when a thirty-week strike was defeated; the Greek workshops were "working day and night" keeping the market going and offering an alternative to the embattled Jewish enterprises.[60] This experience led to a discussion in the Joint Board on the necessity of organizing the unorganized Greek labor force. If not, the union would not be able to secure its power over the "organized" workshops, since the "unorganized" ones would be able to secure bigger and bigger orders thanks to the intensive exploitation of labor and the overall lack of any regulation in their part of the sector. As a union organizer wrote in June 1925, "the real problem lies in the Greek contract workshops, which up to now the union has not been able to organize."[61]

For years this prospect belonged in the realm of fantasy. "Their souls belong to their priest and their bodies to their employer. They do not speak a word of English. They have no idea what a labor union is!" This was the response from an exasperated and experienced union organizer to a suggestion concerning the organization of Greek workers.[62] On the other hand, a younger generation of communist unionists who were actively engaged in the New York Joint Board leadership were determined to carry on. The New York Joint Board reduced membership fees for Greek workers to one third and established, with the help of Greek American communists, a Committee for Greek workers.[63] The results were encouraging: by the fall of 1925 around 420 men and 300 women had been organized.[64] The next step was the decision to strike. On 27 October 1925 picket lines were formed blocking the entrances of Greek-owned fur workshops. The strike had been carefully planned. If it lasted long enough, the small Greek workshops were in danger of losing valuable orders for the winter high season. This determined the outcome, as individual owners came to an initial agreement with the Joint Board. The strike was called off, and the two sides agreed to initiate a discussion on a collective agreement for the whole sector in January 1926. It was a significant success for the union and the communists responded with enthusiasm.[65] In response, the Greek employers established the United Fur Manufacturers Association (UFMA), in order "to protect the interests of the association's members."[66]

The Joint Board communist leadership believed that this initial success would pave the way for the expansion and consolidation of its power across the sector.[67] Following the Greek strike, it began preparations for a general strike. The list of fourteen demands focused on securing steady employment for union members throughout the year and the adoption of a forty-hour workweek, which would be reduced to thirty-two hours during low season.[68] Compared with the significant rollbacks in labor demands during the 1920s, the Joint Board's goals—which included, for instance, an unemployment fund paid for by employers—were remarkably ambitious. The socialist *Jewish Daily Forward* accused the communists of pursuing utopian demands that equaled the complete appropriation of the means of production.[69] The competition between socialists and communists added more complexity to the already complicated world of labor. Greek and Jewish workshops and workers, organized and unorganized workshops and workers, ties of ethnicity and ethnic competition, class antagonism and common ethnic interests, differentiations between skilled workers, gender diversity, and ideological differences—all defined the extremely dynamic and fluid fur industry.

The general strike was scheduled for 16 February 1926. It evolved in the words of Benjamin Gitlow into "a very bitter struggle."[70] For the next four months, until June, the Lower West Side witnessed frequent clashes between strikers, scabs, mounted policemen, and goons in the service of the workshops' owners. The concentration of so many small workshops in a few city blocks defined the form of the conflict. The strikers did not gather outside factory gates and were not supervised by the police, as they were when a strike was announced in the big factories, but rather unfolded in a constant hide-and-seek. A tip about a scab workshop would result in a raid by a group of strikers. After a certain point, the outcome of the strike depended on which side would have physical control of the "fur market." The mainstream immigrant press, such as the Greek-language *Ethnikos Kēryx*, covered the strike on a daily basis, mentioning the number of workers wounded or arrested and whether any "clubs and other weapons" had been used.[71] What is interesting here is not merely the frequency of these incidents but that both sides chose to escalate the conflict, indifferent to the presence of law enforcement, who appeared on the scene when things had spiraled so far out of control that it was impossible to remain absent.

Ben Gold, the communist superstar of the fur workers' union, had warned employers that they were in for "a lesson they would never forget."[72] Armed striker squads were making good on his promise. "The previous week, the whole district between the 6th and 7th avenues, from the 8th street all the way up to the 34th, was literally terrorized by Greek strikers who raided shops suspected of employing scabs," boasted *Empros*.[73] The violence reflected the accumulated tensions in the small workshops. Greek workers, the same ones who had been thought "unorganizable," appeared to be the militant vanguard of the Joint Board. In his retrospective anticommunist memoir, Benjamin Gitlow remembered them as "fearless and adept fighters, exceptional users of the knife, the razor, and other weapons."[74] The language of the Joint Board Greek Committee employed military analogies, with its members being "brave and fearless warriors" in a protracted confrontation between the armies of labor and capital.[75] Even though it is not always easy to discern, this militancy seems to be the product of years of interethnic exploitation combined with cultural affinities between workers and employers. In the world of the fur workshops, the (always male) boss was not a distant figure; his presence was felt on a daily basis, his injustices were felt as personal insults, and the ethnic ties he shared with workers underlined their feeling of being treated in an unjust manner.

Fur Workers or Greek Fur Workers?

As the 1926 general strike unfolded, one thing was certain: the Greek fur workshops would be organized. The question was along what lines. The Greek American communists, who had been instrumental in the unionization drives up until then, believed that the only way forward was the organization of Greek workers in the New York Joint Board. This would signal the end of ethnic autonomy in the sector, as the Greek-owned workshops would be obliged to follow the rules that applied in the rest of the industry. For the United Fur Manufacturers Association, this would be catastrophic. The Greek employer association promoted a different plan—a separate labor union for Greek workers based on the idea of the shared interests between workers and employers of the same ethnicity. The tension between the two proposals encompassed two incompatible understandings of the relation between ethnicity and class. The communists spoke in the name of a single working-class "nation," and the Joint Board operated as a meeting point of transethnic solidarity. The Greek American employers responded to this by invoking the familiar idea of common ancestry and common interests against the enemies of the nation, who, in the fur industry, happened to be not only "Reds" but "Jews."

The radicals were familiar with the man who took up the task of confronting the Joint Board. Ioannis Rompapas, native of Kastoria and erstwhile editor of the *Revolutionary Almanac*, in his new role as president of the UFMA, argued in favor of a "separate" organization for Greek workers. His rationale was based on the "distinct" position of Greeks in the fur sector.[76] Without referring explicitly to Jewish employers and workers, Rompapas claimed that "foreigners" sought to control Greek business ventures and, in order to succeed, took advantage of the workers' legitimate complaints. In this context, the strikes and the prospect of Joint Board control over the Greek workshops would inevitably marginalize Greek presence in the industry. In order to avoid this, the UFMA proposed the establishment of a separate Greek local, which would ensure the prosperity of everyone, employers and workers.

Rompapas was not speaking in a void. Despite the Joint Board success, the Greek fur workers were divided. "Patriotism" appealed to workers who were either indifferent or hostile to the communist unionizing efforts. This becomes evident in consistent Joint Board efforts to equate the idea of shared ethnic interests with exploitation: "It means fifty hours of work per week and wages that are not enough to buy food. . . . [P]atriotism cannot fill an empty belly."[77] Responding to Rompapas, Ioannis Papagiannis, a labor organizer for the Joint Board Greek Committee, underlined that Greek and Jewish employer associations had worked together during the strike and therefore workers were doing exactly the same, seeking unity based on their material interests.[78] A *Daily Worker* special strike issue called on workers to "not be fooled" by the Greek employers' appeals to workers' "honor," but on the contrary to use that "honor" in the service of class solidarity.[79] The Joint Board appropriated the employers' vocabulary as well as the Greek tradition of *filotimo* (honor), but they recontextualized the ethnicity aspect, attempting to link immigrant descent with class organization.

The shared ancestry and familial networks, the participation of workers and employers in the same local ethnic associations, and the fluidity between workers and employers all formed a network of relationships that functioned completely at odds with the communists' perception of a clear-cut antagonism between capital and labor. Immigrants' Old World backgrounds proved to be pivotal in the development of unionizing activities. Research carried out by Joanna Karvonides-Nkosi has demonstrated that in 1925, among the organized Greek fur workers, only 10 percent had any connection with the vicinity of Kastoria.[80] By contrast, workers from Asia Minor and elsewhere proved much more receptive to the ideas of union organization as they did not have to face employers who came from the same vicinity as them. Seventeen of the twenty-two known members of the 1925 strike committee were from Asia Minor and the east Aegean islands.[81]

Despite appeals to workers from Kastoria to break ties with the UFMA, the idea of a separate Greek union was gaining ground.[82] Events unfolded quickly following the end of the strike in June 1926. The result was a major victory for the Joint Board. The settlement (which included a separate agreement with the UFMA) provided for a forty-hour workweek, wage increases, regulation of overtime work, prohibition of contract workshops, and layoffs for scabs.[83] The moment of triumph though was followed by an internal crisis as the conservative American Federation of Labor (AFL) turned against the communist-controlled Joint Board. The publication of a telegram by Charles Ruthenberg to Benjamin Gitlow, stipulating how the Joint Board should react at a critical juncture of the negotiations, signaled the beginning of the end of the sector's communist leadership.[84] On 19 July 1926, the AFL commenced a long legal and political tug-of-war for control of the Joint Board.

At the same time, Greek workers started to feel anxious about the future. The June agreement targeted contract workshops; if it were implemented in September, when production would start in earnest, hundreds would be left without work. The defeat of the communists in the Joint Board gave rise to a systematic anti-communist campaign in the Greek-language press that quickly took on an anti-Semitic hue. "The problem of the Greek workers is to organize in their own interests and not in the interest of the Jewish Association," wrote a leading member of UFMA in the conservative *Atlantis*.[85] In August 1926 a new union was born: the Brotherhood of Greek Fur Workers. The Brotherhood challenged the jurisdiction of the Joint Board Greek Committee, and this permitted the UFMA to claim exemption from the terms of the June 1926 agreement.[86] In the meantime, the new anti-communist Joint Board leadership recognized the Brotherhood as a separate Local (Local 70) under the jurisdiction of the Joint Board, implementing the Greek employers' wishes for a separate regulation of their relations with their workers.

Local 70 admitted workers from workshops whose owners were either Greek or of Greek descent—a vague requirement that grew vaguer still with every passing year. In practice, its establishment inaugurated a ten-year-long period of close relations (often with a financial bent) between unionists and employers based on the idea of common ethnic interests. Apart from hailing from the same vicinity in Greece, the new leadership of Local 70 had one more thing in common with the employer association, the United Fur Manufacturers Association—a distrust of "Reds" and "Jews." Both the UFMA and Local 70 attacked the "Bolsheviks," thus contributing to the emergence of a persistent anti-communist vein within the Greek American community. This was based on the perception of communism as a double threat: a threat against Greek interests, as in the case of the fur strike, and a threat against the Greek presence in the United States. When, during the 1926 strike, *Ethnikos Kēryx* announced that it would stop carrying announcements by the communist-led Greek Workers Educational Associations, Dimitrios Kallimachos emphasized the perils of communism. "A small number of anarchists are trying to . . . fool law-abiding Greek workers," he wrote, and as a result "Greeks are up there on the Black List of America!"[87] The significance of these columns transcends the narrow limits of the fur workers' strike. Kalli-machos was laying the foundations of Greek anti-communism in the United States. According to him, radical practices were inherently anti-American, and as such they put in danger the integration of Greek immigrants into the United States. In this context, the outcome of the 1926 strike was ideal. The organization of the workers under the conservative leadership of the AFL served as proof of their Americanization, while the establishment of Local 70 emphasized the common interests between Greeks, regardless of class.

Faced with these developments, the communists were left with limited choices. The initial efforts by the Joint Board to convince Greek workers not to join the Brotherhood of Greek Fur Workers met with limited success, especially after the expulsion of Gold and his associates.[88] In Local 70, Greek American communists formed an opposition group, but their influence was limited. On the other hand, the strike activities in the fur industry brought for the first time Greek American communists into contact with hundreds of workers, men and women. The organizational gains were obvious: fur workers became the backbone of Greek American communism. Among them, there was a new protagonist, the female workers who did most of certain stages of production such as sewing the linings. Hundreds of Greek women had joined the union in 1925. Up to that point, they were invisible—mentions of them in the mainstream immigrant press are virtually nonexistent. With this in mind, the fact that four women were among the twelve signatories of the Joint Board Greek Committee's strike procla-mation in February 1926 was a turning point.[89] For the first time, female labor was becoming visible, challenging a long tradition that perceived women's work as occasional or supplementary to men's. At the same time, the union's vocabulary, as well as that of the communists, highlighted limits and contradictions. "Manliness," a synonym for militancy, consistency, and an uncompromising stance, was the measure according to which women workers were judged and praised during the strike's day-to-day activities.

The wider picture emphasizes the existence and development of multiple contradictions. The Greek employers and workers perceived the Jews as antagonistic, the relatively larger units in the fur industry were hostile to small contract workshops that appeared and disappeared seasonally, and in the Joint Board the clash between the socialist old guard and the younger communist workers played right into the hands of the AFL. Moreover, in the fur sector's tightly knit society, the distance between the specialized "operators," who sewed the different fur pieces on a garment, and the rel-atively less specialized "cutters," who cut the raw material into pieces, was growing because of the differences between those who defended the labor union and those who believed that their interests were the same as their employers.

Faced with these contradictions, the Greek American communists attempted to counter them by invoking a rhetoric of ethnic solidarity and class unity. The Greek strikers celebrated their victory in October 1925 wearing their traditional folk costumes, while the establishment of the Joint Board Greek Committee recognized the significance of shared ethnicity. At the same time, it sought to transcend it, by organizing Greek workers in a multiethnic labor union. What the militant union organizers had failed to take into account, or had grossly underestimated, was the ingenuity of Greek employers in suggesting an alternative way of organizing the workers: a separate Greek local that would remain under their control. This development caught the communists by surprise, since it challenged one of their basic assumptions—that workers' organizing could only lead to *taxisyneidēsia*, to working-class consciousness.

Nonrevolutionary Times

Between 1919 and 1929, American communism changed significantly. The earlier Socialist Party years and the 1919 split concerned fewer and fewer people, the world of ethnic communism was striving to adapt to the policies of Americanization, and Bolshevization had deprived the communist movement of the adventurous spirit of earlier radical traditions. However, the most important change was the shift concerning the prospect of a social revolution. "The tactic of corrupting parts of the working class will continue and will drive parts of the working class to the right," noted Bertram Wolfe, director of the Party School in New York City (and later, during the Cold War, an anti-communist theorist). "This situation will continue as long as American capitalism is on the up-grade and continues its briberies."[90] American communists were trying to reconcile their faith in an imminent financial crisis with the undeniable reality of high growth rates, lower unemployment rates, and the spread of mass consumption. Was American capitalism an exception to the general rule of postwar transition? This question provoked an interesting debate within the movement. Its outcome, though, was decided outside the United States.

In early 1929, the leadership of the, recently renamed, Communist Party of the United States of America (CPUSA) visited Moscow to appear before a Comintern committee commissioned to examine the "American question." The latter's members revealed the importance that the global revolutionary headquarters ascribed to developments in the engine of global capitalism. Presided over by Joseph Vissarionovich Stalin, the Comintern heard opposing arguments regarding the prospects for the American economy. Stalin's speeches on the matter indicated the abandonment of earlier Comintern positions on the impetus and momentum of postwar American capitalism. "I think the moment is not far off," the Soviet leader said with his customary didactic tone, "when a revolutionary crisis will develop in America."[91] This readjustment was not based on some prediction of the 1929 Wall Street Crash; it had more to do with the internal strife in the Soviet Communist Party and the defeat of Nikolai Bukharin. Nonetheless, it produced a clear result: the expulsion of Jay Lovestone, the party's general secretary who had argued that American capitalism did not face an imminent crisis and was sympathetic to the positions of Bukharin.

These developments had an impact on the microcosm of Greek American communism. The question of the Communist Party's Americanization had already sparked different opinions, leading to an internal crisis in the Greek Bureau. The rise of antagonistic communist groups (Lovestone formed the Right Opposition, while a Left Opposition followed Leon Trotsky's line) intensified centrifugal forces and led to the fragmentation of the Greek American communist movement. At the end of the 1920s, it was divided in three main factions: the CPUSA Greek Bureau (which published *Empros*); a Greek American Left Opposition group centered around food workers in New York City; and a Lovestone group formed by Louis Chriss, the former editor of *Empros*, and Giannis Papagiannis, a fur worker. These factions revealed the crisis of a movement that had stumbled on an uncomfortable truth. Its potential audience was not enamored with the end of capitalism but with its imminent triumph. The typewritten "investment" pamphlets circulating at the time, promising to reveal the secret about "How to Get Rich," carried their own "revolutionary" promise: a promise that appeared to appeal to many more than those interested in the communists' revolutionary program.[92]

Notes

1. John Pepper, "Problems of the Party," *The Worker*, 26 May 1923, 5.
2. Draper, *American Communism and Soviet Russia*, 59.
3. Communist Party of the USA, *Thesis and Resolutions*, 80; Zumoff, The Communist International, 172–77.
4. Workers (Communist) Party of America, *The Fourth National Convention*, 87.
5. Zangwill, *The Melting Pot*, 37; Lenin, "Capitalism and Workers' Immigration," 454–57.
6. *Ē Phonē tou Ergatou*, 28 April 1923, 4.
7. "To What Extent Do the Language Press Reflect the Party Campaigns?" (1930), RGASPI, f. 515, op. 1, d. 2003, l 20; Communist Party of the USA, *Thesis and Resolutions*, 81.
8. "Away with Group 'Psychology,'" *The Party Organizer*, March 1930, 12.
9. Draper, *American Communism and Soviet Russia*, 187.
10. "How Communists Work amongst the Foreign Born," RGASPI, f. 515, op. 1, d. 1221, l. 4.
11. "Statement to the National Executive Committee of the Workers Communist Party," (September 1926), RGASPI, f. 515, op. 1, d. 694, l. 131.

12. YDIA/MFA, 1928/A/2/A.
13. Stinas, *Anamnēseis*, 115.
14. YDIA/MFA, 1927, 4.3.
15. *Rizospastēs*, 29 December 1927, 4.
16. "The Work of the Communist Fractions in Fraternal Organizations" (1929), RGASPI, f. 515, op. 1, d. 1682, l. 22.
17. Ellis Chryssos to Jay Lovestone, n.d., RGASPI, f. 515, op. 1, d. 1049, l. 54–55.
18. M.S. Pandiri to Charles Ruthenberg (12 May 1926), RGASPI, f. 515, op. 1, d. 689, l. 18–20.
19. Chriss to Charles Ruthenberg (July 1927), RGASPI, f. 515, op. 1, d. 1049, l. 45.
20. Storch, *Red Chicago*, 87.
21. "On the Right-Wing Opposition in the Lithuanian Publishing Associations" (1931), RGASPI, f. 515, op. 1, d. 2247, l. 72, and "Central Control Commission Resolution on Factional Situation in the Armenian Fraction in New York" (1931), RGASPI, f. 515, op. 1, d. 2338, l. 78.
22. Klehr, *The Communist Experience in America*, 70.
23. Sakmyster, *Red Conspirator*, 13.
24. Minutes of Central Control Commission (19 June 1934), RGASPI, f. 515, op. 1, d. 3506, l. 43–44.
25. "Plan of Work of Greek Buro [*sic*] of the CC," *Party Organizer* 10 (October 1933), 30–31.
26. *Empros*, 4 September 1926, 1.
27. "Questionnaire to Language Fraction Bureaus" (1927), RGASPI, f. 515, op. 1, d. 1179, l. 12–15.
28. M.S. Pandiri to Charles Ruthenberg (12 May 1926), RGASPI, f. 515, op. 1, d. 689, l. 20.
29. "Dramatic Performance," *Saloniki-Greek Press (Chicago)*, 1 February 1934, 4.
30. "Help Victims of White Terror in Greece," *Labor Defender*, March 1929, 61.
31. RGASPI, f 515, op. 1, Delo d., l.3; Draper, *American Communism and Soviet Russia*, 196.
32. Kraditor, *The Radical Persuasion*, 22.
33. Stalin, "The Foundations of Leninism," 194.
34. Minutes of the Greek Bureau of the Workers Communist Party of America (10 March 1925), RGASPI, f. 515, op. 1, d. 560, l. 51–52.
35. "Comrade Theodore Tiriris," *Labor Defender*, June 1930, 48.
36. Georgios Katsiolis and Joe Marko, "The Labor Movement of Greece," *Industrial Pioneer*, September 1921, 38–40.
37. Katsiolis, *Ta eglēmata tou politismou*, 8.
38. Marcy, *Oikonomologikes Kouventes*, 1.
39. *Organōsis*, 15 September 1923, 2.
40. *Empros*, 1 January 1927, 1.
41. "Why I Joined the Communist Party," RGASPI, f. 515, op. 1, d. 2945, l. 11–16.
42. *Empros*, 6 November 1926, 6.
43. *Empros*, 4 December 1926, 5.
44. *Katastatikon tou Ergatikou Kommatos tēs Amerikēs*.
45. Fried, *Communism in America*, 44.
46. *Ē Phonē tou Ergatou*, 13 January 1923, 3.
47. Weitz, *Creating German Communism*, 279.
48. Brown, *Kommounismos kai Christianismos*.
49. Kivisto, *Immigrant Socialists*, 152–54.
50. *Empros*, 26 April 1927, 5.
51. "A Little Self-Criticism," RGASPI, f 515, op. 1, d. 2211, l. 215–21.
52. *Empros*, 30 October 1926, 4.
53. *Ē Phonē tou Ergatou*, 3 February 1923, 4.
54. *Ē Phonē tou Ergatou*, 19 and 26 May 1923, 4.
55. Jay Lovestone to John (17 November 1925), RGASPI, f. 515, op. 1, d. 443, l. 52.
56. Rand School, *The American Labor Yearbook 1927*, 101–2.

57. Cohen, *Making a New Deal*, 162–83.
58. Greek Section (1925), RGASPI, f. 515, op. 1, d. 446, l. 19.
59. Karvonides-Nkosi, *Greek Immigrants in the Fur Manufacturing Industry*, 305.
60. Foner, *The Fur and Leather Workers Union*, 96.
61. Karvonides-Nkosi, *Greek Immigrants in the Fur Manufacturing Industry*, 402; Rand School, *The American Labor Yearbook 1926*, 143.
62. Gold, *Memoirs*, 41.
63. Foner, *The Fur and Leather Workers Union*, 161.
64. Karvonides-Nkosi, *Greek Immigrants in the Fur Manufacturing Industry*, 420.
65. Ben Gold to Charles Ruthenberg (1 November 1925), RGASPI, f. 515, op. 1, d. 514, l. 183.
66. *Atlantis*, 30 October 1925, 5.
67. Report (6 January 1926), RGASPI, f. 515, op. 1, d. 816, l. 1.
68. Foner, *The Fur and Leather Workers Union*, 180.
69. Schneider, *The Workers (Communist) Party and American Trade Unions*, 82.
70. Benjamin Gitlow to Charles Ruthenberg (4 February 1926), RGASPI, f. 515, op. 1, d. 713, l. 10.
71. *Ethnikos Kēryx*, 19 February 1926, 3; 15 March 1926, 3.
72. "Meeting of the CEC Needle Trades Committee" (4 February 1926), RGASPI, f. 515, op. 1, d. 814, l. 57.
73. *Empros*, 6 March 1926, 1.
74. Gitlow, *I Confess*, 347–48.
75. *Ethnikos Kēryx*, 18 February 1926, 3.
76. *Atlantis*, 27 February 1926, 4.
77. *Empros*, 25 September 1926, 5.
78. *Ethnikos Kēryx*, 6 March 1926, 5.
79. Karvonides-Nkosi, *Greek Immigrants in the Fur Manufacturing Industry*, 430.
80. Karvonides-Nkosi, *Greek Immigrants in the Fur Manufacturing Industry*, 440.
81. Karvonides-Nkosi, *Greek Immigrants in the Fur Manufacturing Industry*, 500.
82. *Empros*, 13 March 1926, 5.
83. Foner, *The Fur and Leather Workers Union*, 240–41.
84. Charles Ruthenberg to Benjamin Gitlow (14 April 1926), RGASPI, f. 515, op. 1, d. 713, l. 20–21.
85. *Atlantis*, 12 August 1926, 5.
86. Minutes of National Committee of Needle Trades (3 March 1927), RGASPI, f. 515, op. 1, d. 1200, l. 7.
87. *Ethnikos Kēryx*, 22 March 1926, 4.
88. *Empros*, 18 September 1926, 1.
89. *Ethnikos Kēryx*, 18 February 1926, 3.
90. Draper, *American Communism and Soviet Russia*, 278.
91. Communist Party of the USA, *Stalin's Speeches on the American Communist Party*, 20.
92. *Atlantis*, 1 October 1928. National Daily Greek Newspaper Records, Box 26.2, Greek Banking Corporations, 1929–1930, HSP.

CHAPTER 3

CRISIS AND REVOLUTION

The Arthritis Doctrine

"The Great Depression changed everything," Vassiliki Lyberopoulos reminisced years later. She went on to say that "for most of us who was poor, the Depression was like this damned arthritis I got. Nobody get real excited about it because it don't come all of a sudden, like a heart attack. It come slow and you always hope it's going to go away."[1] The Great Depression affected the everyday life of the Lyberopoulos family. Up to that point, Apostolos and Vassiliki Lyberopoulos were proud of the fact that they had attained the American Dream. During the 1920s, Apostolos, like many others, had taken advantage of the favorable financial climate to open a small restaurant in a working-class suburb of Chicago, leaving behind a life of wage slavery spent in shoeshine parlors and kitchens. "The Great Depression," though, "changed everything."

The crisis initially affected the restaurant's patrons, but it soon became apparent in the small establishment's meager earnings. Faced with imminent bankruptcy and eviction from the tiny apartment they lived in with their children, Vassiliki Lyberopoulos disregarded her husband's objections and started working in the restaurant. This brief episode is merely a miniscule piece in the grand mosaic of events that ensued after the 1929 stock market crash. However, it provides an insight into the myriad changes in the lives of millions, and into the alternative strategies they had to employ in order to survive in an environment of prolonged deprivation. The Great Depression truly "changed everything," including radically altering the social and political milieu in the United States.

For millions, the Great Depression did not begin on the day of the Wall Street crash but much later, when its consequences were felt in their day-to-day affairs. This was especially true of immigrant communities. Even though Wall Street news monopolized the front pages of immigrant newspapers, the general feeling was that they concerned a distant reality. As a rule, immigrants did not invest in the stock exchange. Within a few months, however, a new word would enter the vocabulary of journalists and newspaper readers alike—depression.

This word, transcribed in Greek (*dēpressio*), first appeared in March 1930, in a correspondence from the industrial town of Toledo, Ohio.[2] It was a crucial month, since industrial conglomerates announced the first pay cuts, and it was then that the number of layoffs for the first time exceeded the number of new jobs created.[3] The journalist probably had no way of knowing all this but could discern that "things were not rosy." The decline in workers' income placed enormous stress on small Greek businesses because it limited the buying power of the working class that the immigrant shops catered to. This early appearance of the word "depression" in the immigrant press was followed by the emergence of new clichés underlining the change that was underway. The stereotypical news reports concerning the elections and the dances of local associations were now embellished with equally stereotypical allusions to "these difficult times." Doctors received "destitute patients free of charge" due to the "general financial difficulties," and suicides were not attributed exclusively to unrequited love but also to dire financial straits.[4]

These gradual changes in everyday life drove to doubt many of those who once believed they had succeeded in the United States. At the end of the 1920s, the predominant narrative promised lasting prosperity, to the point where Herbert Hoover, president of the United States, felt safe to claim that "we in America today are nearer to the final triumph over poverty than ever before in the history of any land."[5] In hindsight, the financial crisis casts these reassurances in a light that is both tragic and ironic. The precipitous drop in industrial production, the explosion of unemployment rates, the general feeling of insecurity, and the images broadcast daily showing masses of people going to charity organizations in order to obtain the necessary means for their survival all turned the United States from the international paragon of capitalist prosperity into a cautionary tale of its catastrophic consequences.

"Now please answer my question: Who is to blame about my present condition and what should I do?" wondered G. A., a reader of the *Ethnikos Kēryx*, who sent a letter to the paper from the industrial town of Yorkville, Ohio. Previously, he had recounted his story:

> I've been working at a steel mill for fifteen years now. I came here to "work and save." I managed to earn enough money to support my parents. Then I took a Greek wife so that our children would get a Greek education. I gave a thousand dollars from my savings to buy a

plot of land, based on columns in the Greek newspapers, and today it's not even worth the taxes I pay on it. Then my wife got sick and I paid 700 dollars for her operation. Then I got a hernia and I paid another 300 dollars for my operation. After all this misfortune, I still had 3,000 dollars put away in the bank of our town, which went bankrupt and gave me only 47.5 percent of what I had in my account and there's no chance they will give me the rest. Today I'm forty-five years old and the father of three, and according to company policy they do not hire anyone over forty-five and I'm considered useless.[6]

This letter describes a common immigrant experience in the Depression era, combining the effects of the financial crisis, the absence of social security, the rising unemployment in the steel industry, and the exclusion of older workers. For years, and especially in the 1920s, US capitalism seemed like it was promising the immigrant workers a stable social contract. A contract based on the value of hard work and cash savings. The "work and save" program that the letter writer describes pertains to a certain era: the era of employers' Americanization programs, of admonitions in the Greek press against radicalism, and of the belief that in the New World hard work would always be rewarded. These assurances were tested during the Great Depression years. The question "Who is to blame for my present condition?" that was asked by anonymous letter writers in the immigrant press ushered in social changes and ideological transformations. "Hoover, you got us!" were the final lines in "Me tis Tsepes Adeianes" (With empty pockets), a popular song by Giorgos Katsaros, which described the erosion of 1920s immigrant prosperity while at the same time pointing a finger at the main culprit for this "catastrophe."[7]

Community Troubles

The crisis assaulted the foundations of ethnic economy. The seemingly secure immigrant microcosm, structured around small business owners, Greek banks, and community functions, proved to be no match for the financial crisis's relentless onslaught. The Great Depression made abundantly clear that immigrant life was now a part of American life. From this perspective, the observation of *Ethnikos Kēryx* on 31 December 1930 was spot on: "We are not immigrants anymore." The columnist's aim was to highlight the Greeks' integration, but the observation, coupled with the onset of the Great Depression, also revealed the limits of community self-sufficiency.[8] When the first immigrants arrived in the beginning of the twentieth century, the strictly delineated community model had a protective function that now proved insufficient. The Greeks of the United States were facing, like every other immigrant community, a financial crisis against which every safety precaution, whether national or communal in nature, would prove wanting.

The "colossal . . . synthes[is] of communities, schools, churches, [and] associations," as the editor in chief of *Ethnikos Kēryx* expounded with enthusiasm on New Year's Day 1929, had all but disappeared within a few years.[9] A sharp decrease in membership dues meant that the various communities could not keep up with their obligations to the banks that had financed the acquisition of their magnificent buildings, those same buildings that had so impressed newspaper reporters during the 1920s. In San Francisco, the Greek community's real estate as well as the Greek Orthodox cathedral were put on auction; in Chicago the church of Saint Basil was foreclosed, while in smaller communities the financial crisis signaled the end of community organization.[10] A steady stream of news about foreclosures on many communities' real estate confirmed what the Greek ambassador had said on the matter: "Virtually every community is in dire straits, saddled as they are with large mortgages."[11]

One of the visible effects of the financial crisis was that the community's mutual aid practices suffered greatly. During the first decades of the twentieth century, immigrant communities had developed mutual aid programs offering financial support to those in need. The Great Depression forced them to cut back on such endeavors. At the end of the 1930s, Mary Antoniou, a young sociologist, recorded the activities of the Greek mutual aid societies in Los Angeles. She concluded that decreases in community income were related to the inability of the various societies to provide relief on a regular basis. As Mary Antoniou noted, "it becomes clear that none of the society's activities . . . is satisfactory."[12] In stark contrast, between 1931 and 1933, around 130 "Greek families" had entered the registers of Los Angeles welfare services. In a similar vein, a correspondent of *Ethnikos Kēryx* observed that in Cleveland "for the first time . . . many of our countrymen are in need of aid by the various American welfare institutions."[13]

These and other observations challenged the comforting reassurances printed in the newspapers, which insisted in presenting the Greek American communities as self-sufficient entities, able to weather the crisis without need of external aid. On one hand, these reassurances expressed a mentality quite prevalent among immigrants, according to which recourse to welfare services signaled personal failure and shamed the entire community in the eyes of "Americans." On the other hand, these columns should be seen in light of the underlying unease, especially in more conservative circles, that recourse to American—and thus non-Orthodox—institutions undermined the community's cohesion and contributed to its ultimate assimilation.[14] Such concerns (apparent, for example, in the diplomatic reports that discuss the risks of letting thousands of poor and orphaned Greek children fall into the care of United States welfare services) betray a reluctance to accept the gradual disengagement of those in need from the traditional channels of community mutual aid, even when the latter were in no position to fulfill their role. This disengagement sprang in large part from the collapse of the local mutual aid channels as well as the striking idleness exhibited by the major institutions of the Greek immigrant community in general.

The crisis in community self-sufficiency is on full display in the various complaints against Greek employers. The letters column in the *Ethnikos Kēryx*, until the beginning of the 1930s, served mainly as a forum for questions about legal and bureaucratic matters. From the beginning of 1931, though, a new kind of letter appeared: serious complaints about work conditions in Greek-owned businesses. The letter writers signed with their initials or under a pseudonym and rarely mentioned by name the "Greek businessman" who "has gone beyond the pale of respectable human behavior." The common denominators of their complaints were pay cuts, bullying behavior, and indifference toward the problems of the people working for them.[15] These charges challenged the idea of common Greek interests, which in the past had functioned as the connective tissue of immigrant entrepreneurship. The shift from "compatriots" to "exploiters," who are indifferent to the plight of the countrymen they employ, provides insight into the uncharted strata of small Greek-owned businesses. The letters to *Ethnikos Kēryx* paint a tragic picture of everyday life, recounting brief tales of exploitation from the back rooms of Greek-owned kitchens:

> I work in a restaurant for twelve and thirteen hours a day and for seven days a week. Since the crisis, my wages have been cut three times; I work in a restaurant. . . . My initial wages were 22 dollars. The first cut made it 18, then 16, and recently it went to 12 per week; I'm a Cypriot and work like a slave in a Greek restaurant. I work thirteen hours for 12 dollars. My boss does not allow me to eat fresh bread or three meals a day; I work in a Greek boarding house. . . . Now they get mad at the smallest things and they swear at me because business has slowed; the Greek owner is very stingy, despite brisk business, however he employs Greek sailors and treats them as slaves, especially the dishwashers, whom he pays $12.50 per week for twelve to thirteen hours of hard work and does not provide for them adequately, he even forbids them to drink a glass of milk.[16]

The isolated voices of protest from the depths of immigrant-run restaurants and boarding houses are the sole indications left to us concerning labor relations. In that particular milieu there were no collective agreements and no formal contracts between employers and employees. What we know about the Greek fur workshops shows that businessmen who ran into trouble tried to cope by reducing labor costs, and that more successful businessmen tried to secure their position using the same method. In the beginning of 1932, the United Fur Manufacturers Association (the Greek employer association) and Local 70 held a meeting to negotiate a new collective agreement for the sector. During this meeting, the employer association proposed pay cuts in accordance with "the present financial situation of the country," while overtime pay "would be equalized with the normal pay of the workday."[17] In the fur sector the median wages between 1927 and 1933 had seen a reduction of 38 percent; however, being skilled workers, the fur workers' wages still remained far above the wages of those who worked, for example, in the kitchens of immigrant restaurants.[18]

During the 1920s, the Greek American press had presented Greek-owned businesses as proof of the increased social standing enjoyed by Greek immigrants, and also as proof of the immediate reward of hard work. This line of thinking was predicated on a traditional outlook that saw immigrant entrepreneurship as the meeting point between innate national virtues and the ideal conditions for personal prosperity provided by the cornucopia of the United States. In the new reality of the Great Depression, the Greek American businesses were painted in a completely different light. "They founder, they fade, and they fall" was the refrain of a regular commenter in the pages of *Ethnikos Kēryx* just one year after the stock market crash.[19]

The predicament of Greek American businesses was laying waste to the dominant notions of success in the United States. The problems faced by small ethnic businesses could be largely attributed to the way they had flourished. Like the community's real estate holdings, they owed their existence to mortgages taken out in the 1920s. They consequently had little room to move since they had to deal both with the sharp decline of consumption by their working-class clientele and the tremendous pressure by banks and suppliers to fulfill their financial obligations. Restaurants provide an illustrative example of how the decline in revenues and the nature of consignments rendered small business owners captive to suppliers, dissolving what little capital they had. In New York alone, half of all Chinese restaurants closed down in the first year of the Great Depression.[20] We do not have similar statistics for the Greek-owned restaurants in the city, but the situation cannot have been very different.

The concomitant shifts in mass consumption and the expansion of big business made matters even worse. "Chain store fever," as Lizabeth Cohen called it, had started to spread into working-class and immigrant neighborhoods, changing "immigrant workers' patterns of consumption in Chicago."[21] The pressures on the owners of small shops and businesses were severe: Vassilios

Tsimbidis, president of the American Hellenic Educational Progressive Association (AHEPA), spoke for many of them when he described "the threat of chain stores" and the complaints of "independent" businessmen.[22] Sales, advertising campaigns, and above all much lower prices lured away the regular clientele of small ethnic businesses, plunging into despair what had been, up to that point, the representative examples of Greek American success. The image of the owner of "one of the best patisseries" in Boston, "bent over his counter with tears in his eyes," "losing business with every passing day" was not an exception in the pages of *Ethnikos Kēryx*.[23] On the contrary, its repetition contributed to the emergence and formulation of a widespread attack against monopoly, led by the owners of small businesses who lambasted "chain stores" and "organized department stores."

Evripidis Kechagias, when he became president of the company that published *Ethnikos Kēryx*, in the summer of 1933, wrote of the need for a new viewpoint, since "the most important lesson that four years of crisis has taught us Greeks, as well as other peoples, is the lesson of collective action. . . . Individualism served well the Greek in the past, but it has the ability to harm him in the future, unless it is combined with a spirit of cooperation."[24] The Great Depression highlighted the limits of immigrant self-sufficiency and functioned as an accelerator of those processes that had already been set in motion since the end of transatlantic immigration. The inability of communities and shared ancestry to protect those in need during the crisis undermined the case for a unified Greek front and, by extension, the power wielded by its proponents. At some point, fifty unemployed men decided to pay a visit to *Ethnikos Kēryx*, asking the newspaper to intercede on their behalf in order to find work in Greek-owned businesses. This was seen as a traditional way of solving everyday problems.[25] However, the fact that their request could not be granted reveals what amounted to a momentous crisis in community self-sufficiency and the familiar solidarity networks.

Drachmas, Dollars, and Bank Panics

An unlikely turn of events challenged further the foundations of community solidarity. On 29 July 1932 the Greek government, led by Eleftherios Venizelos, announced without warning the forced conversion into drachmas of "all obligations in foreign currency."[26] More specifically, the pertinent decree stipulated the conversion of all foreign currency obligations dated before 26 April 1932, when Greece left the gold standard, into drachmas at the rate of a hundred drachmas per dollar. In actual terms, this meant that bank deposits in dollars lost one third of their value overnight, since the conversion rate per dollar in July 1932 was 154 drachmas.

In early August 1932, Leland Morris, the United States consul in Athens, sent a memorandum concerning the "forced conversion of foreign currency into drachmas."[27] Under the restrained tone of a diplomatic communiqué, one can easily discern his annoyance at a measure that greatly affected US organizations and companies operating in Greece, as well as Greek Americans who had entrusted their savings to Greek banks. The consul's memo also reveals that the Greek government resorted to the forced conversion into drachmas when it realized the adverse effects the 1929 crash and the ensuing depression had on Greek American remittances. The year the forced conversion was put into effect, remittances were down to one third of what they had been in 1930, and in 1934 they were down to one fifth.[28] Faced with steep declines the Greek government tried to recoup the losses by appropriating, through forced conversion into drachmas, part of the Greek American deposits in Greece. This conversion became known as "drachmatization."

When drachmatization was put into effect, it met with furious opposition. The forced conversion of immigrant deposits affected both deposits from individuals and capital maintained by various local societies that were underwriting welfare initiatives. It was not long before an unprecedented wave of protest flooded the Greek diplomatic services. Many paid a visit to the diplomatic authorities. As attested by the reports of Charalambos Simopoulos, the Greek ambassador in the United States, they were "protesting, and unfortunately without the appropriate objectivity, against the measure in question."[29] Meanwhile, hundreds of letters started flooding into the offices of immigrant newspapers containing complaints, requests for clarification, personal stories, and a general sense of betrayal by the Greek state. The ambassador's reports to the Greek Ministry of Foreign Affairs reveal that the combination of the Great Depression with the forced conversion significantly affected the everyday life of immigrants. "Many of the deposit holders, if not most of them, belong to the working class, and this is what grants their protestations even more urgency, given the crisis that is unfolding here."[30]

After a few months, a string of new revelations concerning the affair caused a scandal. During the summer of 1932, following the announcement of the forced conversion, the immigrant press assured its readers that the measure would affect only the deposits made in banks in Greece. The newspaper *Atlantis* sent out the same answer to those worried readers who had reached out: "The deposits that have been made to the American branches of the Hellenic Bank Trust Company and the Athens Trust will be unaffected by the drachmatization measures initiated by the Greek Government, since the aforementioned banks function as autonomous American institutions."[31]

These were the local branches of two major Greek banks, the National Bank of Greece and the Bank of Athens, which had opened their doors at the end of the 1920s in New York. *Ethnikos Kēryx* and *Atlantis* had hailed this as a positive development, as it opened a new chapter in the strengthening of ties between Greek Americans and their country of origin. Likewise, the Greek banks' decision to expand to the United States confirmed the importance of Greek Americans' savings, and by extension the success story of Greek immigrants in the New World. These enthusiastic assessments betrayed, apart from the columnists' nationalistic fervor, the somewhat more tangible links between the banks and the publishers of *Ethnikos Kēryx* and *Atlantis*. The two Greek banks allocated considerable funds to spend in advertising campaigns. The National Bank, for example, made an advance payment of twenty-eight thousand dollars to *Atlantis*, covering daily advertising costs for the next three years, 1931 to 1934.[32] It was in this context that the Greek American press encouraged its readership to entrust their savings to the Greek banks.

Besides, they had one important argument in their favor. In the immediate aftermath of the 1929 Wall Street crash many American banks had defaulted. The bank runs that followed mainly involved small and medium-sized banks, which had absorbed most of the immigrants' cash deposits during the 1920s.[33] It was a time when savings were seen as a mark of Americanization, whereas the frequent loans that had been handed out had fueled the rise of small immigrant businesses.[34] The bank defaults terrified those who held modest deposits and were reading, for example, news about the "hurricane" brought about by the collapse of the New Jersey National Bank, which "dragged down with it every business owner in the Greek community there."[35] It was partly for this reason that the immigrant press encouraged the public as well as Greek American associations and societies to turn to "the friend of the Greek immigrant," the "secure and robust Greek Banks whose headquarters are in New York," and assured their clients that all deposits were held "in dollars, in the United States."[36]

The assertions that the Hellenic Bank Trust Company and the Athens Trust—subsidiaries of the National Bank of Greece and the Bank of Athens respectively—were American institutions and so were not affected by the enforced exchange were proven to be utterly false. The immigrants were startled to discover that the two banks had funneled their reserves back to their parent institutions in Greece, and hence their savings fell under the decree of drachmatization. This latest development multiplied the number of people who saw their savings devalued by the day. It also had further implications. Deposits that had been made in New York City or in the cooperating institutions or agencies of the two banks in the United States were now frozen back in Greece.

Thousands of people with small accounts suddenly found themselves faced with the evaporation of their life's savings. Many of them pressed charges against the executive boards of the two banks and the newspapers that had published misleading information, but the slow progress and the various complications of the case frustrated all prospects of remuneration. On the other hand, this affair signaled the disgraceful end of all Greek banking presence in the United States. The City of New York authorities turned against the Greek banks since their actions had violated state laws regulating the activities of financial institutions. As a result, the banks' permits were revoked.

In 1940, *Fordham Law Review* published an article about the relations between the US public sector and the foreign banks operating in the United States. The article commenced with the case of Vasilios Eliopoulos. Eliopoulos was poor and received welfare benefits in the United States. But he had also maintained a savings account with the National Bank of Greece, and the US authorities had pressed charges of fraud. The defendant explained his actions by claiming the loss of his deposit due to the drachmatization and subsequent freezing of his account. The author of the article notes:

> Eliopoulos was telling the truth. The National Bank of Greece had received deposits in New York illegally. He was only one of thousands of Greeks throughout the United States who had entrusted their savings to this bank. Upon receipt of these funds the bankers moved them back to Greece, where they now remain frozen by currency restrictions. Most of these funds, estimated as high as $25,000,000.00, remain unpaid to this day.[37]

The enforced conversion of dollars to drachmas resulted in a grave breach of trust between Greek immigrants and the Greek state. It also increased the visibility and appeal of those who were critical of established community leaders. When, early in 1932, *Ethnikos Kēryx*, with the support of AHEPA, announced an ambitious fundraiser for the acquisition of "a Greek educational institution and boarding house for the Archdiocese," the results were disappointing.[38] After six months of constant front-page promotion, the total raised was only one sixth of the original goal of sixty thousand dollars, and the main donors were the Greek banks, the Greek Orthodox Archdiocese of America, and the newspaper itself. The readers' disappointing response reflected first and foremost their own financial difficulties. But there are other reasons that contributed to their unwillingness to contribute to the charity drive. A long history of mismanagement, and their recent experience with drachmatization, increased their reservations concerning initiatives by the Greek government, such as this particular fundraiser.

The appallingly low level of ethnic solidarity, the decline of Greek-owned businesses, and the role of the press during the banking crisis constituted the pieces of a new mosaic, whose boundaries were defined by the new era that was just beginning, that of the Great Depression.

Hungry Revolutionaries: The Unemployed Councils

On the evening of 16 January 1930, Stefanos Katovis left his apartment in the East Bronx and proceeded to Miller's Market, a local restaurant. Thirty of his comrades waited for him there to protest some layoffs. The life of "Red Steve" was inseparable from the labor movement: he joined the Communist Party in 1921 and had distinguished himself in organizing workers on the West Coast before moving to New York. The protest outside Miller's Market would have passed without incident and would have remained a local affair if constable Harry Kiritz had not shot and mortally wounded Stefanos Katovis. The Greek immigrant, born in Tyrnavos in 1890, died a week later, on 24 January, at a time when it was felt that the United States was entering a period of uncertainty and social unrest.

"We are plunging into a crisis, the full depths of which are still to be explored," observed the introduction to the *Communist*, the theoretical journal of the Communist Party of the United States (CPUSA), in the first days of February 1930.[39] It was an accurate assessment. The days immediately before and after Katovis's funeral had been marked by clashes around the Communist Party headquarters in Union Square, between the police and irate protesters. Katovis's body was displayed there for four days, surrounded by wreaths of red flowers, watched over by a huge portrait of Lenin, and attended by an honor guard.[40] Katovis was declared a martyr for the cause who gave his life for the emancipation of the masses. "[He casts] in blood the shadow of the world-proletarian revolution," was how *Steve Katovis: Life and Death of a Worker*, an English-language "proletarian biography," concluded.[41]

Coincidentally, on the day of the violent clashes outside Miller's Market, the Executive Secretariat of the Comintern in Moscow called for an international day against unemployment.[42] The massive turnout on 6 March 1930 in protests across the United States surprised first and foremost the organizers themselves. Over a million people responded to the call.[43] The mass protests so soon after Katovis's death augmented the martyr's aura. The cover of the *Labor Defender*'s March issue, published by the International Labor Defense, featured a street in New York City packed with hundreds of people gathered in protest and with a lone policeman standing in the middle of the crowd, under the slogan "Fight or Starve!" Inside, a photo collage combined photos from the funeral of Katovis with those from the mass demonstrations against unemployment.[44]

On the day after the mass protests of 6 March, the number of the unemployed was close to two and a half million; by the end of the year it had doubled to five million.[45] In 1931, in Chicago, the unskilled workers' unemployment rate was 57 percent and skilled workers' was 40 percent, while in 1933 the wages of the lucky few who had not been fired had shrunk to one fourth of what they had been in the beginning of 1929.[46] In 1933, at the height of the Great Depression, one in four Americans was out of work. Until the end of that year, in Toledo, Manchester, Birmingham, and Cleveland, those who held a steady job were fewer than the masses of the unemployed or those who were working occasionally.[47] The statistics show a trend of constant deterioration, but they also demonstrate the uneven distribution of the Depression's impact, as the brunt of it was borne by the residents of small industrial towns, unskilled workers, and young immigrants.

A study that was conducted at the time calculated that if the face of every unemployed person in New York City under the age of twenty-five was projected on a movie screen for one second, the result would be an unbroken procession of faces that would last for four straight days.[48] Every second, every single one of those 350,000 unemployed men and women had a story to tell, a story of poverty, family tensions, eviction, debt, and going out to search for work or even for food. The specter of hunger, either as a symbol of destitution or as excruciating reality, appeared in the pages of the immigrant press. For example, here is what P. P. wrote early in 1931: "There are many Greeks, some of us educated, who are without work for over two months now and our money is running out. . . . We are looking for work in the east and the west. We are wandering night and day and we cannot even make enough money in a day to buy a loaf of bread."[49] He was not exaggerating. For millions of people, the first years of the Great Depression were marked by a rapid descent into poverty and a plunge into the depths of society. The denizens of the slums that sprung up, the thousands of transients looking for work (like the heroes of John Steinbeck's *Grapes of Wrath*), and the imposing photographs showing whole queues of homeless people waiting outside soup kitchens turned the unemployed into a visible political subject of the new era.

For the communist movement, the masses of the unemployed were tangible proof of the contradictions at the heart of capitalism; they gave a face to all those who now had "nothing to lose but their chains." The American communists started organizing the unemployed, linking the pressing demands for relief measures with the preparations for "the bigger battles and, finally, for the overthrow of capitalism."[50] Most members of the party did not need any convincing since they were themselves unemployed and were at the forefront of the spontaneous and furious protests of the unemployed that broke out every day demanding "bread and work," as the headlines of *Empros* declared. The American communists brought their organizing know-how and their undeniable passion, and they led the emergence of a many-faceted movement characterized by spontaneity, fury, and practices of immediate action.

"Break down the doors and put back the furniture," the "fearless" Georgios Kellis told protesters who had gathered to block the eviction of an unemployed family. The reoccupation of homes was a favored tactic of the unemployed movement. When the bailiff showed up, the neighbors gathered outside the building where the eviction would take place, waiting for him to depart. When he did, they broke down the locked door and put back in the few pieces of furniture, while the people outside waited for the arrival of the policemen. "When [the landlord] comes, tell the children and women to sit down on the floor so that the policemen and landlord can't get in," Kellis continued.[51] These everyday occurrences often ended in protests that could spiral out of control, since hundreds would join the initial group to protest an eviction or the exemption of a family from social welfare. There was no centrally organized plan of action but rather a convergence, according to E. P. Thompson, "between the grievances of the majority and the aspirations articulated by the politically conscious minority."[52]

The unemployed councils occupied public buildings, demanded food handouts and the provision of welfare services, and defended families who were in danger of eviction. The main advantage of the communists was their ability to turn a feeling of shame, felt by those who were forced to vacate their own homes, into a collective demand with clear-cut goals: annulment of eviction, rent control, and a guaranteed residence for every working-class family. In this context, an isolated incident, such as two policemen going into a working-class neighborhood to evict a family, could quickly escalate into a protest march to the local city hall.[53] They blamed the inherent vices of the capitalist system for the masses' impoverishment and at the same time drew attention to the misfortunes of the working class. The unemployed councils fought for the creation of unemployment offices and unemployment benefits, contrary to the long-standing tradition of the American labor movement, which viewed any state or federal aid with suspicion.

When the Greek American communists, following the party line, proposed the creation of an unemployed committee, they were not just trying to compensate for the absence of institutions in ethnic communities; they were also challenging that feeling of shame that prompted many of the letter writers in *Ethnikos Kēryx* to conclude their stories of misfortune with the request that the editors "please print my letter without a name or address." The rhetoric of the communist movement turned unemployment on its head: from a personal failure it became a public condemnation of the capitalist system.

Workers' Mutual Aid

The Greek American communists encountered for the first time an audience that had nothing in common with the tiny communist circles of the 1920s. Determined party cadres toured incessantly the web of industrial towns between Michigan and Chicago that had been hit especially hard by a double crisis in the automobile and steel industries. The Greek Language Bureau records include orders for consecutive trips, which reveal their efforts to be present wherever there was even the hint of an adequate number of Greek workers or Greek unemployed. The life of a touring revolutionary was not easy; in their reports they gave vent to constant complaints about frequent moves, undelivered party wages, and the circumstances of their everyday life.[54] Nikos Economos (or Economakos) described the organization of unemployed committees in towns and cities such as Milwaukee, Hegewisch, Pullman, and Gary. These committees were often linked with other forms of organizing, such as local workers' associations and the Greek chapters of the International Worker Aid. At the center of all this activity was the unemployed council of Chicago, which was hosted in the Greek Workers Educational Association and numbered six hundred members.[55]

Steve Nelson was a Croatian communist who was responsible for organizing the unemployed movement in eastern Pennsylvania. His most valuable ally in this undertaking was Gus the Greek, a shadowy figure who had contacts in various remote communities such as Mahanoy, Pottsville, Mount Carmel, and Shamokin. The origins of Gus's extensive network were soon revealed. The Greek immigrant had been for years a professional card player and had traveled to working-class communities, where "leisure" denoted the green felt on the coffee shop table. Gus told Nelson how he came to see the error of his ways. It is a story that demonstrates the power that the communist movement attributed to the educational and revelatory aspects of workers' education: a dishwasher had recommended to him "some good books written by a man called Karl Marx."[56]

In urban centers, the Greek American communists had managed for the first time to work with some local associations. "The greater part of Greek families and single men are suffering; they lack even for their daily bread. . . . It is imperative that we all act together to help those afflicted." This was how a committee in Detroit utilized the vocabulary of community mutual aid.[57] Despite these attempts, the "Reds" faced deep suspicion from institutions and communities. In New York, the first meetings for the creation of a Greek unemployed council met with overwhelming success: dozens of local associations answered the call, and even the local diocese sent an observer. However, the search for a golden mean between the communists' anti-capitalist rhetoric and the priorities of the associations proved elusive. The Greek communists believed that if only they proved that the leaders of these associations were not working toward a revolution, the mass of their members would follow the communists. Usually, though, what happened was the exact opposite. In one instance the majority of participants walked out after a few meetings and labeled the communists' interest in the unemployed movement as hypocritical, claiming that the meetings were in essence "a Soviet conference."[58]

Equally scathing in their critique, but from a different angle, were the Trotskyite groups, who discerned in *Empros* further proof of the party's conciliatory policy. Aristodimos Caldis wrote about how Greeks of the CPUSA had contacted a few priests in Philadelphia and were using the church of Agios Georgios to hold the meetings of the local unemployed council.[59] Initiatives such as this, which in the eyes of the fiery Trotskyite revolutionary proved the ideological decline of "Stalinists," illuminate the unemployed movement's circuitous path, as well as the willingness of party cadres to go beyond accepted practices. This is corroborated by party directives, which, in ways that would probably have surprised Caldis, were equally critical of many local initiatives. "This appeal must be condemned, it puts our movement to shame," wrote the Greek Language Bureau in New York City about an invitation sent by a local organizer to the Greek American organizations in Detroit.[60] His explanation reveals the complexities of the wider objective of creating a mass movement: the comrade was trying to enforce the party line and attract "Greek workers, be they members of fascist groups or church organizations."[61] The communists were finding out the hard way that the celebrated "mass work" concealed many, often unanticipated, obstacles.

Party admonishments point to the fact that for many communists the day-to-day operation of the councils was challenging long-held convictions and mentalities. The 1920s "Bolsheviks" had addressed mostly smaller audiences of like-minded people, focusing on matters of party education or the ideological struggle between opposing trends in the revolutionary movement. In the unemployed councils, the Greek American communists soon discovered that the mass turnout was not based on an ideological alignment with the communist movement but on a search for immediate solutions to their problems. When Steve Nelson went into the packed Greek Workers Educational Association in Chicago to give a speech about organizing the unemployed, the head of the meeting warned him: "We don't have to tell them about Lovestone's expulsion from the Party; these people know nothing about it, and we have more pressing things to discuss."[62] Countless similar occurrences contributed to a shift inside the communist movement. The new party mentality was more favorable to the effectiveness of political actions and recognized the importance of each demand separately, a position that up to that point was often seen as bean counting, and was considered detrimental to the future of the revolution.

This shift was quite evident in the establishment of the International Workers Order (IWO). The IWO was a mutual aid organization aimed at providing low-cost health insurance to workers and the unemployed. Founded by Jewish Communist immigrants in the beginning of the 1920s, the IWO had about 3,000 members. The IWO membership exploded in the space of a few years. By 1933 it had increased tenfold, and at the end of the decade it was the largest organization on the American Left, with close to 150,000 members.[63] Its success was mainly due to low insurance costs and to the fact that it did not discriminate against workers with a high risk of accident or precarious working conditions. At the same time, the IWO expressed the shift of the Communist Left toward immediate and tangible relief for those who were afflicted by the deepening crisis. The IWO proclamations put it succinctly: it was a "mutual aid society built on the principles of welfare to all members and support of the worker's struggles."[64] The first Greek IWO branches were founded in Chicago and Detroit in 1931, with a membership of a few dozen each, drawn mainly from workers and the unemployed already organized in the local workers' associations. Greek American communists on the other hand hesitated to follow the party's directive in transforming mutual aid associations under their influence into IWO branches. As they were just establishing, for the first time, ties to local working-class associations, they were unwilling to go forward with a move that would confirm the public's fears about the malign intentions of the "Reds."

This could easily be discerned, for example, in the refusal of the Greek Language Bureau to enforce the conversion of the Pancyprian Brotherhood of New York (a mutual aid association of workers with a Cypriot background) into an IWO branch. "The split" of the Pancyprian Brotherhood "must be avoided at all costs," noted the Greek Language Bureau, which acknowledged that most of its members were probably unconvinced about the goals of the merger.[65] This reluctance was connected with the increase of communist influence in the Cypriot organization, whose members were mainly workers in restaurants and big hotels. The move was spearheaded by Michalis Savvides, who had been born in Larnaca, Cyprus, and had come to the US in 1927 from Uruguay, where he had previously emigrated.[66] Savvides found work at Teachers College in Columbia University and soon formed a group of Cypriot workers who participated in the "Red" food workers union.

This group of radicalized workers was very active in the Pancyprian Brotherhood. In the elections of 1931, Savvides was voted in as president and the communists held the majority in the brotherhood's board.[67] This was the first time that the Left had taken control of a local association. It reflected the communists' ability to link in a convincing manner the financial crisis in the United States with developments in other parts of the world. Savvides and his group had insisted on bolstering mutual aid practices in the brotherhood to coincide with political developments in Cyprus. In the wake of the October 1931 uprising against the British authorities, the Pancyprian Brotherhood organized a fundraiser for the financial support of prisoners and their families. In this context, the communist movement's anti-imperialist and anti-colonial program took on a new, timely significance. The communists offered a radical perspective on the developments in Cyprus by emphasizing the impact that the worldwide financial crisis had on colonial powers.[68]

In this way, the protests of the unemployed in New York City and the uprising in Cyprus were recontextualized as separate expressions of a single global confrontation, and the Pancyprian Brotherhood was transformed into a link that connected them. Likewise, young Latino workers and intellectuals in Harlem neighborhoods were linking eviction resistance with independence movements in the Caribbean, while in San Francisco, Chinese communities reacted to the news of the Japanese invasion of Manchuria by forming groups supporting the Kuomintang.[69] These initiatives were important in two distinct ways. On the one hand, these diasporic activities further reinforced anticolonial movements, offering material support and connections with radical demands and practices; on the other hand, the conversation around the colonies revitalized the debate raging within the communist movement on the national question. The crisis of the old empires appeared to be entangled with the financial crisis, strengthening the belief in an imminent and final confrontation.

Soviet America

"The wheels of History are turning fast," wrote a theorist of the CPUSA.[70] For the communist movement, the emergence of new forms of labor organization and the changes in the day-to-day life of the working-class masses could only lead to one thing: a revolutionary uprising. The 1929 crisis had restored communists' trust in the laws of historical development. During the difficult 1920s, the communists had prophesied, against all evidence to the contrary, that the capitalist economy was a giant with feet of clay. It was a prediction that was based mainly on their faith in history's deterministic course, and not on some farsighted analysis of the traits and trends of American capitalism. The Wall Street crash and the events that followed it allowed them to take pride in the fact that they were the only ones who had predicted what was coming, contrary to all those who "believed in the 'stability of American prosperity' and in 'American exceptionalism.'"[71]

Indeed, the future of capitalism in the United States seemed uncertain. Images of unemployed people filling city streets and of starving farmers in the country revealed the severity of a social problem in a country that up to then had taken pride in the fact that it managed to avoid the obstacles that plagued European nations. The financial crisis emphasized the unpredictability of the present, and the prospect of a great revolutionary transformation was gradually gaining ground. In May 1930, in the wake of mass protests by the unemployed, Congress approved the establishment of the Fish Committee, which would investigate communist activities in the United States. This initiative echoed what had taken place in the years after the October Revolution and the antiradical persecutions of 1919–21. Revisiting the idea that immigrants, and especially those who came from eastern Europe, were responsible for the dissemination of revolutionary ideas in the United States, the Fish Committee proposed various measures against those who would question the existing social and political order.

These worries were exaggerated. Even those who were active in the protests and the unemployed councils did not necessarily share the communists' strategic goals. However, there was no room for calm and objective assessments. The sheer magnitude of social unrest, coupled with similar developments elsewhere in the world, where the financial crisis was followed by political destabilization, caused mounting concern to those who were anticipating a similar cataclysmic event in the United States. "If the Army must be called out to make war on unarmed citizens," commented the *Washington News* with skepticism, "this is no longer America."[72] A few days prior, on 28 July 1932, the National Guard had attacked a demonstration of war veterans who were demanding early disbursement of their welfare benefits. The attack on the veterans' camp, in the center of Washington, DC, left behind two dead and the sense of an imminent and general upheaval. If democracy was turning against its own heroes, what did the future hold for the nation?

In this climate, the future did not bode well for American democracy. The reassurances that the crisis would quickly go away had been proven false and the collapse of the European democracies gave rise to doubts about whether the country would emerge from the Great Depression unharmed. Political and financial analysts increasingly sought an authoritarian turn that would serve as a counterbalance to the unforeseen developments fostered by social unrest. The call by *Barron's*, the weekly financial bulletin, "for a mild dictatorship [that] will help us over the rough spots in the road ahead" was not an isolated or extreme opinion in the public discourse of that time.[73] On the contrary, it fit right into the general sentiment that democracy was the "sick man," whose treatment called for extreme measures. According to this way of thinking, the objective was economic recovery and the containment of social unrest, since its perpetuation would lead, sooner or later, to a communist revolution.

The distance between fears of an imminent social revolution and the organizational realities of the Communist Party is impressive: from 1929 to 1932 the Communist Party's actual membership ranged from nine to twenty thousand.[74] Most of the members had joined after 1929 and were usually unemployed young men of immigrant descent. At the same time, the statistics revealed a fundamental problem. The Communist Party failed to keep these people who had enthusiastically joined its ranks; they soon left it, tired by day-to-day life inside the party. In a rare moment of humor and self-criticism, a cartoon in the *Party Organizer* showed a meeting in which new members who could not follow the proceedings due to the many acronyms and party jargon said, "But they must be speaking Chinese!"[75] Between 1931 and 1933 almost thirty thousand people joined the Communist Party.[76] Less than ten thousand, one in three, still remained after their first year. But the people who worried about the communist threat gave no thought to mere numbers. The events that had taken place in Russia in 1917, and the news of the rapid spread of National Socialism in Germany, which until recently had been a marginal political force, gave rise to fears of a sudden eruption in which fringe radical groups would take advantage of widespread social unrest.

Communists, for their part, shared this view of things. The protracted length of the financial crisis and the frequent incidents of police violence were to them proof of an imminent revolutionary upheaval. This belief was further encouraged by the Communist Party's global strategy, which was summarized in the famous slogan "class against class." According to it, the economic recovery of the 1920s was but a brief interlude before the final crisis of the capitalist system and the inevitable revolutionary transformation. Consequently, since recent developments were reinforcing those predictions, the communist parties around the world were to prepare for the revolution's arrival. In this context, the CPUSA between 1931 and 1933 announced various campaigns to turn "every factory [into] a fortress of communism."[77] Despite ambitious goals and similarly grandiose statements, the results were poor. The campaigns usually ended in miserable reports that as a rule attributed the insufficient growth in membership to various party members' shortcomings and, of course, the destructive impact of ideological deviations from the correct line. What was impressive was not the failures themselves but American communists' repetition of the effort time and again, reminding one of a bad pupil who every Friday promises that on Monday he will do his best, only to fail again.

What they lacked was the ability to question long-held convictions and acknowledge the new realities of the financial crisis. The organizing snags in heavy industry were partly due to the dissolution of the labor movement during the Great Depression, when the financial crisis and high unemployment rates eroded the trade unions' power. Membership in trade unions was falling constantly, union organizers were the first to be laid off, and members were unable to pay their dues. Meanwhile, the employer associations seized the opportunity to dissolve collective agreements, eroding further the unions' power. One look at the huge queues of the unemployed waiting outside the factories for a day's work was enough to stop a labor protest before it even started. The few strikes during the first years of the crisis (only 810 in 1931 and 841 in 1932) were defensive in nature—the percentage of strikes protesting pay cuts increased from 25 percent in 1930 to 50 percent in 1932—and rarely met with success.[78] In short, the specter of unemployment, fear of layoffs, and the gigantic, all-too-visible "reserve army" of unskilled workers, whose ranks were patiently waiting day after day at the factory gates, had struck a decisive blow against the labor movement, which had already been weakened in the 1920s.

The American communists had been seeking the potential revolutionary subject among the industrial proletariat, without taking into account that factories, which had been hit hard by the recession, had fallen under a shroud of silence—a silence imposed by employers and by the realization among workers that any labor demand would have no effect. In this context, the party's recruitment successes were mainly to be found among unemployed people, not in the much-sought-after beating heart of the working class. This was also reflected in the party membership's constant ebb and flow. The unemployed appeared in committee meetings and then disappeared. They were attracted by immediate action and not by long-winded party meetings, and they wandered from town to town looking for work, falling out of the CPUSA membership lists.

Despite their organizational shortcomings, the American communists had a distinct advantage: the allure of the Soviet model. News of the five-year plans' wild success in the Soviet Union, which had remained unaffected by the worldwide financial crisis, brought communist ideas to the center of public discourse. "Today, all roads lead to Moscow," Lincoln Steffens concluded in 1931.[79] Steffens, a pioneer of investigative journalism, eloquently expressed the influence of the Soviet model. He had visited the nascent Soviet Union in 1919 and became an enthusiastic supporter, but what he wrote expressed a deeper admission. The word "today" was alluding to what anyone could see when comparing the conditions in the

United States and the Soviet Union at the time. It was a comparison that proved instrumental in the emergence of a new generation of intellectuals, following in Steffens's footsteps, who were fascinated by the Soviet model without automatically joining the ranks of the CPUSA. In the magazine of the International Labor Defense, the 1931 year-in-review was presented through a juxtaposition of two sets of photographs. In the left column were the propaganda images of smiling Soviet workers along with USSR statistics, and in the right column were photographs depicting the results of the capitalist crisis in the USA.[80] If, during the 1920s, such a comparison would have alienated many workers, by the beginning of the 1930s many of them could easily identify with the statistics of poverty and the images of destitution.

This comparison did not play only into the political activities of American communists. During the first eight months of 1931, the Soviet Union trade delegation in New York City had received a hundred thousand applications by people looking to work in the Soviet Union.[81] As we now know, many of those who emigrated to the Soviet Union, especially the American Finns who settled along the USSR-Finland border, met a tragic end in the late 1930s, when they found themselves embroiled in Stalinist persecutions.[82] Aware of the conclusion of this world-spanning journey, from New York City to the Soviet gulag, we can discern a melancholic and tragic poignancy in the applications of party members requesting permission to realize this journey themselves. Steve Pappas had been born in 1885, in Trebizond, Turkey, and had emigrated to the United States in 1913, where he worked as a tailor and ironer. He became a member of the Socialist Party in 1919 and rejoined the Communist Party in March 1931, when he attended the funeral of Ellis Chryssos, the Trebizond-born editor in chief of *Empros*. In his application for a party permit to work in the Soviet Union, he stressed: "When I leave the US I will buy a round-trip ticket. . . . I will come back and continue my work here."[83]

Pappas's insistence on making clear that he was going to come back to the United States revealed the Communist Party's reluctance to approve member permits, since this would further erode organizational capability. Members of the CPUSA should not pursue their own personal salvation in the Soviet Union, the thinking went, but should work toward transforming the USA into the United Socialist States of America. *Toward Soviet America*, a book by William Z. Foster, who was a candidate for the CPUSA in the 1932 presidential elections, offered a "way out of the capitalist jungle" by describing in more than three hundred pages the historical crisis of capitalism, the inevitable social revolution to come, and the emergence of a "New World."[84]

The apocalyptic tone of the book alternated with an equanimity enabled by the codified certainties of interwar Marxist thought, with the United

States presented as ripe for socialist transformation. The "great problem before the workers," Foster wrote, "is to get the political power."[85] Foster's book reflected the positions of the Communist International's Third Period (1928–33). The two key tenets were expressed in the slogan "class against class" and in comparison of socialist trends with fascism. A lack of originality went hand in hand with entrenched convictions about America's explosive social problems—the solution was a new Soviet America. The book featured a detailed analysis, from the socialization of the means of production to the "new cultural revolution," and compared the USA with the Soviet Union, the country that seemed to have escaped the fallout of the 1929 stock market crash. Foster's proposal made waves both within and outside the narrow limits of the CPUSA. Besides, the fact that the book was published by a mainstream publisher, and not by one of the party presses preaching to the choir, reflected, apart from the target group the writer aimed at, a wider interest in the Soviet example.

The prospect of a "Soviet America" attracted the interest of intellectuals and writers who were looking for a different, and tangible, way out of the Great Depression. When the Communist Party announced that its candidates for the office of president and vice president, in the 1932 presidential elections, would be William Foster and James Ford, an African American, both of them well-known authors and intellectuals, public figures such as John Dos Passos and Sidney Hook expressed their enthusiastic support. The communists' election campaign was characterized by a fiery self-assurance and political voluntarism. "Soviet America," the campaign's main slogan, denoted both a social revolution and a change in the map of the United States through the "self-determination of the black regions" in the Southern states. It's not difficult to connect this position with the Communist International's positions at the time concerning the national question and minority groups. At the same time, however, such demands, which today seem outlandish, bear witness to the fluid nature of that historical moment. Amid the general unrest, the African American population in the South, oppressed in manifold ways, became, as far as the communists were concerned, the principal revolutionary subject.

The New Deal

The outcome of the 1932 presidential elections revealed the Left's limited influence. In the preceding months, many had listened attentively to the programs of the Left—both to the communist calls for revolution and the socialist calls for reforms. But when the time came to vote, the results were disappointing: communist candidates got only 100,000 votes, and socialist candidates got 900,000. Compared to the recent past, these numbers exhibited a relative increase. For example, in Chicago, the emblematic city of unemployed councils, the socialists garnered four times more votes and the communists six times more than in 1928. However, the combined percentage of the vote won by the parties of the Left was around 3 percent.[86]

These numbers seemed, and without a doubt were, insignificant compared to the twenty-two million voters who heeded Franklin Roosevelt's somewhat vague call for a new social contract. Discontent over President Herbert Hoover's feeble policies led millions of voters to support the New Deal. It was the moment when "the forgotten people at the base of the social pyramid," whom Roosevelt routinely addressed in his speeches, rushed onto the political stage. Many of those "forgotten" people were first- or second-generation immigrants, and up until that point as a rule they had been indifferent to the US presidential elections. When they cast their ballots, they inaugurated a long tradition of immigrant communities' support for the Democratic Party and revealed the successive transformations that had taken place during the 1920s and the Great Depression. The effects of the crisis turned presidential elections into something that would have immediate repercussions in their own lives, instead of distant events they were quite indifferent to. "It is imperative to vote for the Democrats in order to better our lot," wrote a reporter for *Ethnikos Kēryx* from Detroit.[87]

The election results also betray a greater shift that would play an important role in the course of the 1930s: the increasing visibility of immigrants on the political and social scene. Proof of this trend was that first- and second-generation immigrants were being elected to high office. Anton Cermak, born in Austria-Hungary, was elected mayor of Chicago in 1931, garnering the support of thousands of immigrants who heard him respond to accusations of un-Americanness with an ironic remark about his ancestors not being on the 'Mayflower,' but "they got here as fast as they could."[88] His victory, as well as the victory of Italian American Fiorello La Guardia in the 1934 New York City mayoral elections, was a sign of an emerging social alliance that combined immigrant descent with labor-leaning rhetoric and support of the New Deal.

As a Republican representative in Chicago put it, "unemployment is by far the most important factor" defining the vote.[89] In the city's immigrant neighborhoods, turnout in the elections increased by two thirds between 1924 and 1936, and this novel interest in political participation favored the Democratic Party.[90] This increase could largely be attributed to committees that were very active in registering voters, organizing fundraisers, and mobilizing "fanatically in favor of Roosevelt and Garner, and the Democratic Party in general, from whom we expect a betterment of the situation."[91] The Greek-Democratic Club of Chicago was at the forefront of registering voters in three different districts and set up a roster of representatives for each of the fifty wards of the city.[92] The final result showed clearly the interplay between class and voting patterns. In immigrant neighborhoods, Roosevelt took more than 70 percent of the vote, while in Anglo-Saxon neighborhoods he got 49 percent.[93] A few days before the election, the managing editor of *Ethnikos Kēryx* had declared, in an article written in English, that "Greek workers and small business owners are among the 'forgotten people,'" and that this was why they should support the Democratic candidate.[94] The day after the election, the newspaper's headline declared: "Triumph for Roosevelt."[95]

In traditional historiography, 26 March 1933, the day Roosevelt was sworn into office, stands as the point when liberal democracy vanquished those who sought to undermine it. Even though Roosevelt did on that day famously say that "the only thing we have to fear is fear itself," the path to the New Deal was not without fear.[96] An "existential anxiety" over the survival of civil democracy was the driving force in the search for a new social agreement in the 1930s. This anxiety defined and redefined the New Deal. Meanwhile, though, as has been shown by Ira Katznelson's retrospective view, fear for the future of democracy—the sense, that is, that popular unrest could lead to an uprising—led the New Deal to exact significant concessions from conservative elements, such as the racist Democrats in the Southern States.[97] In any case, when Roosevelt came to power, in March 1933, no one knew what would follow.

The intensive legislative work carried out in the first few months, the consolidation of presidential power, and especially the fiscal policies of state intervention all gave free rein to comparisons with recent developments in Europe, given that Roosevelt's victory coincided with the rise of Adolf Hitler. "A silent revolution is taking place in America, through the implementation of new laws," the Greek ambassador wrote in his report in May 1933, "not unlike an authoritarian regime."[98] In one of his reports to the Ministry of Foreign Affairs, he included a newspaper cartoon, in which President Roosevelt is pictured as a magician pulling rabbits out of his hat and impressing a child, who represented the American people.

Despite those who saw in it the transatlantic counterpart of European fascism, the New Deal created a shining example whose influence persisted for decades across the globe, shaping in no small part the Western world after World War II. The New Deal was unprecedented. It implemented considerable state interventions to the economy, acknowledged the need for centralized regulation of the relationships between capital and labor, and fostered economic recovery through the support of wage earners and the increase of mass consumption. Even though these disparate elements were not all that clearly defined in the pivotal year of 1933, it soon became clear that the United States had entered a new era, that of "a reasoned experiment within the framework of the existing social system," as John M. Keynes wrote on the last day of Roosevelt's first year in the White House.[99]

That same month, the leadership of the CPUSA was in Moscow for the thirteenth enlarged plenum of the Comintern's Executive Committee, where they described Roosevelt as "leading the United States in the direction of fascism."[100] Earl Browder's speech captured the spirit of the Comintern's Third Period, according to which there was no room for solutions within the existing social order. The American communists escalated their attacks on the New Deal based on the conviction that the stabilizing measures would act only as a temporary stopgap to the intensifying social conflict. Without a doubt, it was a speech whose main political points were hard to reconcile, since party cadres as well as members were trying to prove the reactionary nature of the new laws, such as ones aimed at supporting the unemployed—laws that were satisfying the demands of the movement they themselves had led.

"Certain workers *temporarily* have had their wages increased, some workers have received jobs," said Israel Amter, before attacking those comrades who thought that capitalism had survived the worst. "A new early crash ... will follow," he went on.[101] It was a prediction that would be proven entirely wrong. Despite the New Deal's ups and downs and the sluggish recovery of economic indicators, the "new crash" never arrived. The communist movement was facing something unprecedented, and the theoretical tools at their disposal could not make sense of it. The historical crisis of capitalism produced new policies, which ensured a relative stability and, at the very least, a postponement of the impending revolutionary moment. The situation was further complicated by the explosive appearance of spontaneous and militant movements with radical demands. The strikes of 1934 unleashed a momentous creativity in the forms of organization and protest, while at the same time calling for implementation of the New Deal laws, which had recognized the right to organize.

The chronology of events leading from the New Deal labor legislation to the rebirth of the labor movement brought the communists face to face with a new reality. Contrary to their long-cherished predictions, labor protests had not erupted in the first years of the Great Depression, when the US economy's catastrophic decline was felt by nearly everyone. From 1930 to 1933 labor opposition had been minimal. The 1934 strike movement arose at a time of relative stabilization, when the New Deal's first hundred days were promising a return to a sense of financial normalcy. As a consequence, this stability empowered workers and boosted their self-determination. But if this was true, then the whole thinking of a revolutionary outbreak during a deepening crisis should be, and had to be, modified to arrive at a different

strategy: the revolutionary moment would arise out of the gradual development of the labor movement in conditions of political and social stability.

The Greek Language Bureau's report from March 1934 shows these
trends. Twelve Workers Educational Associations boasted 1,500 members,
the Pancyprian Brotherhood had 150 members, three IWO branches had 50
members each, two youth leagues had 200 members in total. All together
these organizations formed the organizational constellation of Greek American communism.[102] The increase of *Empros*'s circulation to 6,000 copies
(3,650 of which went out to subscribers), the shift to a twice a week publication, and the establishment of the Federation of Workers Educational
Associations clearly indicated a powerful shift, especially when compared to
the first years of the Great Depression. In its address to the national bureaus,
the Eighth Congress of the Communist Party praised the successes of the
Greek Language Bureau and the increase in the circulation of *Empros*,
which represented, in absolute numbers, the largest among the immigrant
party newspapers.[103]

But there was another change taking place, which was far more important. The 1934 report had been signed by someone new. Pete Harisson
(Petros Harisiades) was thirty years old when he assumed the leadership of
the Greek Language Bureau at the end of 1933. Born in Samos in 1903, he
had come to the States in 1916 and had worked various odd jobs, head-
ing inland like many immigrants before him. When he joined the party in
the beginning of the 1920s it was because of these experiences, as can be
deduced by his participation in labor strikes and a few run-ins with the law.

Harisiades, contrary to many of the older cadres, had been radicalized
in the United States and was a proponent of the idea of Americanizing
the party, which had left an indelible mark on US communism during the
1920s. As a consequence, his ascension to the leadership of the Greek Language Bureau signifies the appearance of a younger generation of cadres,
free from the shackles of ideological strife and personal differences that had
plagued the Greek Language Bureau from its establishment in 1925.

Amazingly, one of the contributing factors to the rapid changes in party
leadership was *Ethnikos Kēryx*. In February 1932, Petros Tatanis and Dimitrios Kallimachos, editor in chief and managing editor respectively, pressed
charges against *Empros*. As a result, Karolos Solounias and Konstantinos Kristis, managing editors of *Empros*, were arrested, and a court fight
ensued.[104] The charges concerned a series of articles in *Empros* that claimed
that the editorial board of *Ethnikos Kēryx* had embezzled funds raised by
a Greek American charity fundraiser for the refugees of the Greco-Turkish
War. Similar accusations were frequently launched in the tiny and antagonistic world of ethnic journalism. But *Ethnikos Kēryx* went on to reveal the

identity of the author of the anonymous—and damning—articles. His name was Kleanthis Vasardakis, a journalist for the royalist newspaper *Atlantis*.

The roots of the affair could be traced back to a curious incident early in 1926. The managing editors of *Empros* had organized a big event in New York City against *Ethnikos Kēryx*, accusing the liberal newspaper of mishandling a fundraising campaign. The main speaker had been Vasardakis.[105] The next round of hostilities began when *Empros* printed the anonymous, slanderous articles by Vasardakis. The 1932 court proceedings confirmed the collaboration, and *Ethnikos Kēryx* found the opportunity to launch a passionate attack on the "vulgar, riotous, bourgeois newspaper . . . that is steered from the shadows not by intellectual, class-conscious workers, but by well-known members of the bourgeoisie."[106]

The fiery columns in *Ethnikos Kēryx* questioned the integrity of Greek American communists and attempted to eliminate their participation in labor protests at the time. The stereotypical invocations of "clueless workers" and "deception" emphasized a concern that was quite common at the time: the links between communists and workers' discontent. In this climate, the liberal newspaper routinely advocated for workers to join the conservative AFL unions rather than the unions that were under the control of the "Reds," which were suspected of criminal activities.

These articles had an immediate result. The party cadres who had colluded with the royalist Kleanthis Vasardakis were summarily expelled. Regardless of whether the motives for this unique collaboration were financial in nature, as *Ethnikos Kēryx* trumpeted daily, or a clumsy attempt to exploit the conflict between the two newspapers, as Solounias claimed in his apology, this affair led to the expulsion of the Greek Language Bureau members, who insisted on the need to focus on Greek community life. The expulsion of Solounias from the CPUSA as "a petit-bourgeois liquidationist and opportunist" ushered in a new era for the Greek Language Bureau.[107] However, as its history shows, such organizational changes meant nothing on their own. The crucial factor that changed the form, function, and content of party activities was the radicalization of wage workers who had no previous ties to the communist movement.

The Great Turmoil

On 24 January 1934, the patrons of the luxurious restaurant in the Waldorf Astoria Hotel in New York City witnessed an unprecedented event. Suddenly and without warning, hundreds of hotel and restaurant employees left their posts and picketed the entrance of the magnificent building.

This wildcat strike by a diverse workforce, from porters to chefs, immediately drew a lot of publicity, since it took place in one of the most coveted haunts of the New York elite. *Ethnikos Kēryx* covered the developments from the start.

> Once more, the argument of the plebeians of Rome is confirmed, who went on strike to prove to the patricians that, despite the latters' intellectual superiority, they could achieve nothing without the muscle of the plebeians. Today's plebeians differ greatly from those of yore, who were completely uneducated, because they possess both intelligence and organization. If not, the maître d' hôtel, the famous Oscar, would not have been caught off guard. His employees declared war before he even knew what happened.[108]

Plebeians against patricians: the wave of strikes that surged across the United States in 1934–35 was a sign of the widening social inequalities during the Great Depression, as millions of workers fought for the right to organize and renegotiate the relations between labor and capital. It was a singular moment in the decade of the Great Depression. The spontaneous strikes in 1934 and 1935 were not connected to the official labor movement and its moderate demands. The strikes had been dominated by small radical associations and were bolstered by the participation and ingenuity of workers without any prior experience in trade unions or radical organizations. The statistics show an impressive increase in the number of strikes (1930–32: 2,289 strikes, 849,000 workers involved; 1933–35: 5,565 strikes, 3,760,000 workers involved) but cannot provide an accurate sense of their intensity and scale.[109] During the ten-day strike at the Waldorf Astoria, when six hundred employees left their posts, approximately thirty thousand employees in hotels, restaurants, and food chains marched in the streets of New York City, calling for the implementation of New Deal promises for a new social contract.[110]

These strikes were triggered by the accumulated pressure of the experiences and hardships of the early years of the Great Depression. The protests were further intensified by other factors. For example, the strike in the New York hotels and restaurants erupted immediately after the Christmas holiday season when alcohol was again legal, and so consumption had skyrocketed, following the end of Prohibition in December 1933. Finally, the strikes' unfolding and organizational characteristics often coincided with the activities of radical unions and organizations on the Communist Left. Aristodimos Caldis, a Trotskyite, played a leading role in the Waldorf Astoria strike, where he convinced a hundred Greek and Cypriot employees to leave their posts in the hotel's kitchens and restaurants.

But we should not seek the catalyst that unleashed the labor movement's full potential only in the plans laid by the radical unions. It is also to be found in the first ambitious attempt of the New Deal to renegotiate the relations between labor and capital through central regulation. The National Industrial Recovery Act (NIRA) and its creation, the National Recovery Administration (NRA), were only two of dozens of acronyms that demonstrated the New Deal's intense legislative work in 1933. The NRA legislation provided for the allocation of a "code" to each sector, which would regulate in exhaustive detail working conditions, production, and distribution. It was an ambitious corporatist program, allowing for agreements between employer associations, government committees, and labor unions, with the goal of increasing production and lowering unemployment rates. The increased role of wage labor was set in article 7a of NIRA, which recognized, for the first time in US history, the right of workers to organize in unions, free from the interference of employer associations. Despite the fact that drafting the law was one matter and implementing it was quite another, this declaration became an important milestone in the history of the labor movement.

This can be seen following the NIRA announcement in the emergence of local workers' initiatives, which were not associated with the trade unions, anticipating the debate for the allocation of the eagerly awaited "codes." *Ethnikos Kēryx* ran some brief announcements that invited Greeks to meetings "with the sole aim of defending their interests and supporting the fight for their existence."[111] Such activities cannot be attributed to the central planning of trade unions, either reformist or revolutionary. They expressed the general enthusiasm and expectation caused by the NRA. "Now with the En-Ar-É [NRA] I will buy you a canapé (sofa)." This was what a proud worker promised to his high-minded belle, in the Greek American cover of a popular Greek song.[112] In similar ways, the New Deal promised a centralized regulation of the relations between employers, workers, and consumers.

The steel workers who gathered in October 1933 in the hall of the Greek Democratic Club in Baltimore to "fight together for the rights and privileges of the NRA," or the Boston restaurant workers who gathered in August 1933 in the Dēmosthenēs Club "to establish a labor association to defend their interests," demonstrate the allure that organizing held for the public during the Great Depression.[113] The links between these meetings and the outbreak of strikes over the next few months are not always clear. The strikes were not announced in advance and often did not obey the traditions of the official labor movement. They happened spontaneously. Factories that up to that point were under the employers' complete control were turned into battlefields between strikers, scabs, goon squads, and the police. This was what happened in Weirton, West Virginia. The town's fortunes were tied to the growth of the Weirton Steel factory and the whims of its owner—who, unsurprisingly, was named Ernest T. Weir. On 18 October 1933, ten days after a steel workers' meeting in Baltimore, two thousand Greek workers employed by Weirton Steel became the key players in the first strike that challenged the industrial feudalism that prevailed in the region.[114] At the heart of the debate was the recognition of the right to associate, according to the terms of the NRA. After an initial success, and a strike that was marked by frequent clashes and many arrests, the workers realized that the employers adapted rapidly to the new circumstances. Weirton Steel responded by organizing a company-controlled union that fulfilled the provisions of labor legislation and was directed against the rising tide of militant unionism.

Such initiatives went hand-in-hand with the efforts of big companies to control and suppress procedures that would lead to the collective organization of their workforce. Corporations and companies put up a fierce fight, since they stood to lose everything they had achieved in the 1920s, when employers' programs, administrative restructuring in the companies, and repression had led to the banishment of trade unions from heavy industry. Faced with a radical labor movement, they resorted to violence. In May 1934 in Minneapolis employer associations formed armed groups against a tenacious trade union, which sought to organize the workers in the transport sector.

Meanwhile, in Toledo, workers in the automotive industry fought for the recognition of their trade union so that it could participate in the drawing up of the NRA code for this crucial industry. The battle of Toledo, a large-scale confrontation that exploded after a general strike was announced in the city and the National Guard was called in, resulted in the murder of two workers. A few weeks later, in San Francisco, protest by the port's stevedores soon expanded into a general strike. The city was in a deadlock for days, and the few skirmishes between the strikers and the police soon escalated into daily street battles on the barricades. The dry account of the events that unfolded on 5 July 1934, given by Paul Eliel, head of industrial relations in San Francisco's Chamber of Commerce, conveys the warlike atmosphere in the city: "When the final toll of the victims of strike rioting was taken the casualties were reported as two dead and 109 injured."[115] One of the two men that died that day was the "martyr of labor ideology," the Greek communist Nikos Kountourakis (Nick Bordoise).[116]

The escalation of the street battles was quite far from the intentions of the people who had drawn up NIRA. The law, which aimed to facilitate dialogue between social partners and to allow for a central regulation of the relations between labor and capital, had served as the spark that ignited the tensions and class differences that had accumulated during the Great Depression. At the forefront of this transformation were young workers, often second-generation immigrants, who demanded political and social equality, in the same way that the first-generation immigrants had brandished the Stars and Stripes in the years of labor unrest before World War I.

Those same places now saw the emergence of new forms of labor protest. In Lowell, Massachusetts, in 1933, the Greek workers of the Laganas Shoe Company participated in a general strike of the region's shoemakers and afterward joined a local trade union, the United Shoe Protective Union.[117] Their activities alarmed Christos Laganas, the owner of the factory and a benefactor of the Greek community. In the beginning of 1935, his refusal to recognize the trade union led to clashes in the factory entrance between split factions of Greek workers, which ended with the arrest of a group of strikers.[118] When the case went to court in February, Laganas, accompanied by Greek workers, appeared in court to testify against the strikers. The ages of the defendants demonstrate the leading role that young workers of immigrant descent played in the rebirth of the labor movement. Next to Nikolaos Sabatakos, 46 years old, sat John Jiannoulis, 19 years old, and Georgios Petridis, Aggelos Syggellakis, Georgios Sabatakos, Spyros Kelepouris, Nikolaos Kolitsis, and John Emerson, all of them 20 years old.

It was the young workers, men and women, who played the leading part in the strike wave that followed the announcement of the NRA, those "forgotten people" that up to that point were inhabiting the margins in the immigrant newspapers. They were not the "usual suspects" in the Greek communist groups or the class-conscious workers in radical trade unions. Their presence is often fleeting and can be detected only by their implication in a violent incident or their participation in the leadership of the ephemeral labor collectives that organized the strikes: Dimitris Sarkias and Giorgos Marmaras were convicted in the town of Danbury for assaulting scabs; Peter Gatsis, an organizer of the Greek Striker Committee, was stabbed by company security guards outside the National Biscuit factory gates while demanding union recognition; Thomas Kastas was the representative of a hotel workers' committee in Detroit; Pavlos Skaliotis (Paul George) was arrested in New York and was taken to Ellis Island for deportation.[119]

The workers' radicalization dovetailed with the activities of the Greek communist organizations. In New York, a group of Trotskyite union members in the food sector played a decisive role in the organization of a general strike, especially after that first protest in the Waldorf Astoria. In the Greek fur market, the communists and supporters of Jay Lovestone—among them one Giannis Papagiannis—were fighting with each other and at the same time against the conservative leadership of Local 70. The members of the Greek Workers Educational Associations forged ties with the local workers' initiatives, inviting them to hold meetings in their buildings and coordinating their various activities. In the industrial town of Gary, Indiana, 65 steel workers who were members of the local Greek Workers Educational

Association had also joined the Steel and Metal Workers Industrial Union; in Pittsburgh the local association had enlisted 300 hotel and food workers in the growing Food Workers Union; and in New York City, Spartacus, a workers' association, reported that 250 Greek workers had joined the Food Workers Union.

1934 was a transitional year. The reappearance of labor protests and the new forms of labor organization brought once more to the forefront an old idea: the organization of workers in industrial trade unions. The notion of industrial unionism—the organization of every worker in a particular sector into one union no matter what their position in the hierarchy—had deep roots in the history of the United States. It was a long-standing demand and a favorite proposition by radicals of all stripes, who sought in it a way out of the fragmentation and conservatism of the recognized AFL unions. The spontaneous labor protests, because of their tenacity and the fact that they accepted all workers, regardless of their place in the production line, reopened the conversation around the establishment of a new national federation of trade unions. It would express the new spirit of labor organization, of workers in every sector joining unified trade unions. This model was not new. The radical miners' unions were based on the model of the industrial organization of all workers, regardless of their position, in one unified trade organization. The new labor movement aimed to apply this everywhere: one union for every automotive worker, for example, and one federation that would coordinate the industrial unions of different sectors.

The active groups on the Greek American Left participated in these conversations and contributed to the establishment of local initiatives and workers' organizing at the heart of heavy industry. The Greek American communists had never seen anything like it. The increase in members seemed to validate the party's claims about the potential to radicalize workers. At the same time, it served as a revitalization of the party audience and helped establish communists in immigrant communities that up to that point had been indifferent or outright hostile to them. Demosthenes Nikas described his activities in Philadelphia, and he mentioned 30 new members of the Greek Workers Educational Association and 150 new subscribers to *Empros* as proof of the influence that the ideas of labor organizing had on the people. He also mentioned something that an observer had said as proof of the visibility and respectability that his comrades were enjoying: "Excellent work, Bolsheviks, you did well."[120]

This new acceptance in the community was something that the Greek American communists had been waiting for years. During the Great Depression, their feverish activity finally seemed to bear fruit. That was one way of seeing things. The other was a paradox that was soon be revealed to them. Many of the people who participated in the struggle did not share the same strategic goals—overthrowing the capitalist system—but were looking, through militant forms of organization, for a new and radical regulation of the relations between labor and capital.

NIRA was one of the stillborn initiatives of the first period of the New Deal. Faced with excessive bureaucracy and a program that was unrealistic from the start, this corporatist endeavor floundered until its final rejection as unconstitutional in May 1935. But its effect on the social geography of the United States of America was profound. The labor protests between 1933 and 1935 brought into the spotlight new social dynamics, which would prove extremely influential in the further development of the United States. The new forms of organization, which contrary to the traditional structure of the AFL were dominated by newly established industrial unions, were linked with the resurrection of the labor movement. The establishment of the Congress of Industrial Organizations (CIO) in 1935 was the direct result of organizing unskilled industrial workers and workers in the service sector—professions that up to that point had been beyond the reach of trade unions. These developments reflected the changes taking place inside the United States working class, and especially the leading role played by second-generation immigrants; these developments were based on democracy, elected representatives, and a new culture of unity regarding the idea of organization.

The new geography of organized labor largely dictated the results of the interim elections of 1934 and the 1936 presidential election, mobilizing millions of voters who cast their votes depending on each candidate's position in labor matters. The slogan "Vote Labor" resounded everywhere, from local elections all the way up to the assurances by Roosevelt that the new social contract would continue to be refined and upheld. The fact that the "forgotten people" of the Great Depression were now visible on the political and social stage created a new circumstance in American society, but also ons the American Left, which came face to face with class-conscious people who, for the most part, had never before encountered theories of class consciousness.

Notes

1. Constant, *Austin Lunch*, 32. This is a transcription of an oral testimony and thus the errors in the quote.
2. *Ethnikos Kēryx*, 6 March 1930, 4.
3. Olney, "Avoiding Default," 325.
4. *Ethnikos Kēryx*, 26 November 1930, 5; 23 June 1931, 4.
5. Wecter, *The Age of the Great Depression*, 1.
6. *Ethnikos Kēryx*, 29 September 1930, 8.
7. On Giorgos Katsaros's song "Me tis Tsepes Adeianes", see *Geia sou periphanē kai athanatē ergatia*, 135.

8. *Ethnikos Kēryx*, 31 December 1930, 4.
9. *Ethnikos Kēryx*, 1 January 1929, 1.
10. *Ethnikos Kēryx*, 21 June 1933, 4; 9 December 1932, 4; 21 February 1933, 4; Papoulias, *Anamnēseis*, 83–84.
11. Report, 21 December 1933, YDIA/MFA, 1934/B/10/BA.
12. Antoniou, *Welfare Activities Among the Greek People*, 62.
13. *Ethnikos Kēryx*, 3 November 1932, 4.
14. Report, 14 October 1936, YDIA/MFA, 1937/60/3.
15. *Ethnikos Kēryx*, 31 May 1931, 6; 20 July 1931, 6.
16. Excerpts from letters published in *Ethnikos Kēryx*: A. A., 19 October 1930, 8; N. B., 7 July 1931, 8; Anagnostis, 11 February 1932, 8; D. K., 31 May 1931, 8; K. O., 20 July 1931, 8.
17. *Ethnikos Kēryx*, 22 January 1932, 2.
18. Karvonides-Nkosi, *Greek Immigrants in the Fur Manufacturing Industry*, 191.
19. *Ethnikos Kēryx*, 19 May 1930, 4.
20. Song, *Shaping and Reshaping Chinese American Identity*, 34.
21. Cohen, *Making a New Deal*, 116.
22. *Ethnikos Kēryx*, 21 May 1931, 4.
23. *Ethnikos Kēryx*, 14 December 1931, 4.
24. *Ethnikos Kēryx*, 29 August 1933, 1.
25. *Ethnikos Kēryx*, 22 April 1933, 4.
26. *To ergon tēs kyvernēseos Venizelou*, 276.
27. Leland B. Morris to Secretary of State, "Forced Conversion of Foreign Currency into Drachmas," 7 August 1932, National Archives and Record Administration (NARA), 868.5151/104.
28. Valaoras, *O ellēnismos tōn Ēnomenon Politeiōn*, 59. Immigrant remittances in millions of "stabilized drachmas": 3,134 (1930), 2,504 (1931), 1,154 (1932), 1,085 (1933), 677 (1934).
29. Report, 15 September 1932, YDIA/MFA, 1930–1934/A/14/1.
30. Report, 10 August 1932, YDIA/MFA, 1930–1934/A/14/1.
31. *Atlantis* standardized response to letter writers, *Atlantis*, National Daily Greek Newspaper Records, Box 25.4, Decree of Greek Drachmatization (1932), Historical Society of Pennsylvania.
32. "Agreement between National Bank of Greece, New York Agency, and Atlantis, Inc. New York" (19 June 1931), *Atlantis*, National Daily Greek Newspaper Records, Box 26.3, Greek Bank Advertising Contracts, Historical Society of Pennsylvania.
33. Cohen, *Making a New Deal*, 230–31.
34. Cohen, *Making a New Deal*, 75–83.
35. *Ethnikos Kēryx*, 27 June 1932, 4.
36. *Ethnikos Kēryx*, 18 October 1931, 11.
37. Abraham, "State Regulation of Foreign Banks," 343. See also press coverage of the trial: "Hellenic Bank Head Questioned," *The New York Times*, 8 December 1937, 6; and "Greek Bank Looses Plea," *The New York Times*, 11 January 1938, 38.
38. *Ethnikos Kēryx*, 9 February 1932, 4.
39. "Notes of the Month," *The Communist*, February 1930, 99.
40. "Reds Plan a Rally at Strikers' Burial," *The New York Times*, 27 January 1930, 20.
41. Magil and North, *Steve Katovis*, 30.
42. Carr, *Twilight of the Comintern*, 9.
43. Klehr, *The Heyday of American Communism*, 33.
44. "To a Fallen Fighter: Steve Katovis," *Labor Defender*, 3 March 1930.
45. Rand School, *The American Labor Year Book: 1931*, 31.
46. Cohen, *Making a New Deal*, 241–43.
47. Rand School, *The American Labor Year Book: 1931*, 39.
48. McGill and Matthew, *The Youth of New York City*, 153.
49. *Ethnikos Kēryx*, 28 February 1931, 8.

50. Klehr, *The Heyday of American Communism*, 49.
51. Manuscript in Greek with a firsthand account of the Great Depression years, no author, John Poulos and Constantine Poulos Papers, Box 9, Tamiment Library.
52. Thompson, *The Making of the English Working Class*, 168.
53. De Caux, *Labor Radical*, 162.
54. Greek Bureau CC to the CC Language Dept, 29 December 1932, RGASPI, f. 515, op. 1, d. 2753, l. 49.
55. N. Economos report, 30 March 1932, RGASPI, f. 515, op. 1, d. 2753, l. 2–8.
56. Nelson, *Steve Nelson*, 113–17.
57. *Ethnikos Kēryx*, 21 March 1933, 2.
58. *Ethnikos Kēryx*, 11 January 1933, 4.
59. A. Caldis, "Stalinists Collaborate with Clergy," *The Militant*, 28 January 1933, 2.
60. Greek Bureau CC, 26 May 1931, RGASPI, f. 55, op. 1, d. 2336, l. 57–58.
61. Communist Party of the USA, District Seven, 10 May 1931, RGASPI, f 515, op. 1, d. 2336, l. 78.
62. Nelson, *Steve Nelson*, 75.
63. Keeran, "National Groups and the Popular Front," 23–29.
64. "International Workers Order," 1931, RGASPI, f. 515, op. 1, d. 2584, l. 9.
65. Minutes of the Greek Bureau, 19 January 1931, RGASPI, f. 515, op. 1, d. 2731, l. 37.
66. Manuscript by Michalis Savvides on the Pancyprian Brotherhood, Michalis Savvides Personal Papers.
67. *Ethnikos Kēryx*, 30 December 1931, 4.
68. Greek Bureau Meeting, 16 November 1931, RGASPI, f. 515, op. 1, d. 2531, l. 59.
69. Zumoff, "The African Blood Brotherhood," 200–26; Fowler, *Japanese and Chinese Immigrant Activists*, 101–19.
70. Moissaye Olgin, "From March Six to May First," *The Communist*, May 1930, 417.
71. S. Mingulin, "The Crisis in the US and the Problems of the Communist Party," *The Communist*, June 1930, 500.
72. Schlesinger, *The Crisis of the Old Order*, 265.
73. Katznelson, *Fear Itself*, 12.
74. Klehr, *The Heyday of American Communism*, 91.
75. *The Party Organizer*, April 1931, 21.
76. Degras, *The Communist International*, vol. 3, 280.
77. "Every Factory a Fortress of Communism," *The Party Organizer*, September–October 1931, 1–6.
78. Bernstein, *The Lean Years*, 341–42.
79. Schlessinger, *The Crisis of the Old Order*, 209.
80. "USSR 1931 – USA 1931," *Labor Defender*, November 1931, 215–16.
81. "6,000 Americans to Work in Russia," *The New York Times*, 24 August 1931, 7.
82. Tzouliadis, *The Forsaken*.
83. "Steve Pappas: Application for Leave of Absence to a Foreign Country: Central Committee Communist Party of the USA," RGASPI, f. 515, op. 1, d. 4143, l. 69–71.
84. Foster, *Toward Soviet America*, vi.
85. Foster, *Toward Soviet America*, 270.
86. Cohen, *Making a New Deal*, 478.
87. *Ethnikos Kēryx*, 25 October 1932, 4.
88. Lipsitz, *American Studies*, 45.
89. Gosnell and Gill, "An Analysis of the 1932 Presidential Vote," 975.
90. Cohen, *Making a New Deal*, 256.
91. *Ethnikos Kēryx*, 4 November 1932, 7.
92. *Ethnikos Kēryx*, 12 October 1932, 2.
93. Andersen, *The Creation of a Democratic Majority*, 100.
94. *Ethnikos Kēryx*, 5 November 1932.
95. *Ethnikos Kēryx*, 9 November 1932, 1.
96. Rosenman, *The Public Papers of Franklin D. Roosevelt*, vol. 2, 11–16.

97. Katznelson, *Fear Itself*.
98. Report, 30 May 1933, YDIA/MFA, 1933 B/8/B.
99. "Open Letter to President Roosevelt," *The New York Times*, 31 December 1933, 1.
100. Degras, *The Communist International*, vol. 3, 293–94.
101. Klehr, *The Heyday of American Communism*, 94–95.
102. "Report Submitted by the Greek Buro [sic] of the CC on the Basis of the Questionnaire of the CC," 20 March 1934, RGASPI, f. 515, op. 1, d. 3491, l. 2–4.
103. RGASPI, f. 515, op. 1, d. 3417, l. 177–93.
104. *Ethnikos Kēryx*, 20 February 1932, 4.
105. *Ethnikos Kēryx* had condemned the event in 1926. See 15 February 1926, 4; 16 February 1926, 4. In 1933 the Greek Language Bureau condemned the same event as an expression of Solounias's "opportunism." See "Report of the Situation in the Greek Buro [sic]," RGASPI, f. 515, op. 1, d. 3171, l. 13–14.
106. *Ethnikos Kēryx*, 26 October 1932, 2.
107. Minutes of the Central Control Commission Presidium, 18 February 1935, RGASPI, f. 515, op. 1, d. 3506, l. 10.
108. *Ethnikos Kēryx*, 24 January 1934, 1.
109. US Department of Commerce, *Statistical Abstract of the United States 1951*, 206.
110. Josephson, *Union House, Union Bar*, 218.
111. *Ethnikos Kēryx*, 27 October 1933, 3.
112. Kostas Dousas, "Ergatēs Timimenos" [Proud Worker], Columbia records USA F-56346, 1946.
113. *Ethnikos Kēryx*, 23 August 1933, 4; and *Ethnikos Kēryx*, 9 October 1933, 4.
114. *Ethnikos Kēryx*, 18 October 1933, 4.
115. Eliel, *The Waterfront and General Strikes San Francisco, 1934*, 112–14.
116. *Empros*, 8 July 1938, 5.
117. *Ethnikos Kēryx*, 12 February 1935, 1; Rocha, "The Lowell Shoe Strike in 1933," 115–25.
118. *Ethnikos Kēryx*, 28 February 1935, 1.
119. *Ethnikos Kēryx*, 26 February 1935, 1; *Ethnikos Kēryx*, 8 June 1934, 1; *Ethnikos Kēryx*, 14 August 1934, 4; *Ethnikos Kēryx*, 14 August 1934, 1.
120. "Demosthenis Nikas Interview," Dan Georgakas Personal Papers.

CHAPTER 4

Turmoil and Compromise

Red, American, and Greek Flags

On May Day 1937, it took the seventy thousand men and women who thronged the streets of Manhattan about ten hours to pass through Union Square. This rally, "a celebration without precedent for size and orderliness," demonstrated organized labor's momentum, following the rise of the industrial unions and the New Deal's pro-labor legislation.[1] A camera crew recorded the careful setup of the march, the impressive floats bearing slogans such as "Organization and Unity," the well-made banners, the young workers wearing white shirts and red armbands, and the crowd's orderly flow.[2] It was a disciplined festival with a single demand: the defeat of fascism. Nothing expressed this more eloquently than the procession of people marching with their fists raised high. The universal anti-fascist salute had reached the United States from Spain, where more than two thousand American citizens were fighting in the International Brigades. However, it was not just Spain that was under threat. The rise of authoritarian regimes in southeastern Europe, the Nazis' revisionist claims, the Italian invasion in Ethiopia, and the Japanese atrocities in China were all transforming anti-fascism into a universal watchword that was consolidating geographically disparate confrontations into a single narrative.

The following day, Earl Browder, general secretary of the CPUSA, addressed a crowd of twenty thousand people. He called on them to form a People's Front "in this country" in order to "wipe [fascism] from the Earth."[3] The fight against fascism was the rallying cry of American communism during the second half of the 1930s. In its political vocabulary, fascism stood for the reversal of historical progress and the resurgence of a reactionary system based on discrimination and oppression. In this sense, there was a battle to be fought inside the United States. The banners on May Day declared that "Fordism is Fascism." This equation did not refer solely to the anti-Semitic beliefs of Henry Ford but to the lengthy history of paternalism and anti-union practices within the Ford Motors industrial plants. In an event that seemed to confirm these allegations a few weeks later, the gates of the Ford River Rouge Complex in Michigan were transformed, on 26 May, into a battlefield when company goons attacked union organizers. The response was the addition of another equation to the slogan: "Fordism is Fascism and Unionism is Americanism."[4]

The appeal to Americanism was evident in the 1937 May Day parade. At the head of the procession, members of the Communist Party were marching in perfect lockstep, brandishing red flags and American flags, behind a banner proclaiming "Workers of the World, Unite!"[5] The image of the American flag in communist hands was the outcome of a radical shift in communist politics following the Comintern Seventh Congress in the summer of 1935. Responding to the global rise of fascism, the communist movement called for a Popular Front, a social and political alliance that would defend "bourgeois democracy."[6] The revolution was set aside and the overtones of class war were replaced with a new dichotomy: the "people" vs. fascists. The new line entailed a new approach to the national question. The nation was no longer a tool in the hands of the dominant classes in order to silence class antagonism but a progressive force that embodied the people's quest for equality and freedom.[7] It was a revisionist approach that, in turn, produced a rewriting of communist historiography. The Popular Front was presented as the contemporary fulfillment of the national and republican revolutions of the past in the eternal fight against oppression. In essence, the communists' proposal was disputing the very core of fascist ideology—that is, the submission of class interests to the interests of the nation—by performing a mental about-face: the communists claimed back the idea of the nation by presenting it as the common ground where unfulfilled democratic traditions met the material interests of the subordinate classes.

Earl Browder became the most vocal supporter of the new line. In early 1936 his book *What is Communism?* began with a sweeping statement: "We are the Americans . . . and Communism is the Americanism of the twentieth century."[8] Even though this claim was considered extreme (Browder dropped the slogan following a reaction by German communists in Moscow), its core rationale was in accordance with the Popular Front policy. The American communists continued to claim the country's revolutionary history—Browder's next book, *Who are the Americans?*, featured the military drummers of 1776 on the cover—and presented themselves as the contemporary representatives of a rich social and political history that challenged imperialism and colonialism while fighting for democracy and liberty. Browder was the ideal candidate for this. He hailed from rural Kansas and had been radicalized in the socialist and messianic movements of the Midwest in the early twentieth century. His presence emphasized the fact that an American could, in fact, be a communist. The results were rewarding. "Today for the first time," reported Fred Brown with restrained enthusiasm in the summer of 1936, "the majority of our Party members are native-born workers."[9]

At the same time, the Popular Front years marked a new era in the approach toward immigrant and ethnic groups. During the 1920s, the communist line was largely dictated by the policy of party Americanization and the tireless quest for a homogeneous working class, free from the shackles of immigrant origin. The Great Depression had revealed that deterministic approaches to assimilation were at odds with reality. During the Popular Front years, communists acknowledged that they had been wrong in their predictions. This was not stated publicly, but it could be clearly inferred by the numerous party articles on "immigrant groups" and their "special needs." By following Soviet handbooks on the national issue and the question of minorities, the American communist movement recognized the resilience of ethnicity based on common immigrant heritage.[10] The immigrant communities had not dissolved; they had evolved with the passage of time.

"We must bring forward the revolutionary traditions and contributions of the national groups," wrote Israel Amter in order to emphasize the differences with the 1920s, when the party perceived work among immigrant communities "as being merely an issue of language."[11] This change of line was not just a reflection of the Popular Front. It was in accordance with a broader transformation that challenged the theories of Americanization. The idea of a multicultural United States, in which ethnic traditions constituted a welcome contribution, was gaining ground in public discourse. Intellectuals like Louis Adamic (an immigrant himself) were promoting a narrative in which American strength was the outcome of the country's diverse immigrant and ethnic communities.[12] The participation of first- and second-generation immigrants in the labor movement and their active support of the New Deal gave prominence and visibility to narratives that emphasized pluralism and diversity.

In September 1936, delegates from the foreign-language bureaus of the Communist Party's Central Committee met in Pittsburgh. The last meeting of this kind had been held back in 1925, and this fact demonstrates the return to an approach that had been lost during the party Americanization years. The delegates were concerned with the rise of fascism and more particularly with "the repercussions of events taking place in Germany, Austria, Poland, and many Balkan countries."[13] These repercussions concerned the appeal of authoritarian regimes among the immigrant communities in the United States. "The language work . . . is a special problem . . . because . . . of the tremendous growth of the fascism influence among these workers," a comrade warned in 1935, noting that immigrants were joining labor unions and at the same time were supporting fascist regimes.[14] In the working-class neighborhoods of New York City one could hear Italian workers yearning for a powerful figure like Mussolini.[15] These were not misplaced judgments. In the 1930s, authoritarian and fascist regimes actively tried to win over immigrant communities. Italy provides an illuminating example. The consular authorities supported the establishment of fascist Italian American organizations, coordinated the operations of secret agents, and monitored the antiestablishment activities of anarchists and communists.[16]

Acknowledging this fact, the Pittsburgh conference dictated a new line. The Language Bureaus were called on to create Popular Fronts within the immigrant communities. More particularly, they were tasked with promoting social and political coalitions that would actively oppose the influence of authoritarian regimes among immigrants and encourage their participation in the progressive movements in the United States.[17] "Which is now our next battle?" was the rhetorical question of *Prōtoporos* (Pioneer), the monthly journal of the Federation of Greek Workers Educational Associations in 1937. The answer was simple: "It is the fight against fascism, which when seen through a wider lens, means the fight for democracy and a united front with democratic and liberal elements."[18] The Greek American communists had already initiated this policy. *Empros* initially removed the hammer and sickle from the frontpage rubric and then from the masthead as well. The motto also changed from "the newspaper of Greek workers" to "the newspaper of all working Greeks," thus alluding to an interclass alliance between the working class, the small business owners, and the intellectuals. One of the first to take note of these changes was Nikolaos Tserepis, the Greek consul in New York City. "The local communists," he reported, "were instructed to avoid extremes and to remove from their local paper the hammer and sickle, in order to better approach the working and lower masses."[19] For Tserepis and other Greek government officials, these changes could only be seen as the machinations of a shadowy communist conspiracy, which sought to dupe ignorant Greek Americans. However, this way of looking at things underestimated a crucial factor. The politics of the Popular Front were interacting with the wider transformations and dynamics that were taking place in the decade of the Great Depression.

When, in August 1936, a conservative politician in Greece, Ioannis Metaxas, imposed an authoritarian regime that quickly escalated into a semi-fascist dictatorship, the Greek American communists responded accordingly. Within the context of the Popular Front, they systematically claimed to be the true representatives of the "Greek nation" while promoting an inclusive historical narrative in which the Greek nation had always fought for freedom and equality against foreign oppressors and their local representatives. Compared to the past, the difference was all too clear. "To hell with a homeland like that!" Sokratis Georganteas had exclaimed, in the mid-1920s, in a proletarian short story recounting his adventures on the Asia Minor war front, where the Greek flag had led soldiers to "a feast for crows."[20] In the 1937 May Day parade, the Greek American communists had procured both American and Greek flags, while among them marched a few men wearing the fustanella, the traditional costume of the Greek Revolution.[21] In the words of *Empros*, the global fight against fascism "teaches us the need to utilize both the international and national means at our disposal," as well as the "democratic traditions of both nations"—the Greek and the American nation.[22]

The Greek American Popular Front

This shift did not take place overnight. It was a lengthy and complicated process that had its origins in the Greek political and social circumstances of the mid-1930s and the impact they had on the immigrant communities of the diaspora. In the turbulent Greek interwar era, the year 1936 stands out. In 1935 an unsuccessful military coup organized by liberal officers had led to the return of the exiled king to Greece and the restoration of the monarchy. This development coincided with social unrest and the growing influence of the Communist Party. In 1936 the results of the parliamentary elections neatly expressed the political impasse: the two main parties (the royalist and the liberal) could not form a government without the support of the communists. The preliminary discussions between the Liberal Party and the Communist Party, an embryonic Greek Popular Front, were followed by a mass strike in Thessaloniki that resulted in bloodshed. The phantom of Spain haunted the political establishment; when Ioannis Metaxas seized power on 4 August 1936, it seemed that order had been restored. And it had been, but at the expense of social and individual liberties. Greece was now a member of the extended family of authoritarian European states.

The Metaxas regime targeted communism as the main enemy of the nation and soon the outlawed party suffered successive blows. In this context, the Greek communist movement developed a flexible political geography. It established networks and organizational centers outside Greek borders in order to coordinate the fight against Metaxas, to provide material support to political prisoners, and to train new party cadres who would invigorate the exhausted party apparatus. The epicenter of this activity was Paris. An experienced group of Greek communists who had been living for years in the Soviet Union traveled to France and, by taking advantage of the favorable Popular Front government there, established a party apparatus that connected Athens with Moscow via Paris. This development coincided with the gradual establishment of links between communists and exiled politicians from the old liberal order in order to form a joint front against the Greek dictatorship. The outcome of these deliberations was the formation of Dēmokratikē Enōsē Ellinōn Gallias (Democratic Association of Greeks in France—DEEG).[23] The DEEG portrayed itself as the fulfillment of the Greek Popular Front, as it was the meeting point of diverse political figures who shared animosity toward Metaxas and had agreed on the "restitution of constitutional freedoms in Greece."[24]

The communist activities in Paris were linked with the coordination of Greeks, from different parts of the world, who were fighting in Spain in the International Brigades. In 1938, Dimitrios Sakarellos, the man responsible for the Greek Communist Party apparatus in Paris, reported to the Comintern: "204 [Greeks] or more—81 from America, 75 maritime workers, 22 from England, mainly Cypriots, 9 from Canada, 8 from the Soviet Union, and 7 from France."[25] For young Greek Americans this was the first time they were meeting communists from other diasporic and immigrant communities—not to mention from Greece. It was a formative experience for them, as Spain became a metaphor for the desire to assist in the struggle against the Metaxas regime. Parallels between the two Mediterranean countries were often drawn, and maybe it was not by accident that in Comintern telegrams "Greece" was the codename for Madrid.[26] In a similar vein, the letters by fighters in the front lines that were published in *Empros* combine the description of wartime events, the lyricism of total commitment to the struggle, and a constant dialogue between the "trumpets sounding from Madrid" and the "call against the Fourth of August [the day Metaxas took power in Greece]."[27]

Spain allowed young volunteers of Italian, Jewish, Greek, Croatian, and Czechoslovakian descent to discover anew a distinct anti-fascist identity, which was related to developments in their—or their parents'—countries of origin. "Don't you understand that we Jews will be the first to suffer if fascism comes?" wrote Hyman Katz, while injured, in a letter to his mother.[28] Back in the United States, the ethnic Left presented Spain as the reenactment of the progressive internationalist tradition of the nineteenth century. In a commemorative photo book published by the Greek Workers Educational Association in New York, the Greek battalion in Spain, named "Rigas Feraios" (after a revolutionary who had envisioned a Balkan federation in the late eighteenth century), became the answer of "the Greek nation to the many Byrons, Fabviers, and Santarosas" who had fought for Greek independence against the Ottoman Empire.[29]

Spain though did not only serve as an ideological point of reference. The meeting of volunteers from the United States with Greek party cadres allowed the mending of the broken links between Greek American communism and the organizational world of the Greek communist movement. The new line of the party and the dictatorship in Greece presented them with a unique opportunity to reconnect with a lost tradition: the diasporic function of immigrant radicalism. Much like a tango dancer, at first tentatively and then with increasing confidence, Greek American communists acquired a new role within the political geography of the anti-Metaxas movement and the Popular Front efforts. After all, they had advantages: a broad organizational network, a biweekly newspaper (*Empros*), a monthly literary journal (*Prōtoporos*), a bulletin for maritime workers, and access to the largest and most significant Greek immigrant community outside Greece.

In August 1937, a four-page pamphlet was circulated, announcing the establishment of the Greek American Union for Democracy.[30] The founding declaration was not signed by the Left's "usual suspects" but by five personalities identified with *Ethnikos Kēryx*: Dimitrios Christophorides, Ilias Tzanetis, Petros Kekes, Georgios Baltas, and Georgios Karaflos. Denouncing the Metaxas regime as "fascist," these prominent liberal figures expressed their willingness to cooperate with the communists in the global fight against authoritarianism and reaction. This spirit of cooperation became evident in the organization's public events, as speakers included labor unionists and intellectuals who were well-known communists.[31] An official statement by the Greek Bureau consolidated the agreement in the usual way of raising some objections in order to conclude that the Greek American Union for Democracy was a positive step in the fight against fascism and the restoration of democratic liberties in Greece.[32]

These developments echoed the formation of a Greek Popular Front in France. In the summer of 1937, *Empros* had reprinted an article from a Greek journal published in Paris that expressed the agreement between communists and exiled politicians on the prospects of an alliance against the dictatorship.[33] This was proof of renewed organizational ties with Greek communism's center in France, as *Empros* had correspondents in major French cities and in the front lines of the Spanish Civil War, while the communist Greek Maritime Workers Union had moved its headquarters to Marseille and had established a "station" in New York. Communication networks of a different kind existed between the liberals in New York and Paris, as evinced by the coordination of Christophorides and his group with the initiatives of exiled politicians in the capital of France. The most meticulous observer of these networks seems to have been Nikolaos Tserepis, the Greek consul in New York, who accurately detected links between the increased activity "among the local Greek communists, democrats, and liberals" and similar activities in France.[34]

In the confrontation with the Metaxas regime, the key argument of the Greek American Popular Front was that the Metaxas dictatorship represented values that went against the foundations of the United States. Fascism was perceived as an anti-American project. When, in April 1939, Vasilios Papadakis, the Metaxas regime's Minister of Defense, scheduled a two-month tour in the United States, the Greek American Union for Democracy appealed to the president and the State Department, requesting that he be declared persona non grata, as his activities would endanger the democratic institutions of the United States.[35] The establishment of the Dies Committee, which was commissioned to look into foreign intervention in American affairs, allowed the anti-fascists to present themselves as conscientious citizens fighting a foreign-imposed threat. Paying no attention to the irony of the whole matter (if one considers how the Dies Committee proved instrumental in curtailing the CPUSA's ties with the Communist International), the Greek American Union for Democracy called on authorities to block any public appearance and propaganda by Greek government officials.

The rhetoric and activities of the Greek American Union for Democracy reveal how Greek American anti-fascists were trying to appropriate the concept of the "nation" and draw parallels between Greece and the United States. They treated the Greek government as "anti-national" by emphasizing its submission to German and Italian interests; for instance, the loans of Greek antiquities to German museums were perceived as an act of treason. At the same time, support for Metaxas was an "anti-American" activity, since this was an authoritarian and fascist regime whose values were the opposite of the founding values of the American republic. In this context, the confrontation between the Greek American Union for Democracy and the supporters of the Metaxas regime highlights the globalizing effect of political anti-fascism—and of fascism itself—as well as the efforts to define Greek reality based on rival perceptions about the nature of contemporary Americanism.

When, in 1935, the Greek Orthodox Archdiocese of America decided to introduce into the Mass the *polychronion* (an older prayer in honor of the king), the move met with strong opposition in many communities.[36] What is important here is the way these oppositional voices were identifying royalism (and what's more, a reference to a foreign King) with anti-Americanism. "Does the ambassador realize that by chanting *polychronia* in our temples we automatically violate the oath we gave as American Citizens?" was the rhetorical question of a letter writer in the pages of *Ethnikos Kēryx*.[37] *Empros* identified a "good American" with an anti-fascist, since "you are either a good American or a good fascist, these two are mutually exclusive—it's like fire and water."[38] In a play by the International Workers Organization, a young Italian immigrant explained to his father that he was ashamed that the other kids were criticizing the politics of Italy, and his father told him that "we are all Americans and we are good Americans because we fight for the sacred traditions of liberty in the country we came from."[39]

These statements reflect how the immigrant Left was trying to recontextualize Americanism as antithetical to the European fascist and authoritarian regimes. It was a successful effort. Immigrant communities did not necessarily feel obliged to follow or support the activities of European governments that were at odds with their own realities. In the Greek American case, the traumatic experience of the enforced exchange of dollars to drachmas in the early 1930s was too recent. Moreover, the Metaxas regime often appeared to promote policies that sounded antiquated, treating immigrants as mere extensions of the Greek state. Things had changed. When Vasilios Papadakis toured immigrant communities, he reported with "regret" that many immigrants labeled the Metaxas regime as "fascist" and "authoritarian," and he discerned a fundamental incompatibility between the regime's ideological foundations and what he considered "the prevailing atmosphere of the 'liberal' American ecosystem."[40] In order to respond to this challenge, he suggested the establishment of an extensive program with the aim of inviting young Greek Americans to Greece. Two years earlier, Ioannis Metaxas himself had attended the official welcoming dinner of a "pilgrimage" trip by young Greek Americans in order to remind them of Greece's fervent wish to reach out to its "children in America."[41] In a similar spirit, Papadakis suggested the launching of Greek American chapters of the Metaxas-inspired National Youth Organization (Ethnikē Organōsis Neoleas—EON). the American Hellenic Educational Progressive Association (AHEPA) responded swiftly leading to the cancellation of the project.[42]

AHEPA was far from a communist organization. However, its positions during the late 1930s highlight the convergence of anti-fascism with Americanism. AHEPA's conventions traditionally stayed away from political discussions, but in 1938 delegates voted resolutions in an anti-fascist vein—against the Italian occupation of the Greek islands of the Dodecanese, against the anti-Semitic campaigns in Nazi Germany, and against authoritarian regimes in general.[43] Things came to a head during AHEPA's presidential elections. The Metaxas government had promoted the candidacy of Vasilios Helis, a self-made entrepreneur involved in oil extraction. Helis had served as consul in New Orleans, and he maintained close ties with Metaxas regime officials, while promising to expand his business activities in Greece.[44] When he made his bid for the presidency of AHEPA, Helis faced organized opposition by the Greek American Union for Democracy, which accused him of being a secret agent for the Metaxas regime.[45] This created an uproar and in the end Helis lost to Vasilios Tsimbidis.

The outcome of the AHEPA convention coincided with the decision of the Greek Bureau of the CPUSA to hire a respectable liberal intellectual as *Empros*'s editor in chief. Dimitrios Christophorides had served for years at *Ethnikos Kēryx*, and he was a vocal supporter of the New Deal and a committed anti-royalist when it came to Greek affairs. From 1935 onward, the liberal daily newspaper was witnessing an escalating internal schism that was reinvigorated by developments both in Greece and the United States. The schism concerned the question of communism. For instance, when the Metaxas regime was imposed, the liberal *Ethnikos Kēryx* maintained a position of "sympathetic neutrality" toward the dictatorship. While the newspaper discreetly disapproved of the authoritarian turn in Greek politics, it routinely repeated the dictatorship's revelations of communist plans to overthrow the political order and acknowledged a unanimous popular support for thwarting the "Reds." This stance was the result of a gradual acceptance of authoritarianism, especially following the decision of Eleftherios Venizelos to recognize the return of King George II to Greece in 1935.[46]

Dimitrios Kallimachos was the key person in promoting a narrative that presented the "Reds" as a potential threat both in Greece and in the United States. An intellectual instrumental in the dissemination of "hegemonic versions of immigrant subjectivity," Kallimachos's writings betrayed his religious roots (he had a degree in theology and had served as a priest) as well as his conservative leanings (before emigrating to the United States he had been editor in chief of an Athenian antiparliamentary journal).[47] Under Kallimachos's direction, *Ethnikos Kēryx* adopted a consistent anti-communist tone in which the "red dictatorship" promoted by *Empros* was presented as "infinitely worse and more depressing and more tyrannical than the simple simulacrum of a dictatorship that has been installed in Greece."[48]

There was only one column where things were different. The daily column of Dimitrios Christophorides on page two was a thorn in Kallimachos's side. When, on 21 July 1936, the main article of *Ethnikos Kēryx* argued that the Spanish Civil War was a "decisive battle between the believers of a conservative republic and the forces of the far left, which aim to install a communist dictatorship," Christophorides counterattacked, decrying the "counterrevolution supported by catholic feudalism and the monarchy."[49] This uneasy coexistence finally ended with the sacking of Christophorides in August 1936, three days before the dissolution of the Greek parliament. What followed was a gradual, but steady, rapprochement between *Empros* and Christophorides, with the latter appearing on the former's pages, something that ultimately led to the announcement of their collaboration in mid-1938.[50]

This agreement was in line with the logic of the Popular Front, whereby the communist Left relinquished control of its daily newspaper in order to promote a "progressive program to fight back the reactionary forces of the oligarchy." Christophorides accepted the position, noting that his decision was based on "the issue of a realignment of progressive forces, of rallying and readjusting to the new historical circumstances." The new period of the emblematic newspaper of the Left was announced with the usual fanfare and was linked, as usual, with the momentous developments taking place everywhere in the world, developments that created the necessity for a new awareness and a similarly readjusted way of thinking and acting. It is clear that this cooperation came to be because of the mutual shift on both sides. The communist Left was seeking alliances in the spirit of the Popular Front, and liberals like Christophorides were in need of a vehicle to express their own opinions, after *Ethnikos Kēryx* aligned or compromised with the Metaxas regime.

From this point onwara, *Empros* became a different newspaper: it carried high-quality features, had correspondents in various communities, was free from tiresomely prolix party announcements, and reported on issues that were of interest to the immigrant communities. The increase in circulation (6,000–8,000 copies) and advertising, and the expansion of points of sale, proved that Christophorides brought to *Empros* his experience and appeal.[51] At the same time, its obvious similarities, both in tone and subject matter, with the dailies of New York City clearly demonstrated a wider transformation, namely that the Greek communists' most successful moment was when they were incorporated into the mainstream conversation by tamping down their own goals. In the fourth congress of the Federation of Greek Workers Educational Associations, in March 1938, the delegates enthusiastically approved the removal of references to class antagonism from their charters, and the subsequent renaming to Greek Educational Associations. This shift signaled the end of an era—the prospect of a revolution had been replaced by the quest for progressive reforms.

Workers' education, which was one of the communists' main concerns during the 1920s, had been replaced by a program that would prepare the children for "the struggle to earn their living in society." *Prōtoporos*, a monthly literary journal, was the vehicle for promoting a "progressive educational platform" questioning the outdated and inward-looking community schools.[52] The program of *Prōtoporos* was not exceptionally radical; the key concept was progress, which had replaced the concept of class antagonism. The Greek intellectuals of the Popular Front years as a rule were conservative in their use of literary forms and they chose carefully their themes. The most renowned was Georgios Koutoumanos, a poet who rose to the position of president in the Federation of Educational Associations. His poetry collections combine the customary immigrant nostalgia with a pastoral lyricism and a grandiose rhetoric on the global battle of titans between progressive and reactionary forces. Theano Papazoglou-Margari, the editor of *Empros*'s women's column, had replaced her class-conscious short stories with advice on proper etiquette and cooking recipes, along with a veneer of moral virtue that was permeated by a pursuit of social acceptability and financial security.

For the anti-communists and supporters of the Metaxas regime, all these were just tricks intending to fool naive workers. In McKeesport, Philadelphia, the local Greek Labor Workers Educational Association and the Steel Workers' Local 1237 had supported the foundation of a Greek school free from the archdiocese's control.[53] Conservative circles were quick to react. "He was hired in order to propagandize Communism" was how the hiring of a teacher was described in a memo to the Greek Ministry of Justice, trying to find out if there were sufficient grounds "to submit a formal request to the American authorities asking for his deportation."[54] In San Francisco, the local newspaper *Kalifornia*, led by the royalist Anastasios Moudanos, cooperated with the local consular authorities against the Greek Workers Educational Association's attempts to forge links with the Greek American communities of the city.[55] In their reports to the Greek government, they repeatedly admit the difficulty in limiting communists' activities, since "they are American citizens" and therefore indifferent to threats of repercussion by Greek authorities.[56]

The Greek state could not provide the answer, either in theory or in practice, to how to combat the influence of Greek American "Reds." Despite the efforts of the Metaxas regime, its success was minimal in portraying the United States as a liberal paradise that communists were taking advantage of. Conservatives (and supporters of Metaxas) had a much more flexible, and perceptive, approach. Given the support of Greek Americans for the New Deal, they tried to emphasize a corporatist connection between Metaxas, who was trying to offer a solution to accumulated social and political questions, and FDR, who strived to eliminate the consequences of 1929. In this analogy, communism was a threat as it derailed the potential for reform. Moreover, it was an anti-American project. *Atlantis*, the royalist newspaper, commenting on strikes, admonished the Greek workers "to become good American citizens, and to avoid communism as they avoid the plague."[57] This was a line of reasoning that related to the active involvement of Greek American workers in the rising tide of the working-class movement.

Working-Class Stories

One summer day in 1937, in Weirton, West Virginia, Mike Tsouvalos's mother paid a visit to her nephew, John Frangakis. She begged him to intercede on her son's behalf and get him rehired in the sorting warehouse of Weirton Steel. On 31 May, a group of workers had attacked Tsouvalos; he fled and did not report back to work. As a result he was fired. John Frangakis was a foreman for Weirton Steel and Tsouvalos's mother had every reason to believe that he could help. But he did not give her any reason to be hopeful: "Aunt, I can't do it for you, because he is a CIO man."[58] The two men belonged to rival unions. Frangakis was a member of the employer-controlled Employee Security League, while Tsouvalos was a member of the newfound CIO (Committee of Industrial Organization) local chapter. From the beginning of May 1937, the foundries, the warehouses, and the corridors of Weirton Steel were witnessing daily tension and clashes between members of the rival unions. Tsouvalos's mother probably had no idea that her nephew had attacked her son. During the night shift on 5 May 1937, John Frangakis had led the attack against workers who had shown up for work with a CIO button on their uniforms. Among the eight Greek workers who had been beaten was his cousin, Mike Tsouvalos.

This is just one of the countless incidents of low-scale violence that marked the CIO's grand campaign for the unionization of steel workers.[59] Even though it is impossible to ascertain why someone like Mike Tsouvalos went to work wearing the CIO button, the result of such choices is much more evident. The reports by the National Labor Relations Board are rife with workers' testimonies on the everyday violence exerted by companies and company unionists against the right of workers to organize. "Did you get back to the mill after?" a member of the committee asked Steve Xindas, one of the men who had been attacked on 5 May. "After the scare I got that night? No. No," Xindas answered. He had left Weirton and despite a painful shoulder injury he had gone, on foot, to neighboring Steubenville, where the Steel Workers Organizing Committee maintained an office.[60] These are incidents of a "complex and often dramatic" nature—in the words of Lizabeth Cohen—that compose in a kaleidoscopic manner the big picture of labor unrest in 1937.[61] That year was marked by a clash between the rapidly emerging militant industrial unions and company-controlled unions. The important question was which of the two would be allowed to sign collective agreements according to the recent New Deal labor legislation. In the year 1937 more strikes were recorded than in any other year in the entire history of the United States (4,740), while the requests to the National Labor Relations Board for mediation reached 12,000.[62] Many of the strikes were successful, contributing to the expansion of CIO-affiliated unions; at the end of 1937 its membership had swelled to almost four million.[63]

Bolstered by Roosevelt's labor-friendly declarations during the 1936 election campaign, as well as the relative stability of the economy at the time, thousands of workers undertook the difficult task of spreading the labor movement's message in the strongholds of industrial feudalism—the great steel mills and the automotive assembly lines. New Deal legislation on the right to organize provided the necessary framework, but it was not just that. The disproportionate price that the working class had paid after 1929 allowed the unions to present themselves as a necessary countermeasure to the injustices inflicted upon the world of labor. At the same time, resentment toward big corporations and those who represented their interests had reached an all-time high. "If you destroy the leisure class, you destroy civilization," replied the banker tycoon J. P. Morgan when it was revealed that he had paid no income taxes between 1930 and 1932.[64] Such statements highlighted class distinctions and served as reminders of the uneven burden of the financial crisis. In this context, the working class was glorified as the unsung hero of social progress, while the New Deal appeared to fulfill the desire for a social reform that would remedy the injustices of the recent past.

The Committee of Industrial Organization (CIO), founded in 1935, had proposed the organizing of nonunionized workers in industrial unions, challenging the craft-based structure of the American Federation of Labor.[65] The idea of industrial organization was not new; it had fueled radical alternatives to the AFL's hegemony but had failed to crystallize into a competitive alternative form of labor organizing. Therefore, many thought that the CIO was doomed to failure. "To mingle highly skilled and lower skilled into one organization," the vice president of the AFL said, "is as impractical as endeavoring to mix oil and water."[66] However, within two years, what at first had seemed impossible started yielding remarkable results. This would not have been possible without the grassroots activities of thousands of workers. Proactiveness and initiative at the local level, the emergence of elected union organizers from the ranks of the workers themselves, and a culture of equality in the various meetings made the CIO's first steps look like an experiment that linked the democratization of the workplaces with the labor movement's democratic practices.

The outcasts of the craft unions were largely responsible for this development; indeed, first- and second-generation immigrants formed the backbone of the new labor movement. For instance, when Republic Steel, in Chicago, fired 656 workers in retaliation for the activities of the Steel Workers Organizing Committee, the names of those fired offered a panorama of the ethnic and racial diversity of the American working class: James Dimitrakopoulos, Frederick di Santo, John Lolito, James Kostaropoulos, Joseph Bruno, Mathew Marentic, Joseph Zarkovich, Auguste Yuratovac, Carl Mostrom, Basil Kardaras, John Durkin, Joe Miller, Edward Conlon, Carl King, George Casteris, Frank Crocilla, and Anton Kerkos.[67] The young immigrants who joined the ranks of the CIO did not seem to share the feelings of inferiority that had plagued the previous immigrant generation.[68]

John Poulos had been born in Lynn, Massachusetts, in 1911, a few years after the arrival of his family in the US from the village of Vamvakou, in Laconia, Greece.[69] His adolescence, during the 1920s, had been marked by his clash with the oppressive environment in the Greek community, which was a nightmare shared by millions of second-generation immigrants. The nightmare included extra lessons after school, in this case Greek language lessons, in the basement of a church or a community building. He was unemployed during the first years of the Great Depression and thereafter occasionally employed in an automobile repair shop. John Poulos joined the Socialist Workers Party, the leftist opposition to the Communist Party. The young radical became a leading member of Local 701 in Lynn, which evolved into one of the first examples of industrial-type organization in the food industry, uniting workers in restaurants, canteens, food chains, and hotels. Poulos's local experience led him to the next step, which came when the CIO hired him as an organizer of industrial unions in Massachusetts.

The industrial unions had realized the importance of ethnic working-class mobilization and therefore worked closely with immigrant communities and political groups. The Steel Workers Organizing Committee (SWOC) invited representatives of Greek American associations and clubs to open meetings in order to strategize how the message of unionization would reach "every Greek district, every Greek household, every Greek settlement."[70] The Federation of Greek Workers Educational Associations was pivotal in providing a solidarity network in Midwestern working-class communities. In Gary, Cleveland, Canton, McKeesport, and Pittsburgh the local Greek Workers Educational Associations organized events, hosted touring organizers, and operated registration offices for local CIO chapters. The communist press followed these developments closely. In Ohio, the towns of Yorkville, Beech Bottom, and Benwood had all seen the establishment of local CIO chapters, thanks to the tireless campaign of Demosthenes Nikas. In Canton, a Greek worker was elected vice president of the local CIO chapter. In Chicago, seven Greeks had been injured in the clashes outside the Republic Steel plant. And in Indiana Harbor, four Greeks were members of the thirty-strong strike committee.[71]

This news turned the public's attention to the remote world—largely invisible to the mainstream Greek American press—of *atsalades* (steel men). In the summer of 1937, the literary journal *Prōtoporos* published a "proletarian short story" introducing its readers to the everyday life of workers in the *teneketzidika* (steel mills).[72] It was a story full of professional jargon, including Greek American adaptations of English words relating to the industrial process (e.g., *alavatiras* for elevator), but most important to the emerging world of organized labor was *yunio*, meaning union. Despite its didactic tone, the story offers an intriguing insight into the main reasons for friction. The "bossie" (boss) against whom the workers organize is not a faceless figure on the board of directors but the production line supervisor. He embodies all the negative qualities of a worker who has renounced his class and acts as a representative of the employer. He determines the rate of production, the hirings and the firings, while controlling the workers' everyday life. From this perspective, the "proletarian short story" reflected the polarization inside steel factories.

In real life things were even more complicated. Weirton Steel had complied with the National Industrial Recovery Act (NIRA) legislation, implementing a program of labor representation under its own control. Moreover, the company encouraged the formation of a citizens' initiative that aimed to protect the right of labor to be free from external pressure—meaning free from the CIO.[73] "We all belong in a great family with common interests," declared the *Weirton Steel Employees Bulletin*, making it clear that the Steel Workers Organizing Committee represented an external threat to a harmonious community.[74] On a broader level, the CIO's militant character, and the activities of communist union organizers within it, stoked the fears of those who believed that the New Deal's stabilizing measures were creating fertile ground for an all-out attack on the sacred right to private property. In the words of a conservative group, "Join the CIO and help build a Soviet America!"[75]

In this climate, Demosthenes Nikas arrived in Weirton to establish a CIO local chapter. Before long, he realized that the leading figures of the Greek American community were in close contact with the company. The local AHEPA and GAPA (Greek American Progressive Association) chapters had signed a citizens' declaration against the CIO, and Weirton Steel had repeatedly responded to AHEPA's and GAPA's financial demands and had recently made a significant contribution for the completion of a Greek Orthodox church.[76] Moreover, a group of Greek Americans who had been among the leading figures of a strike in 1934 were now actively engaged in the company union.[77] For instance, a certain George Ellison (Giorgos Papantoniou), the vice president of a short-lived union following the strike, was now the key organizer for the Hatchet League (a group that was responsible for maintaining order within the plant).[78] In contrast to how things had been in the past, the foremen and line supervisors were not exclusively of Anglo-Saxon descent. Keeping the workers in line was often accomplished by creating systems of control based on shared ethnic origin. The fact that Ellison spoke the same language and shared the same customs with the numerous Greek American workers in the plant was a crucial advantage, since he could address them differently, or use networks of kinship and shared ancestry, to make sure that the undesirables were marginalized and that the obedient were rewarded.

In his correspondence for *Empros*, Nikas described Weirton as a feudal city that proved that "fascism" had already taken root in the United States. Using the playbook from his years in the IWW, Nikas tried to expose Hatchet League members by revealing their names. Traditionally, the communist movement interpreted similar phenomena in light of the concept of the misguided worker. In the new polarized reality, Nikas presented the Hatchet League as a "fascist wasps' nest"—when a worker joined it, it meant that he had crossed the Rubicon. This was a way to shame them in the community and to neutralize their activities against CIO members. His strategy did not yield the expected results. The Greek American members of the Hatchet League were operating in a safe environment; Nikas was the outsider, not them. Tensions remained high, but the CIO failed to challenge the dominance of the company union.

In other cases, violence escalated. National Guard armed units were deployed outside factory gates, goon squads routinely attacked strikers, and armed striker militias responded accordingly. In many cases, physical violence led to casualties. The SWOC's attempts to put a stop to employer control in Little Steel was marked by the death of eighteen CIO support-ers.[79] It was a moment of general upheaval. In early 1937, the CIO organiz-ers had succeeded in occupying the assembly lines of the General Motors factories. Occupying the space of production was an unprecedented tactic, since strikers would traditionally deploy around a factory or plant in order to block other workers from entering. Writing for *Empros* from Cleveland, an anonymous worker described how he became involved in the wildcat strike: "At 11 p.m. we saw all the bosses and factory managers running up and down, agitated like. At noon . . . we learned that the enginehouse had stopped and that the workers were on strike. I was curious and went down to see what was going on. And I saw all the machines idle and the workers walking around between them."[80]

The occupation of the assembly line—immortalized in photos that show workers reading the newspaper while sitting on car seats—carried revolu-tionary connotations that went back to the factory occupations of the post-1917 moment in Europe. Moreover, the prospect of unionizing the workers at the core of capitalist production was a revolutionary break with a long history of employer control and embedded practices that alternated between paternalism and oppression. Finally, the dynamics of the confrontation created a spectacular arena that gave rise to fears and aspirations around a potential overthrow of the existing social and political system. Nonetheless, the strikers' main demand was not to put an end to the wage labor system but to reach a compromise that would recognize and safeguard their right to collective organization and bargaining. In a 1937 sociological survey, the workers of Chicago blamed powerful businessmen and company unions but were reluctant to claim a socialist future. On the contrary, the overwhelm-ing majority preferred "the strengthening of two institutions to rebalance power within capitalist society: the federal government and labor unions."[81]

For the communist movement, this did not represent a betrayal. On the contrary, it seemed in accordance with the Popular Front strategy and the strategic support of the New Deal. A Greek American organizer in the SWOC campaign summarized this position: "Only under a progressive government helmed by Roosevelt and supporting the Wagner Bill, whereby the worker has the right to organize in whatever organization he sees fit, and under the strong leadership of CIO, can we hope to have steady work."[82] The labor movement's trust in state mediation was linked to the industrial unions' support of the New Deal program. In 1932, workers and the unemployed alike had voted for the Democratic Party without much to go on, but in 1936 organized workers had voted for Roosevelt en masse, contributing to his triumphant reelection. The Labor Non-Partisan League expressed the labor movement's politicization and contributed to garnering the votes of more than 80 percent of organized workers.[83] The results in industrial towns clearly demonstrated the alignment of wage labor with the Democratic Party. In Weirton, Roosevelt garnered three times as many votes as Alf Landon; in Homestead, four times; in Pittsburgh, seven times.[84] These results challenged the powerful employer associations that had funneled money into the Republican Party, warning about the dangers posed by the dynamic entry of the labor unions onto the political stage. The outcome of the 1936 elections confirmed that when the many were mobilized, they could counter the influence wielded by the powerful few.

Contrary to the triumphant outcome of the 1936 elections, the results of the labor unions' great organizational campaign in 1937 were mixed. The sharp increase in the numbers of organized workers was attributed to the recognition of the industrial unions in the factories of Big Steel and the main automotive companies, foremost among them General Motors. On the other hand, the Little Steel companies (Weirton Steel being one of them) had managed to counter the labor unions' demands through a combination of preventive and repressive measures. By mid-May 1937, the Little Steel companies had announced pay raises, while company unions unleashed attacks against the dissidents. The murder of ten workers outside the gates of the Republic Steel plant in Chicago demonstrated that the strike had reached its limits, since the SWOC could not further escalate the conflict and its reserves were exhausted. Even so, the big picture had now changed. The CIO unions had succeeded in changing the balance of power and appeared to be a vital component of the New Deal coalition.

Furs: A Greek American Story

"The fur business is almost completely irrational from the trap to the show window," reported *Fortune* magazine in January 1936.[85] This was not a very original observation. The complexities of the fur market routinely produced consternation among outside observers. However, the *Fortune* article had something to add. Despite the Depression, the sector was expanding: the market for fur coats had doubled, the number of workshops (2,101) and employees (9,749) in New York had reached the numbers of the pre-Depression years, and the annual turnover showed that the worst had passed.[86] This resurgence was owed to a turn toward cheap raw materials and affordable products, including low-cost rabbit fur that enabled the miraculous recovery of the fur industry. This development went hand in hand with the expansion of sweatshops using cheap labor. These were usually overseen by an experienced worker and added yet another piece to a chaotic puzzle in which the limits between employers and employees were often fuzzy.

The expansion of the contractor workshops was a constant concern for organized labor. In 1935 a new union had emerged. The International Fur Workers Union was the product of a merger between the "Red" Industrial Union of Fur Workers and the International Fur Workers Association, which belonged to the American Federation of Labor.[87] The new union (which soon joined the CIO) launched a campaign against contract work and aimed to impose a closed-shop system. In this context, the constellation of Greek fur workshops was targeted as an autonomous sphere that threatened the union's potential for regulating and controlling the sector—something that had also happened a decade earlier. This meant that the "ten years of harmonious cooperation between capital and labor"—in the words of the president of the Greek United Fur Manufacturers Association (UFMA)—were coming to an end.[88] Until 1935, the conservative leadership of the Greek Fur Workers' Local 70 relied on its close ties with the Greek employer association and the support of the American Federation of Labor.[89]

This changed in early 1936. What followed was a reversal of what had taken place in 1927. Back then, the union's anti-communist leadership had supported the autonomy of the Greek Local 70 as a counterbalance to the influence of Ben Gold and his communist comrades. Now, the Joint Board leadership challenged the leadership of Local 70 and aimed to impose a leadership that would be closer to the newly established industrial union. The first step toward this end was a decision that "Greek fur workers" would transfer from the Joint Council to Local 70.[90] In practice, this meant the return of communists and sympathizers (who had been barred from Local 70) to the Greek Fur Workers' local. The move yielded immediate results. In 1936 there were two competing groups. The Progressive Group represented the alliance between communists, socialists, and those who were disgruntled with the course that Local 70 had taken; it expressed the Joint Board positions and argued for the compliance of Greek workshops with the terms of employment that applied to the rest of the sector. The Group of Loyal Members defended the logic of class cooperation based on common ethnicity between employers and workers; it defended Greek exceptionalism, it referred to traditional ways of solving disputes, and it cultivated anti-Semitic and anti-communist sentiments.[91] Contrary to the 1920s, though, when these references were merely implied, the visibility of the communist movement led to a much more explicit attack.

"The fight for Local 70 is not a labor issue, as it first seems," argued Ioannis Rompapas. "The struggle is an ethnic one."[92] According to the erstwhile radical, who at that point was also a leading member of the Greek employer association, the survival of the small Greek workshops was largely the result of lower wages, which could be attributed to Local 70's conciliatory politics. Should the workshops comply with the terms of employment that applied to the rest of the sector, they would go under. According to Rompapas's line of thinking, the labor movement was an instrument of Jewish entrepreneurs that sought to eradicate the Greek workshops. In this conflict, racial rhetoric became the norm. At the end of 1936, *Ethnikos Kēryx* carried a series of articles that presented developments in the fur industry as a confrontation between Greeks and "foreigners." "The corruption . . . of the union's Greek character," it was argued, "would result in the gradual disappearance of Greek workers and Greek employers, so that foreigners will build on the ruins."[93]

The ramp-up of damning articles came in the aftermath of a serious blow to the conservative Group of Loyal Members. In December 1936, two members of the board of directors resigned and accused the Local 70 leadership of financial mismanagement and backroom deals. Following this, the Progressive Group appealed to the International Fur Workers Union, condemned the "racist and antisemitic propaganda" of the Local 70 leadership, and requested the union's intervention. The offensive culminated in an inquest ordered by the board of directors of the International Fur Workers Union into the practices of the president and vice president of the Greek local.[94] The findings were damning: the defendants had shown callous disregard for the conditions of work in the Greek workshops, put up with wages below the minimum, allowed for overtime without the relevant remuneration, and led a series of strikebreaking activities.

The response of the deposed leaders is telling. In cooperation with the Greek United Fur Manufacturers Association and with the encouragement of the Greek consular authorities, they petitioned the Greek government and the dictator Ioannis Metaxas. This confirms on the one hand the steadfast cooperation between employers and conservative unionists. On the other hand it reveals a fascist vocabulary in which anti-Semitism and anti-communism went hand in hand. Feeling secure to express their views far from the public eye, they described recent developments as the result of shadowy forces: "Our opponents, who are all Israelites . . . allied with subversive Communist elements . . . [and] a few traitorous Greeks[,] . . . are trying to eradicate us . . . with satanic and terrorist methods."[95]

Furthermore, this line of argument points to an extremely narrow, ethnically determined framework in which the epicenter was the Greek fur workshops and all other social and political actors were just puppets in the hands of "foreigners." In this context, they requested an intervention by the Greek government, connecting the fight for Local 70 with the dictator's efforts to "rid our beloved Greece of the despicable virus of Communism."[96] It is definitely ironic that the conservative unionists and employers could not grasp that an intervention by the Greek government would be considered a "foreign" intervention. For them, the whole affair was a Greek matter.

In the streets of New York City, many violent incidents marked the transition of power in Local 70, sending many to hospitals and others to courtrooms.[97] The tensions, though, soon subsided. The Joint Council appointed a transitional leadership and a new collective agreement was signed. In July 1937, the elections confirmed the triumph of the Progressive Group.[98] From this point onward Local 70 joined forces with the newly established Joint Council (which replaced the Joint Board) in a campaign against contract work in unorganized sweatshops. This entailed mapping out various neighborhoods, surprise attacks by union groups to destroy equipment and raw materials stored in illegal warehouses, and pressuring legitimate "contract shops" to sign the collective agreement. *Empros* urged its readers: "If you know of persons who work at home or in remote locations, notify Local 70 central offices."[99]

Greeks were active in the contract workshops and participated actively in the American Fur Lining Contractors Association. Of the one hundred total members, twenty-five were of Greek descent, three of them had been elected to the board of directors, and one, Apostolos Apostolidis, was the president.[100] By using the seasonal nature of the work as its main argument, the association had obtained a favorable court decision that excluded its members from existing collective agreements. "The Supreme Court forbade Gold's organization to harass the association presided over by our countryman, Mr. Apostolos Apostolidis," announced *Ethnikos Kēryx* with obvious satisfaction.[101] The response of the Joint Council was a strike in the summer of 1937 that targeted the American Fur Lining Contractors Association. The mobilization of women who worked as seamstresses led dozens of formerly unorganized employees in the Greek "contract shops" to join the union. In October 1937, Local 70 could boast that it had more members than ever before: 1,455.[102]

The expansion of Local 70 transformed the gender dynamics within the union. The "finishers"—young women—played a crucial role in the production process, since they finished the treatment of furs by adding, either by hand or with a sewing machine, pieces of cloth, lining, or other cosmetic elements to a garment. Following the 1937 strike, women constituted 52 percent of the Local 70 membership; they were constantly celebrated for being in the vanguard of the movement, but only through the stated or implied comparison with the pioneers, who were all men. On the other hand, the election of three women workers to the Local 70 board of directors indicated a shift; invisible female labor had never concerned the Group of Loyal Members that had dominated Local 70 for ten years.[103]

Encouraged by these developments, the Joint Council decided to escalate its efforts in 1938 by organizing a general strike. The demands reflect the quest for job security: by proposing a thirty-hour, five-day workweek, the Joint Council aimed at an allocation of employment throughout the year, aiming to eradicate seasonal unemployment and the intensification of work during the high season.[104] The strike lasted two months. It was an impressive endeavor, with hundreds of workers, men and women, mobilizing on a daily basis and participating in cultural and educational events aiming to preserve the strikers' morale. In 1926, the strike had been an isolated incident in an era of organized labor retreat, but in the late 1930s it was an integral element of a broader working-class movement. The outcome was comparable to the results of similar campaigns in heavy industry. Some demands were satisfied (eight months of guaranteed work per year for union members and a reduction of contract workshops) but not the crucial issue of reducing work hours.

For Greek American communists, Local 70 was the "the pride of all Greeks in America."[105] In the 1938 election, 1,200 workers voted in favor of the Progressive Group.[106] This success bolstered the communists' confidence further. They were the ones who as early as 1926 had insisted on the necessity of breaking the strong ties between employers and employees, and now they were rewarded. Trying to respond to the new realities, Local 70 strived to offer an alternative form of working-class culture. Its two-story building was open every day and functioned as a meeting point, hosting social and educational initiatives. The customary annual festival was soon complemented by new activities: boat excursions around Manhattan, theater performances, lectures, participation in welfare programs, and summer camps for the members' children. At the same time, Local 70 became the pillar of the Greek American Popular Front activities. It participated in committees for New Deal progressive candidates, condemned the Metaxas regime, and provided financial support to the Second Spanish Republic and to political exiles from Greece.

Its dominance allowed its opponents to regroup and rebrand themselves. The old Group of Loyal Members dissolved and a new opposition was formed, named the Right-Wing Liberal Bloc. This new title expressed the transition from an older, paternalistic practice of privileged relations with Greek employers to the political and ideological polarization of the 1930s. When the communists had first appeared in the sector, in the mid-1920s, their opponents had argued for a unity based on the common interests of Greek workers and employers. These arguments were still in use, but the Right-Wing Liberal Bloc demonstrated an alignment with the unfolding polarization within the American labor movement, between the radical unions of the CIO and the anti-communist unions of the AFL. The Popular Front supporters in Local 70 believed that there was a thread connecting developments in the United States and in Greece; their opponents did not disagree, but they had a different name for it: anti-communism.

A Bitter End

In their year-in-review for 1938, in the issue of 30 December, the editors of *Empros* admitted that "it hadn't been an auspicious year."[107] A number of crucial fronts in the fight against fascism had been irrevocably lost or did not inspire much hope anymore. In Spain, the forces of Franco were advancing in Catalonia, in China the revolutionary forces were fleeing, in central Europe the Munich Agreement confirmed the "appeasement policy" and paved the way for Nazi expansion, while in Greece the Metaxas regime seemed more secure than ever. Naturally, none of the above was painted in such bleak colors in *Empros*. What is more, its editors were not prepared to admit that 1938 had marked the end of the New Deal's prolabor agenda and its conservative turn. A brief depression (following the 1937 strike wave) and a new political alliance between Republicans and Southern Democrats had resulted in a setback for the New Deal's progressive reforms.

After this point, American communists tried to turn back the clock to the magical moment of the Popular Front, but it proved impossible. In the summer of 1939, the Molotov-Ribbentrop Non-Aggression Pact severely undermined their efforts and led to the collapse of the anti-fascist momentum. It was a pivotal shift that would give rise, in the not-too-distant future, to the theory of two totalitarianisms that equated fascism and communism. The communist movement tried to recoup its losses by taking advantage of the public's increasing dissatisfaction with an eventual entry of the United States into the war. However, the anti-war movement was dominated by isolationists, who had no sympathy for the communist movement, while the Non-Aggression Pact rekindled accusations about the Communist Party's control by foreign powers. The Dies Committee, which up to that point concentrated on the activities of fascist groups and investigated their links with authoritarian regimes in Europe, expanded its focus to include the communists and their links to Moscow. This systematic pressure led the Communist International to an unprecedented decision: the CPUSA withdrew from the Comintern. The years 1939 and 1940 were one of the strangest periods in the history of the communist movement.

The Greek American communists were facing additional difficulties. The German offensive in France in 1940 led to the dissolution of the Greek Popular Front activities and the network of diasporic communist groups. In Greece, the Communist Party was being ruthlessly persecuted. In the United States, anxiety over foreign agents created serious problems for leading figures of the movement who, for various reasons, had not yet become naturalized citizens.[108] The Greek American Union for Democracy went into hiatus after the Molotov-Ribbentrop Pact. The communists' response was to rename *Empros*, which had been published under that name for more than fifteen years, as *Eleutheria* (Freedom)—a rather defensive move that did not leave much of a legacy. Giorgos Koutoumanos, president of the Greek Educational Federation, in a letter to his comrade and brother-in-law, Michalis Savvides, observed that "the misinformation of our countrymen has created antipathy and hostility—one could say against us."[109]

The outbreak of the Greco-Italian War in October 1940 further increased the isolation of Greek American communists. Their staunch opposition to the Metaxas regime and their refusal to participate in fundraisers for bolstering the defensive capabilities of Greece made them an easy target for slander in the immigrant press. At the same time, they were also facing one unacknowledged but quite serious problem: the conflicting information that reached the United States concerning the position of the Greek Communist Party on the question of the war. Their predicament is palpable in a resolution approved in a meeting that was held in the Spartacus offices in New York, three days after the outbreak of the Greco-Italian war. The participants declared their support for the "struggle of the Greek people against the fascist invaders" and formulated a demand for the "formation of an all-party government," which would free the country from the two "opposing factions."[110] The tone of the resolution is restrained: there are none of the usual slogans, no mention of the communists in Greece, and most importantly, no mention of the Metaxas regime.

A few weeks later, on 16 December, the cover of the weekly magazine *Life* featured an evzone—a Greek infantryman—blowing the bugle atop the Acropolis, in a photograph that emphasized the link between the ancient Greek past and the contemporary struggle against totalitarianism. In the winter of 1940, news from the Greek-Albanian border elevated Greek Americans to the representatives of a people successfully resisting the fascist threat. This glory-by-proxy (and attendant pride) was combined with worries over the fate of friends and family in the Old World, as well as a rekindled interest in Greece. The opponents of the Metaxas regime, communists and liberals, were facing a paradox. For years they had been certain that the dictatorship would collaborate with the Axis powers, but now the opposite had taken place. What would the world look like after this? One thing was certain: nothing would ever be the same again.

Notes

1. "70,000 Here Mark Orderly May Day," *The New York Times*, 2 May 1937, 1.
2. Tape: CT 1-H-2, Tamiment/Wagner Moving Images Collection, Series III, The Tamiment Library and Robert F. Wagner Archives, New York University.
3. "Mass War Urged to End Fascism," *The New York Times*, 3 May 1937, 6.
4. Kazin, *The Populist Persuasion*, 146; Vials, *Haunted by Hitler*.
5. Tape: CT 1-H-2, Tamiment/Wagner Moving Images Collection, Series III, The Tamiment Library and Robert F. Wagner Archives, New York University.
6. Dimitrov, *The Fascist Offensive and the Tasks of the Communist International*.
7. Eley, *Forging Democracy*, 266.
8. Browder, *What is Communism?*, 19. See also "Reminiscences of Earl Browder: Oral history" (1964), 236, Columbia University Oral History Collection, Special Collections.
9. Fred Brown, "Building the Party During the Election Campaign," *The Communist*, October 1936, 966; Klehr, *The Heyday of American Communism*, 381.
10. Irene Browder, "Problems of the National Groups in the United States," *The Communist*, May 1939, 456.
11. Israel Amter, "Work Among National Groups: A Central Communist Task," *The Communist*, August 1938, 722, 729.
12. Shiffman, *Rooting Multiculturalism*; Brown and Roucek, *Our Racial and National Minorities*.
13. "Decisions of the National Conference of Language Bureaus," *The Party Organizer*, November 1936, 15–18.
14. Anthony Bimba, "Report on the Language Press" (1935), RGASPI, f. 515, op. 1, d. 3742, l. 32.
15. "District Bureau Meeting," 13 October 1934, RGASPI, f. 515, op. 1, d. 3523, l. 292.
16. Ottanelli, "If Fascism Comes to America," 185.
17. "To the Croation Bureau C.C.-To the Croation Fractions of C.P (1936)," RGASPI, f. 515, op. 1, d. 3990, l. 24–26; *Empros*, 1 January 1937, 3.
18. *Prōtoporos*, February 1937, 3.
19. Nikolaos Tserepis's report to the Ministry of Foreign Affairs, 19 May 1936, YDIA/MFA 1936/48/6.
20. *Empros*, 25 September 1926, 4.
21. *Empros*, 23 April 1937, 2.
22. *Empros*, 1 June 1937, 1.
23. Karpozilos, "Apopeires sygkrotēsēs," 37–53.
24. Thrasos Kastanakis Papers, folder 32, "Ellinikē Dēmokratikē Enōsē sto Parisi," Hellenic Literary and Historical Archive Society.
25. Report, 9 May 1938, RGASPI, f. 495, op. 11, d. 130, l. 161–62.
26. Firsov, Klehr, and Haynes, *Secret Cables of the Comintern*, 110.
27. *Empros*, 14 January 1936, 5.
28. Carroll, *The Odyssey of the Abraham Lincoln Brigade*, 17.
29. Ellēnikos Ergatikos Ekpaideutikos Syndesmos Spartakos, *Ellēnes ethelontai eis tēn Ispania: anamnēstikon leukoma*, New York 193[8], 15.
30. Thrasos Kastanakis Papers, folder 32, "Ellinikē Dēmokratikē Enōsē sto Parisi," Hellenic Literary and Historical Archive Society.

31. "Assail Regime in Greece," *New York Times*, 15 November 1937, 3.
32. *Empros*, 1 October 1937, 4.
33. *O Dēmokratēs*, June 1937, 1–3.
34. Nikolaos Tserepis to Ioannis Metaxas, 5 December 1936, YDIA/MFA, 1936/48/7.
35. Request to the State Department, 29 July 1939, by the Greek American Union for Democracy and the Greek Federation of Workers' Educational Associations; rejection, 7 August 1939: NARA, 868.01B II/I4; Greek American Union for Democracy to F. D. Roosevelt, 10 March 1939, NARA 868.00/1076; Christophorides, *A New American Problem in the Light of Nazi Aggression*.
36. Dimitrios Sicilianos to the Ministry of Foreign Affairs, 15 November 1935, YDIA/MFA, 1935/A.A.K.2: Politics.
37. *Ethnikos Kēryx*, 15 November 1935, 4; *Ethnikos Kēryx*, 18 November 1935, 1.
38. *Empros*, 18 May 1937, 4.
39. "Builders of America," 21, Peter V. Cacchione Papers TAM 73, Box 3, Folder 11 "PVC plays: Builders of America, Pageant for Columbus Day," Tamiment Library.
40. Report of Vasilios Papadakis, Nikolaos Tserepis Papers, Hellenic Literary and Historical Archive Society. On EON, see "The Greek Phalange and its Efforts to Obtain Cooperation in the United States," 5 April 1939, NARA, 868.00/1095; Saloutos, *The Greeks in the United States*, 339–40; *Empros*, 15 March 1938, 4; and *Empros*, 10 August 1937, 1.
41. *Tessera crhonia* diakyvernēseos, 237.
42. Papaioannou, *The Odyssey of Hellenism in America*, 170–71; and Saloutos, *The Greeks in the United States*, 341–42.
43. Leber, *The History of the Order of AHEPA*, 314; Saloutos, *The Greeks in the United States*, 336, 432; Christophorides, *A New American Problem in the Light of Nazi Aggression*, 3.
44. Malafouris, *Ellēnes tēs Amerikēs*, 544–46.
45. *Empros*, 12 August 1938, 1; *Empros*, 17 June 1938, 1.
46. *Ethnikos Kēryx*, 4 December 1935, 1; *Ethnikos Kēryx*, 11 December 1935, 1.
47. Laliotou, *Transatlantic Subjects*, 152–58.
48. *Ethnikos Kēryx*, 18 September 1936, 4.
49. *Ethnikos Kēryx*, 21 July 1936, 2, 4.
50. Georgakas, "Demosthenes Nikas," 105.
51. *Empros*, 8 November 1938, 1.
52. *Prōtoporos*, 17 July 1936, 6.
53. *Empros*, 22 April 1937, 1; *Empros*, 14 June 1937, 5.
54. Letter to Ministry of Justice, 17 October 1939, YDIA/MFA, 1939/B/10A/BA.
55. *Empros*, 21 September 1937, 3.
56. Letter to Ministry of Foreign Affairs, 30 November 1939, YDIA/MFA, 1939/B/10/BA.
57. *Atlantis*, 26 April 1935, 8.
58. National Labor Relations Board, "In the Matter of Weirton Steel Company," 1,252.
59. Zieger, *The CIO*, 38.
60. National Labor Relations Board, "In the Matter of Weirton Steel Company," 1,238.
61. Cohen, *Making a New Deal*, 293.
62. Crowther, "Analysis of Strikes in 1937," 11; Stein, "The National Relations Board," 690.
63. Levinson, *Labor on the March*, 315; Fine, *Sitdown*, 22.
64. Schlesinger, *The Coming of the New Deal*, 479.
65. Committee for Industrial Organization, *Industrial Unionism*, 5.
66. McElvaine, *The Great Depression*, 288–89.
67. National Labor Relations Board, "In the matter of Republic Steel Corporation," 145–77; Roediger, *Working Toward Whiteness*, 217.
68. Morawska, *For Bread with Butter*, 266–97.
69. "Lynn," John Poulos and Constantine Poulos Papers, Box 11, Tamiment Library.
70. *Prōtoporos*, August 1936, 4, 22; Keeran, "The International Workers Order," 390–91.
71. *Prōtoporos*, November 1936, 10–11; *Ethnikos Kēryx*, 9 July 1936, 2; *Empros*, 18 June 1937, 1.

72. *Prōtoporos*, July 1936, 14–16; *Prōtoporos*, August 1936, 19, 25; Laliotou, *Transatlantic Subjects*, 105–6.
73. Hennen, "E. T. Weir, Employee Representation and the Dimensions of Social Control," 40; National Labor Relations Board, "In the Matter of Weirton Steel Company," 1,186.
74. National Labor Relations Board, "In the Matter of Weirton Steel Company," 1,179.
75. Kamp, *Join the CIO and Help Build a Soviet America.*
76. Varano, *Forced Choices*, 66; *Empros*, 5 November 1937, 3.
77. "Demosthenis Nikas Interview," Dan Georgakas Personal Papers; Dan Georgakas, "Demosthenes Nikas: Labor Radical," 106.
78. National Labor Relations Board, "In the Matter of Weirton Steel Company," 1,145–267, 1,228–37, 1,252; *Empros*, 19 January 1937, 5.
79. National Labor Relations Board, "In the matter of Republic Steel Corporation," 146–47; Zieger, *The CIO*, 62; National Labor Relations Board, "In the Matter of Republic Steel Corporation and Steel Workers Organizing Committee. Case No. C-184," 318.
80. *Empros*, 8 January 1937, 5; Fine, *Sitdown*, 54–57.
81. Cohen, *Making a New Deal*, 252–53.
82. *Empros*, 19 November 1937, 6.
83. Leuchtenburg, *Franklin D. Roosevelt*, 188–91.
84. Zieger, *The CIO*. 392.
85. "Furs," *Fortune*, January 1936, 66.
86. Karvonides-Nkosi, *Greek Immigrants in the Fur Manufacturing Industry*, 191.
87. Foner, *The Fur and Leather Workers Union*, 447–80; "Report on Fur Elections," 23 November 1935, RGASPI, f. 515, op. 1, d. 3761, l. 88–91.
88. *Atlantis*, 17 January 1936, 4.
89. Foner, *The Fur and Leather Workers Union*, 491.
90. *Ethnikos Kēryx*, 6 May 1936, 5.
91. *Atlantis*, 29 April 1936, 4; *Atlantis*, 13, 14, and 15 May 1936, 4.
92. *Ethnikos Kēryx*, 21 September 1936, 4. *Ethnikos Kēryx* published seven articles by Rompapas between 10 August and 21 September 1936. See also, *Ethnikos Kēryx*, 7 July 1936, 4.
93. *Ethnikos Kēryx*, 12 December 1936, 4.
94. Foner, *The Fur and Leather Workers Union*, 491.
95. Letter by Ioannis Liakos and Georgios Volanis to Ioannis Metaxas, 25 February 1937, YDIA/MFA, 1937/60/3.
96. Letter by Ioannis Liakos and Georgios Volanis to Ioannis Metaxas, 25 February 1937, YDIA/MFA, 1937/60/3.
97. "3 Stabbed in Fight of Union Factions," *The New York Times*, 20 February 1936, 2.
98. *Empros*, 20 July 1937, 1.
99. *Empros*, 8 June 1937, 1.
100. *Ethnikos Kēryx*, 28 January 1936, 4.
101. *Ethnikos Kēryx*, 13 May 1936, 2.
102. Karvonides-Nkosi, *Greek Immigrants in the Fur Manufacturing Industry*, 509.
103. *Empros*, 29 June 1937, 1; Foner, *The Fur and Leather Workers Union*, 504–12; *Empros*, 20 July 1937, 1.
104. Foner, *The Fur and Leather Workers Union*, 517; *Empros*, 29 March 1938, 1.
105. *Empros*, 16 March 1937, 1.
106. *Empros*, 2 August 1938, 1.
107. *Empros*, 30 December 1938, 1.
108. N. Oikonomakos to M. Savvides, 10 July 1940, Michalis Savvides Papers, folder 1.
109. G. Koutoumanos to M. Savvides, 12 September 1939, Michalis Savvides Papers, folder 1.
110. Resolution approved in the meeting of the Greek Educational Association Spartacus on 31 October 1940, Basil J. Vlavianos Papers, Box 154, CSUS; Meyer, "Italian Americans and the American Communist Party," 213–14; Demetrios Christophorides, "What's Happening in Greece," *New Masses*, 26 November 1940, 5–6.

CHAPTER 5

PLANNING THE FUTURE

I Need America, America Needs Me

On 13 June 1942, hundreds of thousands of people attended a huge parade in the streets of New York City.[1] Orchestrated to enhance the communal war effort and to demonstrate the unity of the American nation, the parade's slogan, "I Need America, America Needs Me," placed emphasis on American exceptionalism. Participation in the war effort was not the product of a shared historical past but the conscious choice of citizens belonging to a novel political nation. Its citizens joined the war effort to give back to the country that had guaranteed their individual and civil liberties.

In events such as this one, newspaper reports rarely strayed from the beaten path; as a rule, they adopted a sentimental and enthusiastic tone, and the narrative was embellished with intriguing snapshots, representative moments, and funny incidents. The many pages that the *New York Times* devoted to the parade were no exception. At the same time, though, the usual assertions concerning the resoluteness and communal sprit of the gathered crowd concealed an unacknowledged concern: what were the thoughts and feelings of those citizens who watched the United States wage war on their countries of origin? The *New York Times* reporter described the "cosmopolitan city crowds," emphasizing "loyal German and Italian-Americans" and the presence of "almost every other national and racial strain" as proof of national unity in difficult times.[2]

The vacillations between, on the one hand, a resounding hurrah over the Americanization of millions of immigrants and, on the other, concerns about their loyalties, pervaded American politics during the war years.[3] Empirical evidence exacerbated this ambivalence. In 1940, one year before the United States entered the War, statistical authorities had recorded 25 million residents, one sixth of the country's entire population, who had either been born outside the United States or had at least one "foreign born" parent from continental Europe or Asia.[4] In this context, the documented fascist and authoritarian influence in immigrant communities gave rise to concerns about the existence of a potential fifth column within the United States. A perceptive reader of the *New York Times* would have noticed the lack of any reference to "loyal" Japanese Americans. According to the United States government, they were in short supply. From the beginning of 1942, more than one hundred thousand Japanese—of whom more than two thirds were American citizens—had been transferred from the West Coast to concentration camps inland, where they remained in custody for the duration of the war.[5] This unprecedented, selective restriction of the civil liberties of citizens who were a priori considered a threat to national security challenged Roosevelt's declarations that Americanism "is not, and never was, a matter of race or ancestry."[6]

On the other hand, the "America Needs Me, I Need America" parade illustrates the dynamics of a new relationship between ethnicity and Americanization. According to the parade outline, the 27th float would represent "the foreign-born going through the great symbolic 'Melting Pot' and coming out with [the] designation 'I am an American.'"[7] The analogy to a famous episode from World War I seems obvious. Back then, the Ford Motor Company had launched an ambitious patriotic campaign promoting Americanization, which also entailed a symbolic act: immigrant couples would enter a gigantic pot wearing their traditional costumes, from which they emerged wearing "American" clothes and brandishing American flags. Now, during this war effort, Americanization policies were turning once again to the concept of a momentous transformation in which ethnic communities had to proclaim their organic inclusion in the American nation.

However, there was one crucial difference—ethnicity did not belong just to the past. In the 1942 parade the last floats carried young people of immigrant descent in traditional costumes. The flags they carried were not American but from countries that had resisted the Axis powers. In this instance, the immigrant past was compatible with the American present, and the point where they converged was the common enemy of fascist totalitarianism.[8] The photograph depicting traditional Greek costumes and "pleated skirts" constitutes an example of the resurgence of Old World symbols in this new reality. Immigrant pride was now acceptable, but on one condition: the alignment of immigrant descent with US foreign policy. The parade floats named "Free Greece," "Free Yugoslavia," and "Free Poland" functioned as unofficial ambassadors for resistance movements, governments-in-exile, and the suffering nations of Europe. Immigrant newspapers and organizations functioned as voices of European nations fighting fascism. Greeks, Poles, and Czechs in traditional costumes marched along

Manhattan's Fifth Avenue as proof of the war's globalizing influence and the United States' leading role in it.

"The political life of other nations," a government official noted, "has been transferred to American or British soil" because of fascist occupation.[9] This realization led to the creation of governmental agencies tasked with the collection, processing, and dissemination of information related to immigrant communities and exiled individuals. The Foreign Nationalities Branch (FNB) in the Office of Strategic Services (OSS) acquired intelligence on the activities of "foreign political personalities in the United States" in order to be kept "generally informed about respecting foreign political activities among the nationality groups in the United States."[10] In June 1943, the FNB prepared a classified booklet on each "foreign national group" in the United States. The introduction by DeWitt C. Poole, the FNB's director and an experienced diplomat, emphasized the war's ideological aspect and the United States' exceptional position. The American nation's binding factor was not a shared past but an agreement among its citizens to uphold the values of liberal democracy. This inclusionary rhetoric was in stark contrast with the racial theories of fascism. In such a dynamic interpretation of the United States there was room for everyone. Commenting on the arrival of political refugees and the resilience of immigrant communities, DeWitt C. Poole observed that the USA was operating as a democratic constituency for countries that had lost their sovereignty.[11]

Meanwhile, the priorities of the war effort necessitated the collection of intelligence on the present and future of Europe. This led government agencies to rely increasingly on the skills and expertise of expatriate intellectuals and immigrant community networks in order to monitor what went on across the Atlantic. Second-generation immigrants were instrumental in this effort; one of their chief advantages was knowledge of the required languages, which permitted them to translate the various articles in immigrant newspapers. As a rule, they had grown up in working-class families, obtained their degrees during the difficult years of the Great Depression, and belonged to the New Deal's social and political coalition. They offered their services as journalists, researchers, speechwriters, analysts, and informants, and they found reflected in the resistance movements of Europe their own political and social concerns, rediscovering through the war their own immigrant past.

Constantine (Connie) Poulos was one of them. He was born in Lynn, Massachusetts, got a degree in journalism, and on the eve of the war had published a short-lived but influential review called *Hellenic Spectator*. Written exclusively in English, the *Hellenic Spectator* indicated the emergence of a young and educated Greek American generation who yearned for a radical renewal of discourse within immigrant communities. The journal supported the New Deal and commented on the labor movement, the rights of the "foreign born," and the fight against fascism in the United States and Europe.[12] For Connie's brother, John Poulos, this was not enough. He was a Trotskyite union organizer who recognized his brother's efforts for a progressive liberalism but criticized his lack of a decisive—that is a truly revolutionary—stance.[13] In its own way, it was a valid critique: Connie Poulos was a leftist liberal committed to anti-fascism, not a communist revolutionary.

Connie Poulos's articles soon came to the attention of Louis Adamic, an intellectual devoted to combating discrimination against immigrants and the main figure behind the review *Commonweal*. The January 1941 issue carried an extensive feature on the Greco-Italian War. Adamic's article recounted in brief the history of Greek immigrants in the United States, the immigrants' social pursuits, the American public's recent interest in the Greeks' country of origin, and their contribution to US society. At the end of his article (dedicated to an old Greek American who, despite his financial difficulties, had put his child through college "so that he will help this country"), Adamic made an explicit mention of Constantine Poulos and his *Hellenic Spectator*.[14]

With such recommendations, the young Greek American journalist secured a position in the Foreign Language Division (FLD) in the Office of War Information (OWI). Poulos provided the agency with material from the Greek armed resistance movement against the fascist occupation, including "The Voice of the Greek Underground," a collection of partisans' poems and songs.[15] Initially he was successful in disseminating such material to the immigrant communities and the broader public. Later on, though, he realized that the priorities of the OWI were moving in a different direction. From the beginning of 1943, the OWI adopted a cautious policy when it came to the resistance movements in Greece and Yugoslavia, as they were suspected of being controlled by the respective communist parties. The question of whether the FLD would adopt the positions of national resistance movements or governments-in-exile became a subject of contention.

In April 1944 the armed forces of the Greek government-in-exile in Egypt revolted in favor of the nascent government of the national resistance movement. The OWI's decision to reproduce the statements of the British and Greek governments against the rebels led to the resignation of ten employees from the FLD. Among them was Connie Poulos and a friend of his, Charles Olson—who would go on to become a famous poet. "We were sniped at and gnawed and trimmed and pestered until there was absolutely nothing else for us to do," Poulos wrote to Louis Adamic.[16] A few weeks after his resignation, Poulos left for occupied Greece as a correspondent for the Overseas News Agency (ONA).[17] His example is indicative of how a resurgence of interest in European developments produced a new version of national belonging in the second immigrant generation. Poulos, through his involvement in the war effort, began to think more and more on Greece. His itinerary reflects the course of his thinking. In summer 1944 he went to Smyrna and from there a fishing boat took him to the island of Evia, where he met with OSS agents who were working closely with the Greek partisans.

Visions of a New World

"What are we fighting for?" asked Dean Alfange (Konstantinos Alfantzis) in early 1944, before asserting that "the battle of ideas and ideals which rages beneath the surface of the clash of arms, shall be the real decisive battle of the war."[18] Alfange, who had been born in Istanbul and had emigrated to the United States with his family when he was three years old, belonged to those intellectuals of immigrant descent who had proved their mettle in the public arena. Alfange had authored a distinguished study on the Supreme Court and was one of the main figures in the liberal-left circles of New York City. In 1941, prior to the United States' entry into the war, he had served as vice president of a short-lived initiative that sought—despite its reservations about the Stalinist regime—material support for the Soviet Union.[19] In 1942 the American Labor Party (ALP), the state party of New York that functioned as a meeting point for union organizers, radicals, communists, and supporters of the New Deal's left wing, chose Dean Alfange as its candidate for the New York gubernatorial elections.

The Greek American lawyer's anti-fascist opinions were well known (one newspaper had described him as a "one-man workforce dealing misery to Hitler"), and the fact that he was chosen stressed his party's connections with the immigrant communities.[20] Aiming to be the voice of "Roosevelt supporters, New Dealers, liberals, and progressives," the ALP adopted "Save the New Deal" as its main slogan, and its platform called for a new social contract supporting the working classes, the defeat of the "isolationists," and the opening of a second front in Europe.[21] Dean Alfange got 410,000 votes; that is, he won the support of one in six voters in the state of New York (17 percent). The result was a significant success for the ALP.[22] At the same time, it was a success for Greek American leftists and liberals, who aimed, by drawing attention to Alfange's immigrant descent, to draw attention to developments in Greece.

The "Greek question" had three main elements. The first one had to do with the lengthy history of Balkan rivalries and the quest for a postwar resolution that would guarantee a solution to outstanding minority issues and territorial disputes in the region. The second one was related to the country's economic and political postwar future and whether this would lead to the return of the monarchy or to a republican democracy. The third one, encompassing the other two, was the antagonism between the partisan resistance movement and the Greek government-in-exile. These three elements appeared on the agenda of a public debate hosted by the journal *Free World* in October 1943 on the "Battle for the Balkans". The Greek case in the Balkan debate was presented by Basil Vlavianos, the new editor in chief of *Ethnikos Kēryx* and a member of *Free World*'s editorial board. In his lecture, Vlavianos outlined a plan of international cooperation that would result in a Balkan federation based on the establishment of democratic governments across the region. In the course of the discussion, he defended the policies of EAM (Ethniko Apelephtherōtiko Metōpo- National Liberation Front), a resistance organization in Greece that included communists, socialists, and liberals. For Vlavianos, the EAM could guarantee a smooth postwar transition toward the establishment of a liberal and democratic regime worthy of the sacrifices made by the occupied European nations. The whole discussion moved along similar lines. Despite preexisting tensions between the Balkan states, all speakers emphasized the prospects for a new era of cooperation and stability as they anticipated the establishment of postwar governments committed to a shared platform of anti-fascism and progressive politics.[23]

The year 1943 was marked by a proliferation of plans for postwar reconstruction. The capitulation of Italy, the many successes of the Balkan resistance movements, and the defeat of the German offensive in the Soviet Union all pointed to the same conclusion: the war would soon be over and the question of a postwar settlement would be real. Meanwhile, the self-dissolution of the Comintern, the ramping-up of the Allies' declarations concerning the postwar world, and the first instances of international cooperation toward that end sustained discussion about the dawning future. *Time*, in its annual book review section, detected a new, rapidly growing category: "books on the postwar world."[24] These works (such as *One World* by Wendel Willkie or *Reflections on the Revolution of our Own Time* by Harold Laski) used the present military confrontation as a point of departure and went on to sketch a radically different future based on international cooperation and the implementation of ambitious social reforms.

Within this context, Vlavianos's vision for postwar Greece—and more broadly for the Balkans—reflected the rising popularity of federalist visions that went hand in hand with plans for social reconstruction and a radical new beginning based on the harsh experiences of the interwar financial crisis and the sacrifices of the war. Journals like *Free World* and *New Europe* became forums for intellectual and political exchange while also serving as meeting points for US intellectuals, European exiles, and immigrant groups interested in developments in Europe. They all agreed on the need to redraw the social and political map of Europe, based on the conviction that the experience of wartime resistance movements would be the defining factor for the shape of things to come. For many, communism was not considered to be a concern or, worse still, a potential threat. Vlavianos, for instance, felt at ease defending EAM even though he was not a communist himself. Quite the contrary.

Vlavianos had arrived in New York City in September 1939 to visit the world's fair, accompanied by his wife, Aikaterini Nikolaou. The outbreak of the Greco-Italian War led them to extend their stay in New York, and gradually this temporary solution turned into a permanent reality. The cosmopolitan couple, who had left Athens in 1937 to live in Paris, espoused liberal views and belonged to the upper echelons of Greek society. Nikolaou was the heiress of a prominent shipping family, while Vlavianos, who was himself a man of independent means, had studied law in Athens, Leipzig, and Munich. He had also pursued a degree in psychology and the subject of his doctoral dissertation, which he submitted in 1924, was the custom of the vendetta (or blood feud) in Greek traditional communities.[25]

In the beginning of 1940, Basil Vlavianos became the owner and editor in chief of *Ethnikos Kēryx*. The daily newspaper had run into financial difficulties, so Vlavianos's interest in the endeavor was instrumental for its survival. Vlavianos was accompanied by two close associates of similar background: Stefanos Ladas, a lawyer and diplomat, and Nikolaos Mavris, a doctor.[26] The three men had lived for a time in Paris before moving to New York and belonged to liberal networks that were involved in the discussions for an anti-dictatorship movement.[27] The outbreak of the Greco-Italian War in October 1940 brought these deliberations to a sudden halt. *Ethnikos Kēryx* supported the Greek war effort and criticism against the dictatorship disappeared. However, following the country's occupation, *Ethnikos Kēryx* became a vocal opponent of the Metaxas regime that had collapsed amidst the military defeat. From mid-1941, Vlavianos vocally argued in favor of a final break with the legacy of the dictatorship and denounced the presence of "fascist" ministers in the new Greek government-in-exile. When in February 1942 the Greek government-in-exile formally dissolved the 1936 dictatorship, he could not conceal his enthusiasm: "Free and undistracted by fascist scheming we [can now] work . . . toward a speedy and full Allied victory, and for a free, great, and democratic Greece."[28]

From mid-1943, Vlavianos moved even further to the Left. *Ethnikos Kēryx* covered Greek news presenting EAM in a favorable light. Vlavianos became a vocal supporter of the national resistance movement and his connections in journals and discussion forums were instrumental in raising awareness about Greek developments. He was not the only one. Dean Alfange, Michael J. Politis, and George Mavris (Vlavianos's close associates), as well as the director of AHEPA, George C. Vournas, wrote many articles in a wide array of newspapers and journals discussing what the world would look like after the war. Their writings demonstrate, in varying degrees, the favorable welcome that EAM's program received in the USA and the conviction that the postwar reality would not be founded on a restoration but on a decisive break with the past. In this context, the future of Greece would be determined by the momentum of the resistance movement and the guaranteed right of nations to self-determination.

"EAM was founded a month after the German invasion to coordinate the activities of various forces of the people, patriotic organizations, and civil movements . . . and its aims can be summarized as follows: first, the liberation of the country, and second, the establishment of a people's government following the liberation." Such were the introductory lines of an article Vlavianos published in the *Nation*.[29] Similar assessments frequently arose in the pages of *Ethnikos Kēryx*. In one of their meetings, on the eve of the liberation, the newspaper's editors one by one expressed their support for EAM, whose "cause is just and must prevail," since "it represents progressive ideas."[30] For liberals such as Vlavianos, the platform of the European resistance movements was in accordance with the politics of the 1930s New Deal. They had much in common: social welfare, political freedom, and the central role of organized labor in the drawing up of a new social contract.

Remnants of the "Old World"

On 29 January 1942, on the first anniversary of the death of Ioannis Metaxas, his close associate and former minister Kostas G. Kotzias was lamenting the vagaries of living in New York.

Here there are three kinds of people of Greek descent 1) Greeks with Greek papers, non-naturalized, 2) nouveau-riche American Greeks, and 3) the true Greeks, the pure American salt of the earth. 99 percent of the people populating the first two categories are the worst you can imagine. Supporters of Venizelos and Communism . . . commenced an attack on August 4th calling it Fascist!!! On Metaxas, calling him a Fascist!!! . . . Our life is frugal. . . . I have no sources of income, no support, not even of a moral kind. . . . But I will not yield. The more they strike, the more iron turns into steel.[31]

The tone of the letter betrays a man in the depths of despair. A few days later, Kotzias's worries must have reached a new low. On 4 February 1942, the prime minister of the Greek government-in-exile, Emmanouil Tsouderos, signed a constitutional act that formally put an end to the dictatorial regime that had been imposed in Greece on 4 August 1936. Closely associated with a delegitimized regime, Kostas Kotzias was facing serious problems. His wages were about to be cut off, and he would lose his right to appear as a representative of the Greek government that had resisted the Italian invasion.

Kotzias had arrived in New York City in August 1941 claiming that he wanted to award President Roosevelt the golden medal of the city of Athens as an expression of gratitude for the United States' support to the Greek nation.[32] He did not receive the warm welcome he had hoped for. "Beware of this Greek Bearing Gifts," was the title of an article in *Scoop*. The "handsome and impressive" Kostas Kotzias was called "the Greek Goebbels" in an article that featured two photographs showing him smiling next to Adolf Hitler and Joseph Goebbels himself.[33]

Kotzias was not the only representative of the inner circle of the Metaxas regime in the United States. Anticipating the capitulation of Greece, prominent members of the government had fled to different directions and a core group found refuge in New York City. They could count on their salaries and the support of wealthy Greek Americans. Not surprisingly a number of Greek officials stayed for a lengthy period of time in the luxurious St. Moritz Hotel on the East Side of 6th Avenue. The "St. Moritz Hotel Society" included, among others, the "dishonest" former minister of labor Aristidis Dimitratos, the "fascist" former secret adviser to the regime Ioannis Diakos, and the "corrupt, self-centered, and insatiable" former minister of finance Andreas Apostolidis.[34] These adjectives, which had been liberally applied by the author of a confidential report compiled for the OSS, reveal their predicament: they were trapped between the hostility of liberal and communist Greek Americans and the distrust of American authorities, who treated them as representatives of a semi-fascist regime.

The shift from initial tolerance to marginalization was evident in the case of Aristidis Dimitratos, who had arrived in New York City in October 1941 as a representative of the Greek government in the annual conference of the International Labor Office.[35] Dimitratos, who was the regime's minister of labor, remained in New York after the conference ended and participated in the Central and Eastern European Planning Board, which operated under the aegis of four governments-in-exile.[36] His ousting from the Greek government-in-exile early in 1942 brought him to an impasse. Dimitratos tried to reinvent himself. Posing as the leader of a nonexistent Greek labor party, he stated that he was eager to contribute to "postwar reconstruction in order to achieve Peace and Freedom."[37] Behind these grandiose declarations, though, lay the unease of self-exiled politicians who had been excluded from the discussions about the present and the future of Europe.

Moreover, the Metaxas people were excluded from Greek American initiatives raising support for the suffering Greeks. Greek American organizations expressed their support for the Greek nation using a vocabulary that evoked the idea of "democracy" and challenged the foundations of the Greek dictatorship. "Help Greece—it is an investment in Democracy," ran one of the main slogans of the Greek War Relief Association, which had been founded in November 1940 with the aim to coordinate food shipments to Greece. When Dean Alfange addressed the organization's inaugural event he did not even mention the Greek government.[38] The Greek War Relief Association relied on an extensive network of local committees, it functioned independently of the Greek embassy, and it placed particular importance on publishing its financial sources and the results of its fundraisers. These practices differed from the centralized and opaque models of earlier charity drives organized by Greek governments in immigrant communities.

Building upon the anti-fascist momentum of the 1930s, those who opposed the dictatorship presented the ideas of Metaxas as quintessentially anti-American. When, at the end of 1941, conservative circles close to the Church attempted (once again) to establish a nominally independent organization of Greek Orthodox Youths under the name of EON (Ethnikē Organōsē Neoleas, which had been the Metaxas youth movement acronym), AHEPA (American Hellenic Educational Progressive Association), the biggest Greek American organization distanced itself immediately and condemned the endeavor as foreign to American interests: "Keep foreign creeds and ideas out of the Church, out of the schools, out of the organized social forces. . . . America does not need them—or want them. Is this clear?"[39]

These episodes relate to the broader transformation in the relations between Greek Americans and the Greek state during the 1930s. The "American citizens of Greek descent" had been annoyed by the forced drachmatization of their savings and the tendency of Greek governments to perceive them merely as extensions of their own plans. The Metaxas regime had estranged many who thought that the authoritarian character of the Greek government stood for the exact opposite of American democratic values. Despite the fact that the Greco-Italian War had temporarily quieted the regime's critics, the collapse of the front and the ensuing capitulation resulted in a resurgence of outspoken criticism against the dictatorship. Greek American organizations were reluctant to submit without question to the policies of the Greek government. This process of emancipation and independence reflected the communities' rising self-confidence and the emergence of a novel understanding of the diaspora's role vis-à-vis Greek affairs.

This became evident in the summer of 1941. Following the occupation of Greece, two rival organizations emerged in the United States aiming to defend the Greek nation. Such rivalries were not unprecedented in Greek American affairs, but this time the rift reflected a deeper divergence. The

National Committee for the Restoration of Greece, founded in July 1941, was supported, and according to other sources even encouraged, by the Greek government-in-exile, through the Greek ambassador in Washington, DC.[40] AHEPA's reaction was, again, swift. At its annual conference, in August 1941 in Cincinnati, AHEPA declared its intention to call for a conference of all Greek American organizations in order to coordinate their activities concerning Greece. The result was the establishment of the American Pan-Hellenic Federation. Contrary to the National Committee for the Restoration of Greece, the federation had no ties with the Greek government and was outspoken in its criticism to the Metaxas regime. The future of Greece was framed within the context of democracy.[41] "Hitler has crushed the land where Democracy was born, but not the Democratic spirit" proclaimed, in English, the invitation of AHEPA to the organization's founding congress, concluding that "so long as there is a United States of America, Democracy is not lost. The answer to Fascism and Nazism is more democracy. . . . When Fascism and Nazism are exterminated, democratic Greece shall be free."[42] In this way, the federation was claiming a distinctive diasporic role. "Americans of Greek descent" were enjoying the privilege of political freedom in the United States and thus had the moral obligation to contribute to the liberation of Greece—from the Axis forces as well as from the shackles of the Metaxas regime.

Double Ambassadors

At the end of the 1930s, the Greek American communists had claimed a leading role in the fight against the Metaxas dictatorship. The crisis of the Popular Front policy, the German-Soviet Non-Aggression Pact, and the outbreak of the Greco-Italian War had led to the interruption of all related activities. Now, conditions were once more favorable. The American Pan-Hellenic Federation was founded around the time when the Soviet Union entered the war, and the coincidence allowed the communists to embrace the new initiative and to play a leading part, with their customary zeal, in spreading the federation's message. In early 1941 the Greek American communists launched a new newspaper. *Ellēnoamerikanikon Vēma* (Greek American tribune) was a sixteen- or twenty-four-page tabloid, with pages in English for the "youth." Its editor in chief was Dimitrios Christophorides. The newspaper promoted the activities of the American Pan-Hellenic Federation, whose second congress, in October 1942, brought together groups that signaled the emerging alliance between liberals and communists: labor unions, mutual-aid associations, local associations, and AHEPA chapters. "It's nothing but an accumulation of Reds," Babis Malafouris reported to Basil Vlavianos, without realizing that the editor in chief of *Ethnikos Kēryx* was more than interested in these proceedings.[43]

The American Pan-Hellenic Federation was the first in a series of similar organizations that expressed the alliance between liberals and communists within the Greek American ecosystem. These organizations combined opposition to the Metaxas regime with the values of American democracy. They also added an additional layer as far as the role of the diaspora was concerned: "Americans of Greek descent" announced their intention to contribute to the reconstruction of their country of origin by using their own American experiences from the turbulent 1930s. Postwar reconstruction was seen as an extension of the policies behind the New Deal. When a Greek American Labor Committee was founded in 1943, the declaration, signed by dozens of Greek American unionists, stated that their support for the EAM platform in Greece was an outcome of their experiences during the Great Depression, their belief in the power of organized labor, and the prospect of a democratic regime that would emulate the New Deal policies.[44] Their conviction that workers would become, after the war, the driving force of social modernization in Europe enhanced their support for postwar reconstruction. The Greek Americans aspired to act as double ambassadors—of anti-fascist Greece to the United States, and of "New Deal" United States to Greece.

The rapprochement between liberals and communists became evident in 1942 but gained momentum in 1943 when Basil Vlavianos directed *Ethnikos Kēryx* toward the policies of the EAM in Greece. Initially, the communists were cautious. The past weighed heavily on their minds. During the Popular Front years, *Ethnikos Kēryx* was instrumental in stopping deliberations about a liberal-left Greek American coalition against the Metaxas regime. Moreover, Vlavianos's background did not help matters. The communist *Ellēnoamerikanikon Vēma* presented him as yet one more expatriate political figure who cared more about postwar negotiations than about the pressing priorities of the war itself.[45] In a frontpage cartoon a furious Uncle Sam was excoriating those who were building houses of cards, trying to shape the postwar world while the war was still raging.[46] For the Left, there was only one way to help Greece, encapsulated in the call to "support President Roosevelt and the battle against Hitler."[47] These cartoons were published early in 1942, when American communists were trying to counterbalance the impact of the German-Soviet Non-Aggression Pact by focusing exclusively on the necessity to intensify the war effort. The CPUSA tried hard to pass itself off as the only responsible political and social movement, totally devoted to the war effort; questioning the war was perceived as something that—deliberately or not—supported the Axis powers.[48] In this context, the Greek American communists avoided any discussion of the shape of the postwar world as an unnecessary diversion. It was a policy that hailed from the Popular Front years; immediate anti-fascist priorities trumped strategic questions of socialist transformation. Sometimes, this led to paradoxical situations. In the summer of 1942, King George of Greece visited the United States. When readers of the *Ellēnoamerikanikon Vēma* protested the lack of any organized action against him, Petros Harisiades responded that the future of the monarchy was not at stake at that point and communists should not bring to the table matters that by their nature cause conflict. The main priority was the fight against fascism.[49]

The communists' stance changed during the war. From the end of 1942, and especially from the beginning of 1943, the matter of the postwar arrangements started to play an ever-expanding role in their thinking. *Ellēnoamerikanikon Vēma* cast aspersions on the legitimacy of the Greek government-in-exile and started arguing that the postwar Greek government should reflect the impetus of the national resistance movement.[50] This change in course was combined with news from occupied countries that reached the United States and created great expectations in the organizations of the immigrant Left. A succession of crises in the exiled governments of Poland, Yugoslavia, and Greece led the US communists to establish organizations that would introduce to the United States the positions of the European resistance movements, and would function as a counterweight to the official channels that the exiled governments had access to. The model was the All-American Slav Congress, the brainchild of Louis Adamic, which aimed to familiarize the American public with the Yugoslav resistance movement and to lay the foundations for a postwar federation in eastern Europe. The Congress had been founded in April 1942, and its main goal was the mobilization of Slavic communities in order to exert pressure for the opening of a second European front, which would remove some pressure from the Soviet Union. This model was repeated in dozens of initiatives, ranging from small communities of political refugees, such as the German American Committee to Defeat Hitler, all the way to labor union committees, such the American Polish Labor Council and the National Council of Hungarian American Trade Unionists.

A Greek American Labor Committee was founded in October 1943 and was renamed, on the eve of the liberation, in August 1944, as the Greek American Committee for National Unity. Such committees operated as unofficial ambassadors of the Greek resistance movement and insisted on an accord between the aims of EAM, the Allied proclamations, and the direction that US foreign policy would take. Their success was reinforced by the creation of more connections between the Old and the New Worlds. The establishment of the Greek Maritime Workers Federation headquarters in New York City proved to be a pivotal development. The maritime workers unions were under the control of militant communists, and this army of transnational workers provided the Greek American Left with resources regarding developments in Greece and the government-in-exile that operated out of London and Cairo. At the same time, the hundreds of Greek seamen arriving in New York City provided the Greek resistance movement with increased visibility and momentum. A photograph of the lounge in "Spartacus," in a *Life* magazine feature on the "foreign seamen whom the tides of war bring to New York City," portrays young men wreathed in cigarette smoke, holding discussions and drinking, sitting at the tables under a banner bearing the slogan "Read *Ellēnoamerikanikon Vēma* to be well informed."[51]

By mid-1943 it was becoming evident that support for EAM was gaining momentum. US authorities discerned three main factions within Greek American communities: the royalists, the liberals, and the communists.[52] This was a traditional classification. What was new was the widening rift among liberals concerning their stance on EAM. One manifestation of this division was an internal conflict that arose among the editors of *Ethnikos Kēryx*. When Vlavianos gave his public support to EAM, he angered Dimitrios Kallimachos, one of the newspaper's oldest editors who, during the 1930s, had been at the forefront of the battle against the Popular Front. In October 1942, "due to a change in the paper's national politics," Kallimachos resigned from *Ethnikos Kēryx*.[53] During the Popular Front years, the paper had vacillated on the question of whether to cooperate with the communists, but the outcome had been different: Kallimachos had triumphed. When Basil Vlavianos arrived on the scene, Kallimachos was forced out.

Kallimachos's resignation paved the way for a dialogue between *Ellēnoamerikanikon Vēma* and *Ethnikos Kēryx*. Since the beginning of 1943, Dimitrios Christophoridis and Basil Vlavianos, as editors in chief of their respective newspapers, had appeared together at public events on the present and future of Greece. The cooperation of the two papers formed a space for dialogue between liberals and communists. It began with their shared opposition to British foreign policy and the prospect of the King's return to Greece, but it did not stop there. On the contrary, it coalesced more and more around the defense of EAM's modernizing policies and the prospects of a postwar agreement that would be in line with Allied proclamations concerning the right to self-determination of those nations that had been under fascist occupation.

This development, though, also bolstered the opposition. After his resignation, Dimitrios Kallimachos cofounded a new weekly newspaper. The launch of *Eleutheros Typos* (Free press) in July 1943 finalized the division that was taking place in the liberal camp. The newspaper's militant rhetoric reflected Kallimachos's anti-communism and opposed the collaboration of

Ethnikos Kēryx with the "Reds." *Eleutheros Typos* reported extensively on the clashes between right-wing and left-wing resistance organizations and disputed the Left's communication campaign for the dominance of EAM, while warning of an unfolding communist conspiracy that intended to seize power in Greece.[54]

The increased interest in Greek affairs fanned the flames and divided immigrant communities. The main line of division was the stance on EAM. From mid-1943 there were two antagonistic and relatively equal audiences as evidenced by the circulation figures of Greek American publications. The liberal *Eleutheros Typos* and the monarchist *Atlantis* expressed their support for the Greek government-in-exile, acknowledged—in varying degrees—the monarchy, and above all opposed the Communist Left. Their combined circulation surpassed 22,000 copies (6,000 and 16,000 respectively). At the opposite side, the two newspapers that supported EAM and called for a new social and political order surpassed 19,000 copies (*Ethnikos Kēryx* with 13,000 and *Ellēnoamerikanikon Vēma* with 6,000).[55]

The information war was the rallying point of the supporters of EAM. The first act of the Greek American Labor Committee was to disprove news of an unfolding "civil war" in Greece, while the Greek American Committee for National Unity was founded with the goal of rebutting "misleading information spread by the Greek reactionary circles in Cairo . . . in order to illuminate the Greeks in America as well as the American public on the Greek matter."[56] The committees in support of EAM published books and leaflets circulating news, at times inflated and at others accurate, on the successes of the resistance movement. The published titles, such as *Greece Fights for Freedom*, had high print runs (50,000 copies), most were written in English, and these publications (such as the *Bulletin of the Greek American Committee for National Unity*) were sent to journalists, politicians, and intellectuals.[57] These activities constituted a systematic attempt to influence US foreign policy regarding Greece, demonstrated the influence of resistance movements in certain sections of the US intelligentsia, and showed the emergence of an alternative philhellenism, which aspired to the founding of a Greek republic free from the shackles of the past.

The various pamphlets and bulletins introduced the reader to the accumulated political and social issues that had plagued the modern Greek state since its independence, with a particular emphasis on its dependency on foreign powers and the unpopular institution of monarchy. They then presented EAM as an umbrella group under which heterogeneous political forces worked for the modernization of Greek society and the establishment of a democratic government. The introductory texts insisted that coverage of what went on in Greece was useful not only for understanding developments in Europe but also for helping the USA decide its stance on postwar agreements. By using a widely accepted political vocabulary, where "democracy" was mentioned side by side with "security" and the goal of ensuring "lasting peace," the committees in support of EAM presented it as an integral part of the global drive toward a better future. In a similar context, Basil Vlavianos and Dimitrios Christophoridis made frequent interventions in order to dispute allegations that EAM was preparing a communist revolution.[58] "Communism has no place in Greece," the biweekly *Bulletin of the Greek American Committee for National Unity* assured its readers.[59]

The impact of these ideas was visible in the Greek American communities. The composition of the various committees demonstrated the convergence between the world of organized labor, which had emerged during the 1930s, and the expatriate intellectuals and political figures of prewar liberalism. The leadership of the Greek American Committee for National Unity was made up of experienced political figures, representatives of local associations, prominent individuals in the Democratic Party, and labor organizers from the CIO unions. It was an exciting time for Greek American communists. The discontent that had accumulated over the choices of Greek governments during the 1930s and the prospect of a fresh start was capturing the hearts and minds of a wider audience, which was rediscovering its Greek heritage through its support for the long-suffering people of Greece. The three thousand people who gathered in New York City on 30 January 1944 to listen to a discussion between Basil Vlavianos and Spyros Galanopoulos, a representative of the Greek American Labor Committee, mark the zenith of the Greek American communists, who felt more and more that they were in the epicenter of the immigrant communities' social and political life.[60] Once more, as in the Popular Front years, their increasing impact and their ability to form effective collective movements was based on distancing themselves from the goal of revolution. It was not merely a tactical choice but an actual reorientation that followed the new politics of the CPUSA.

The Unpredictability of History

In the beginning of 1944, the CPUSA announced something previously unheard of in the history of the communist movement: the party decided to dissolve itself in order to further serve the aims of anti-fascist unity. This was the party's response to the Tehran Conference of the Great Powers in December 1943. According to Earl Browder, the conference pointed to a convergence between socialism and capitalism after the war ended—an unprecedented synthesis. Browder called Tehran "history's greatest turning point" and proposed that the Communist Party should transform itself into a political association that would function as a pressure group within the

Democratic Party and the New Deal coalition, supporting close ties with the Soviet Union and a mutually agreed reconstruction plan for the future.[61] "We are departing from orthodoxy," Browder announced to a stunned audience, before he launched into an analysis of the monumental implications of the declarations of the Tehran Conference, thus paving the way for the establishment, in May 1944, of the Communist Political Association.[62]

This radical revision did not come as a bolt from the blue. For the American communists, the Tehran line was the result of a long journey that went from the Great Depression, support for the New Deal, anti-fascist commitment, and wartime belief in the resilience of the alliance between the United States and the Soviet Union. Moreover, their vision of convergence was in dialogue with postwar plans that envisioned similar forms of transnational cooperation that would surpass the national and ideological divisions of the past. Hopes for a postwar synthesis did not appear unfounded, and the European resistance movements played a major part in boosting these hopes. Earl Browder was interested in the European resistance movements' proclamations, be they in France, Yugoslavia, or Greece. Their goals were not geared to socialist revolution anymore, even though the communists had greatly contributed to their development. News from Europe seemed to confirm the prediction that the main confrontation in the world that was dawning would not be between capital and labor but between progress and reaction, that is, between the supporters of the anti-fascist proclamations of the Great Powers and those who opposed them. Developments in Europe and Asia, where communists were leading national resistance movements, captured the imagination of their comrades in the USA, who were once more turning their attention beyond the Atlantic and Pacific Oceans in order to divine the direction of historical progress. History was unpredictable, argued Browder at the end of 1943 in order to emphasize the need for a radical reorientation in the US communist movement. A year later, the events that took place in the streets of Athens, Greece, seemed to confirm Browder's assessment of the unpredictability of historical development, but in the opposite direction.

On 3 December 1944, at 11 a.m., the first waves of a massive protest organized by EAM reached Syntagma Square. Suddenly "the police . . . fired toward the crowd at about 1110hrs. . . . All demonstrators lay prone from the moment of the first volley. At about 1115 hrs, they began to rise and disperse. . . . As the crowd withdrew, a minimum of twelve (positive count, incomplete) bodies lay in the street. . . . Most of these appeared dead."[63] This laconic recounting of the ninety seconds that changed the course of Greek history can be found in the classified report by John L. Caskey, an American archaeologist and OSS official. Caskey had recently arrived in Athens from Izmir, where he directed the OSS regional branch.

In Izmir in the summer of 1944, Caskey had met Connie Poulos, who had been "reading and re-reading the *Grapes of Wrath*," waiting patiently for the signal to board a fishing boat that would take him to the eastern shores of the island of Evia.[64] The two men would meet again in liberated Athens, as members of a small American group staying in the Grande Bretagne hotel.

Caskey and Poulos played, each in their own way, important roles in verifying the details of the fateful morning of December 3rd. The top secret report GA-149, which contains Caskey's observations, placed the blame on the Greek police, who were presented as firing without provocation on protesters who up to that point were "excite[d], but good-natured."[65] Intelligence coming from Athens contributed to the US State Department's cautious stance. On 5 December, the secretary of state, Edward Stetinius, stated that the USA respected the liberated countries' right to self-determination.[66] This statement was followed by a guarded response to the British request for military support as conditions in Athens worsened by the day. The events of 3 December were followed by an escalation of violence; EAM armed supporters clashed with the nascent forces of the first Greek postwar government and with British troops who had landed in Athens after the city's liberation.

When the police started firing on the crowd on the morning of 3 December, Poulos was in Syntagma Square, standing right next to the photographer Dmitri Kessel. Poulos's renown had already spread among the small group of American journalists who came to Athens with the British forces in October 1944. Poulos was already in the city, since he had followed a completely different and much more dangerous route. He had reached Evia in August 1944, and there the Greek American correspondent for the Overseas News Agency had met with three members of the OSS Stygia Mission, which was cooperating smoothly with the forces of ELAS (Ellēnikos Laikos Apelephtherōtikos Stratos-Greek People's Liberation Army). "Comrade-in-arms" Connie Poulos was provided with marching papers by the ELAS 7th Infantry Regiment in Evia, allowing him to follow the rebels' triumphant entry into the liberated capital of Greece.[67] He was the first correspondent to arrive in Athens, preceding the British Army.

Almost two months had passed since that day, and now Poulos was standing next to the man who recorded, with successive clicks of his shutter, the chain of events of 3 December. Kessel's photos remain to this day the only photographic evidence we have of those ninety seconds of gunfire and their immediate aftermath. "Civil war erupts in Greece," proclaimed the Christmas issue of *Life* magazine, which printed photos showing the puffs of dust thrown up by the bullets, the terrified protesters fleeing the square, the dead lying in the street, the flags of the Allied nations carried by the crowd, and the blood-spattered banner held aloft by young women, bearing the EAM slogan "When people face tyranny, they take up the chains or the arms."[68]

At the same time, Kessel's colleagues, "shocked by what they saw," wrote, tore up their copy, and rewrote it time and again, "trying to be impartial."[69] In the pages of the *Washington Post*, Stephen Barber reported closely on the British forces' reaction to the unprovoked attack, the cry of the irate crowd calling for democracy, and the persecution by the Athens police commissioner, Aggelos Evert. "I saw him . . . giving the order to fire," Barber wrote.[70] Accredited by news agencies that disseminated their correspondence to newspapers, reviews, and radio shows, these US journalists were fascinated by the Greek resistance movement. When Kessel did his photo-essay on the tragedy at Distomo, before events escalated in Athens, the images from a ravaged Greek countryside were printed alongside survivor accounts, interviews with ELAS fighters, and a full-page portrait of Aris Velouchiotis, "the guerrilla chief [who] took his name and beard from the ancient god of war."[71] The idealized view of the resistance and clichéd perceptions of Greece as the birthplace of democracy led most of the US journalists to support EAM in the Battle of Athens. The journalists' views had been shaped by their social and ideological experiences from the decade of the Great Depression, an antipathy for British colonial practices, and an idiosyncratic mix of nonconformism and a spirit of adventure. A memorandum by the State Department to President Roosevelt, on 30 December 1944, stated that the American public had been shocked by the violent confrontation and placed the blame on British forces.[72]

The demand for democracy and its betrayal by the reinstatement of the old political establishment, with the support of British guns, was the point on which most American commentators agreed. Using the correspondence from Athens, *Philhellene*, the bulletin of the American Friends of Greece, which under no circumstances could have been considered radical, disapproved of Churchill's criticism of EAM and cautioned that British interference in Greek politics could lead to a civil war.[73] "A war within the war," wrote Frank Gervasi, emphasizing that EAM was promoting a "democratic revolution" and not a communist takeover of power.[74] Gervasi's articles published in *Collier's* reflected a general impression that the postwar transition that was taking place in Athens was nothing like what the Allied powers had pledged. Writing in the *New York Post* from Rome, in the beginning of February 1945, star correspondent Leland Stowe described Athens, which he had just left, as "the saddest city in Europe."[75] At the same time, he estimated that the events in Athens represented a serious departure from the spirit of the Tehran conference, using one of the main arguments of the American Left on the matter.[76]

Stowe's line of argument relied on historical analogy. If the Spanish Civil War had paved the way for World War II, the fighting in Greece could spread to the Balkans, Italy, France, and the Netherlands, leading them once more to totalitarian regimes and to the reinstatement of interwar political elites. Thus, the Battle of Athens ceased to be an exclusively Greek affair and brought to the fore all those questions and contrasts that would determine the shape of the world after the war. Stowe's reasoning was simple: the United States should have intervened during the first phase of the crisis in Greece, ensuring a smooth postwar transition. This view, that the United States should act as a counterweight to Great Britain, was not exclusive to the events unfolding in Greece. The Greek case seemed to be the point where the Left and the liberals ran out of patience regarding Great Britain, which was further blamed for its stance against the national resistance movements during the war and its reluctance to commit to a solution of the colonial matter during the Great Powers conferences in 1943 and 1944.

The demand for a forceful US diplomatic intervention mobilized diverse political forces in the United States. This demand had been put forth right after the liberation of Athens. On 14 October 1944, in an open letter to Roosevelt, Vlavianos stressed that the American policy of neutrality concerning the events in Greece would practically benefit "those who are trying to impose unpopular persons upon the Greek people, persons who could never keep power in Greece without the aid of fascist methods."[77] Vlavianos implied that a return of the king to Greece with the support of Great Britain was entirely possible, and he petitioned the USA to adopt a stance that would ensure, on the one hand, the free choice by Greeks of their system of government, and, on the other, the country's economic reconstruction. Vlavianos carefully timed the appearance of his open letter. He printed it a mere month before the presidential elections, hoping to leverage the votes of Greek Americans to change the course of US foreign policy. His endeavor met with limited success, since the matter of American-British accordance, which was at stake at that point, was of paramount importance.

However, up to the announcement of the Truman Doctrine in March 1947, the Left and its liberal allies steadily declared, either in mass events or in meetings with senators who lent a sympathetic ear, that there was room for a positive US intervention.[78] During the Battle of Athens, this position was interpreted as a possible series of US diplomatic initiatives that would put an end to the hostilities. Thus, the usually cautious AHEPA bought out a full-page ad in the *Washington Post* to demand, through its supreme president George C. Vournas, that the United States rethink its wartime policy of agreement with Great Britain, since American weapons were being used against "the Greek patriots—the very men who fought Hitler for 4 years—not Communists . . . by British colonial troops in the city of Athens."[79]

This strong anti-British sentiment was particularly prevalent during the postwar transition. "Our prestige and authority in Greece has to some extent been undermined," Churchill admitted, "by the American Press, reporting back."[80] This was clear in the opinion surveys carried out on the American public. A memorandum by the United States Department of State specified that among those who were dissatisfied with the cooperation of the "Big Three" (around 30 percent of the sample), disappointment in the British choices had soared from 33 percent (April 1944) to 54 percent (December 1944), while the respective percentages concerning the Soviet Union were 44 percent in April and 18 percent in December.[81] In this context, controlling the information that came out of Greece was of prime importance.

The US correspondents in Athens refused to reproduce the official version of events, and this created daily tensions with the British authorities. On 5 January 1945, eleven correspondents issued a memorandum requesting the intervention of the United States government—the only one who did not sign was A. C. Sedgwick of the *New York Times*, a known anti-communist—so that "the deeply interested American public may be enabled rightfully and without any infringement of British military security to hear occasionally part of the EAM view of the present conflict."[82] This was an initiative by the supporters of national resistance movements, such as Connie Poulos and Leland Stowe, but among the signees were some more moderate colleagues, such as Marcel W. Fodor and George Weller. This act of protest infuriated the opposite side. Some conservative correspondents such as Richard Capell of the *Daily Telegraph* did not hide their contempt for the "recently Americanized" journalists (a comment that alluded to some of them being of immigrant descent), who had no battle experience but were so passionate about it.[83] A few days later, Connie Poulos found his hotel room in disarray and received threats by far-right circles. He decided to leave Athens and go on an extended tour of the Balkans and eastern Europe, where he observed the postwar transition along with the Red Army's advance. A similar course was followed by most of the US correspondents, who went on to Italy or the Middle East to continue their work.

An OSS report from Athens, in the aftermath of the December events, reported a widespread "secret hope" among the population that the Soviet Union and the United States would not "let EAM fail."[84] Of course, this was a groundless hope, because if there was something on which the two great powers agreed, it was their cautious stance regarding the events of December 1944, which at no point resulted in tangible aid to EAM or any serious diplomatic pressure on the British. In hindsight, these expectations and hopes become mere historical footnotes. However, any deterministic interpretation presenting the transition from World War II to the Cold War as something almost linear in nature contains a serious flaw. It underestimates the momentum of the alternative views, trends, and debates that existed at that point, at the point of transition. The "secret hope" in the streets of Athens may seem today like a failed reading of international relations and of the Allies' priorities in the war effort; however, these frustrated expectations offer a view into the experiences and perceptions of the period, which show us that the outcome was not as foregone as we like to think.

The "secret hope" concerning Greece knew no borders. The American Left, and more specifically the Greek American alliance of communists and liberals, had based on it the idea of postwar cooperation between the USA and the Soviet Union. The Greek crisis provided an excellent opportunity to illustrate this idea, as can be inferred from the frenzy of activity by the committees in support of EAM, who wanted to inform the public and exert as much pressure as they could on the decision-makers of US foreign policy. The correspondence by US journalists offered the evidence that the EAM supporters needed. The pamphlet *Greek Liberation*, published by the Greek American Council for National Unity, contained excerpts from the correspondence of Frank Gervasi, Leland Stowe, and the Greek American journalist Panos Morphopoulos, along with transcriptions of two popular radio shows whose hosts belonged to expatriate anti-fascist groups that had come to the USA in the 1930s: Lisa Sergio, from Italy, and Johannes Steele, from Germany.[85] The aim of this publication was to provide an overview of the triumphant liberation of Athens and to inform the public on the prospects of EAM.

By inundating major newspapers with letters of complaint about erroneous reporting, by organizing events, and by translating and reprinting articles about the crisis into Greek, the Greek American Committee for National Unity reiterated an essential argument: the events in Greece demonstrated the need for a United States diplomatic intervention, which would safeguard the self-determination of the liberated nations of Europe. "Rally to the support of our State Dept . . . for free political action in Greece" was the main slogan of an American Labor Party event in New York, whose speakers included Petros Harisiades from *Ellēnoamerikanikon Vēma* and Basil Vlavianos from *Ethnikos Kēryx*. In Greece, the EAM people were raising similar demands by stressing their agreement with the New Deal. Petros Roussos, a leading figure of KKE (Kommounistiko Komma Elladas-Communist Party of Greece), spoke highly of the United States, and Connie Poulos was more than eager to report this: "Greek people feel assured not only that America can help us in this hour, but she will do so without attempting to interfere in our domestic political life."[86]

The streets of Athens provided a more tangible version of this expectation. Numerous commentators, ranging from communist authors to American military officers, noted the preponderance of American flags among the crowd of protesters on 3 December, and the fact that many of the protesters ran to the American embassy to seek help. William Hardy McNeill, who went on to become a celebrated historian, succinctly summarized a shared sentiment. The protesters, he wrote, made "a definite effort to distinguish between the American and British policy. They shouted 'Roosevelt-Roosevelt,' constantly, and carried vast numbers of American flags. There were also many Greek flags, a few Russian, but no British."[87] Of Kessel's photos, the only one that *Life* printed full-page showed two protesters holding a "homemade American flag," while in the background two protesters could be seen lying dead or wounded. [88]

When Kostas Karagiorgis arrived in New York City, in April 1945, the EAM supporters in the States turned it into the latest and most significant attempt to promote the prospect of US intervention in the Greek matter. Karagiorgis, editor in chief of *Rizospastēs* and a leading member of the KKE (Kommounistiko Komma Elladas-Communist Party of Greece), was the ideal candidate. He had lived in France and Germany during the interwar years, he was a cosmopolitan intellectual and professional revolutionary, and he could assume the role of ambassador of the Greek resistance movement in the aftermath of its recent defeat during the Greek December. Karagiorgis remained in the States for close to three months, touring incessantly and making many public appearances, culminating in the United Nations founding conference in San Francisco, which he attended as a delegate of EAM.[89]

Karagiorgis's tour had been organized by the Greek American Council, the committee that succeeded the Greek American Committee for National Unity after the Greek December. Karagiorgis's meetings and contacts reveal the intellectual networks of the EAM supporters in the USA as well as the resilience of the communist-liberal alliance in the immediate aftermath of the Greek December defeat. Eva Palmer-Sikelianos brought Karagiorgis in contact with liberal Jewish circles in New York City, where he discussed the persecution of Greek Jews. Georgios Vournas, the President of AHEPA, organized his radio appearances, enlisting the help of Drew Pearson, his close friend and an extremely popular columnist, who during the Greek December had accused the US government of providing silent support to the British intervention. Basil Vlavianos, using his title as a member of the Greek delegation in the UN founding conference, assisted Karagiorgis in San Francisco. Finally, Dimitrios Christophoridis interceded so that the opinions of the Greek Left would find their way into the pages of the American Left's newspapers and reviews.[90]

Everywhere he went, Karagiorgis described the Greek December as an aberration of the postwar transition because it violated the right to self-determination. His reasoning reiterated the basic tenets of EAM—that there was no question of a communist revolution, that the resistance movement's program contained proposals to modernize the system of governance, and that the attack of December 3rd constituted a premeditated provocation intending to disrupt the momentum that EAM had built up in recent years. In this climate, the celebrated Greek communist managed to divide the United Nations into two opposing camps. One was defending the principles of the Tehran Conference and the other was trying to revise them. Karagiorgis placed Churchill squarely in the revisionist camp, while on the opposite side, next to Joseph Stalin, he placed Harry Truman, the American President who had just been sworn into office.[91]

"The winds will blow from all sides and scatter the fascist tatters," Karagiorgis wrote in a column in *Rizospastēs* when he returned from what he called the "North American democracy with a population of 140 million."[92] His optimism in the fair winds of history would soon be proven false, in Greece and the USA alike. The conclusion of the Greek December dealt a decisive blow to the EAM alliance in Greece, and likewise to the momentum of its "ambassadors" in the United States. This development was not merely a transatlantic reflection of Greek affairs but a far more complex and serious process of transformation that was linked with the emergence of the USA on the global scene and the appearance of a new equilibrium on the eve of the Cold War.

The most serious setback, though, was a shift in the public discourse in the United States. If in recent years the support for the national resistance movements could appear compatible with the wider goals of anti-fascist unity and winning the war, the war's conclusion signaled the end of this line of thinking. The shift took place gradually, following the transition from a spirit of anti-fascist unity to the global split of the Cold War. The events in Athens played an important role in this transition. The armed conflict left behind grave concerns about the possibility of a smooth postwar transition. These concerns resulted in successive organizational crises within the Greek American Council for National Unity. However, this turn of events did not concern exclusively the Greek Americans' support to EAM. The Greek example was gradually transformed into the ideal proxy for the confrontation between the USA and the Soviet Union, and pretty soon the "Greek question" became a shortcut for the building Cold War.

The tensions that accompanied the postwar transition in southeastern and eastern Europe gave rise to anti-communism within immigrant communities. "Here's how the red Hitlerites are preparing the new conspiracy," was one of the headlines of *Eleutheros Typos* during the days of the Red Army's march on Berlin.[93] As the spirit of anti-fascist unity was fading, such views could be expressed with increased urgency. This was further helped by the reestablishment of the anti-communist state apparatus in Greece. The papers of Basil Vlavianos reflect a change of atmosphere in the aftermath of the Greek December. Hundreds of letters to the editors of *Ethnikos Kēryx* betray disappointment and disillusionment; many portrayed EAM in bleak colors, as news from friends and family offered an insight into the violent clashes in Athens. Some of them could have never been printed, since they were full of delirious insults, especially against Vlavianos for his stance on the Greek December. Many of them, however, had been sent by traditional readers who notified the paper about canceling their subscription, saying that they felt cheated by the proclamations of EAM, which had shown its true face in December 1944. "Now that I am certain of events in Greece, I want to notify you that I'm canceling my subscription," began the letter of a reader from Chicago. Another reader from Tacoma completed his thought, writing, "I am not a friend of the king nor a friend of dictators but I do not appreciate communism, which you support these days."[94]

These letters, written in unsteady hands and full of spelling mistakes, show a reorientation on the issue of communism. As early as the mid-1930s, the matter of cooperation with the communists had divided US liberals as well as the Greek American supporters of the New Deal. The postwar transition was marked by the retreat, and at some point by the collapse, of the alliance between liberals and communists. The causes were manifold. Chief among them was disappointment in the postwar transition in Europe, which was dominated by the example of the eastern European countries, where single-party governments emerged under the control of the Red Army. Greece, too, served as proof of the communists' true intentions. This disappointment was clearly visible in the articles of intellectuals on the anti-Stalinist Left, as well as among the liberals who had cooperated with the communists during the War. However, apart from certain famous public disavowals of "Red totalitarianism," there were also the average readers of an immigrant newspaper, who believed that communism constituted as much a threat for the USA as for the country they had left behind a few decades earlier.

Faced with developments they could have never foreseen, the US communists had to confront the fact that their choices were being cast in doubt by Moscow. In April 1945, the same month that Kostas Karagiorgis arrived in New York City, the leadership of the US communist movement was informed that the academic journal *Cahiers du Communisme* had published an article on CPUSA's decision to dissolve the party. The article contained an unpleasant surprise for Earl Browder.[95] Jacques Duclos, the leader of the French Communist Party during the occupation, had written a searing indictment of Browder's choices and accused him of misconstruing the importance and substance of the Tehran Conference. "In our opinion, there is nothing that could justify the self-dissolution of the CPUSA," Duclos wrote—and everyone knew that "our" referred to the Soviet Communist Party. This episode signaled the end of the American Popular Front. The US communists, with their customary and impressive ability to change opinions and still preserve their self-confidence, decided to reconstitute the CPUSA, to oust Browder (who was unrepentant, along with his supporters), and to predict that the next—and final—historical crisis of American capitalism was on the horizon. In a sense, this prediction constituted a return to normality for the US communist movement. The consequences would soon be made apparent.

Notes

1. "I Need America, America Needs Me: The Plan of the Demonstration," Transport Workers Union of America Records, WAG 235, Box 11a, Folder 32, Tamiment Library.
2. "Millions Hail Marchers Here," *The New York Times*, 14 June 1942, 1, 38.
3. Lees, "National Security and Ethnicity," 114.
4. Foreign Nationalities Branch, *Foreign National Groups in the United States*, xi.
5. Ngai, *Impossible Subjects*, 175.
6. "Japanese Americans in the Victory Program," Japanese American Committee for Democracy, 1943, Transport Workers Union of America Records, WAG235, Box 31, Folder 17: "Japanese-American Committee for Democracy," Tamiment Library.
7. "I Need America, America Needs Me: The Plan of the Demonstration," Transport Workers Union of America Records, WAG 235, Box 11a, Folder 32, Tamiment Library.
8. "Scenes During Yesterday's Demonstration," *The New York Times*, 14 June 1942, 39–40.
9. Lees, "National Security and Ethnicity," 120.
10. William Donovan to F. D. Roosevelt, 20 December 1941, see Vlanton, "Documents," 32.
11. Foreign Nationalities Branch, *Foreign National Groups in the United States*, v.
12. "The Issue in the '40 Elections," *The Hellenic Spectator*, September 1940, 1–5.
13. John Poulos, "Constructive Criticism," *The Hellenic Spectator*, March 1940, 18.
14. Louis Adamic, "Greek Immigration in the US," *The Commonweal*, 31 January 1941, 368.
15. "The Voice of the Greek Underground," John Poulos and Constantine Poulos Papers, Box 5, Tamiment Library.
16. Lees, *Yugoslav-Americans and National Security*, 161–62.
17. Connie Poulos to Louis Adamic, 28 July 1944, Louis Adamic Papers, IV. Subject Files, A. Nationalities: Germans-Hungarians, Box 58, Manuscripts Division, Department of Rare Books and Special Collections, Princeton University Library.
18. "Text of Address by Dean Alfange at Dinner in his Honor Given by the Emergency Committee to Save the Jewish People of Europe at Commodore Hotel," 26 January 1944, Dean Alfange Papers, Series 2, "Articles and Speeches," New York Public Library, Manuscripts and Archives Division.
19. "A Program of Action, Radio Address by Dean Alfange," 15 June 1941, Dean Alfange Papers, Series 2, "Articles and Speeches," New York Public Library, Manuscripts and Archives Division.
20. "AHEPANS in the News," *The Ahepan*, September–October 1942, 22.
21. For campaign materials, see Basil J. Vlavianos Papers, Box 154, California State University, Sacramento, Special Collections and University Archives; "Alfange's Clear Stand," *Daily Worker*, 27 August 1942, 2.
22. "Big Alfange Vote Makes ALP a Powerful, Permanent Force," *New York World-Telegram*, 4 November 1942, 2.

23. "Battle for the Balkans," *Free World*, November 1943, 425–39.
24. "The Year in Books," *Time*, 20 December 1943, 33.
25. Richardson, "The Basil John Vlavianos Papers," 95–96.
26. Basil J. Vlavianos Papers, Box 145, CSUS.
27. S.P. Ladas, "Programmatic Thoughts of the Three New Directors of the National Herald," *The Hellenic Spectator*, October 1940, 4.
28. *Ethnikos Kēryx*, 7 February 1942, pg. 4.
29. Basil Vlavianos, "The Greek United Front," *The Nation*, 6 November 1943, 527.
30. Meeting, 10 July 1944, Basil J. Vlavianos Papers, Box 145, CSUS.
31. Kostas Kotzias to Theologos Nikoloudis, 29 January 1942, Theologos Nikoloudis Papers, Hellenic Literary and Historical Archive Society (ELIA).
32. "President to Receive Greek Medal," *The New York Times*, 9 August 1941, 16.
33. "Beware of this Greek Bearing Gifts," *Scoop*, n.d., 38, John Poulos and Constantine Poulos Papers, TAM 114, Box 20, Tamiment Library.
34. "Greek Politics in the United States," 15 December 1943, in Vlanton, "Documents," 88–95.
35. "US Woman Arrives on Clipper," *The New York Times*, 28 October 1941, 12.
36. Patrikiou, "Apeikoniseis tēs Gēraias Ēpeirou," 196.
37. "Greek Labor Party and Trades Unions, May Day Manifesto," Basil J. Vlavianos Papers, Box 246, CSUS.
38. "Address by Dean Alfange, Past Supreme President of the Order of AHEPA," 5 December 1940, Dean Alfange Papers, Series 2 "Articles and Speeches," New York Public Library, Manuscripts and Archives Division.
39. Saloutos, *The Greeks in the United States*, 341.
40. "Articles of Association," 24 July 1941, Basil J. Vlavianos Papers, Box 13, CSUS.
41. Saloutos, *The Greeks in the United States*, 347.
42. "Invitation to Pan-Hellenic Congress," August 1941, Basil J. Vlavianos Papers, Box 13, CSUS.
43. Babis Malafouris to Vlavianos, 31 October 1941, Basil J. Vlavianos Papers, Box 13, CSUS.
44. "Greek-American Labor Conference," 21 November 1943, Transport Workers Union, WAG 235, Box 31, Tamiment Library.
45. *Ellēnoamerikanikon Vēma*, 23 January 1942, 1.
46. *Ellēnoamerikanikon Vēma*, 13 March 1942, 1.
47. *Ellēnoamerikanikon Vēma*, 6 February 1942, 1.
48. Howe and Coser, *The American Communist Party*, 408. See also, *Ellēnoamerikanikon Vēma*, 18 December 1942, 1.
49. *Ellēnoamerikanikon Vēma*, 19 June 1942, 4.
50. *Ellēnoamerikanikon Vēma*, 20 November 1942, 6.
51. "Foreign Seamen," *Life*, 28 September 1942, 62.
52. "The Greek Community," June 1943, in Vlanton, Issue 1,"Documents," 81.
53. Demetrios Kallimachos to Demetrios Michalaros, 26 March 1952, Callimachos Demetrios Papers, Greek American Collection, Immigration History Research Center, University of Minnesota.
54. *Eleutheros Typos*, 8 April 1944, 4.
55. Georgakas, "Constantine Yavis," 123–26.
56. "Greeks Here Dispute Reports of Civil War," *The New York Times*, 20 October 1943, 5; Documents on the foundation of the Greek American Committee for National Unity: Basil J. Vlavianos Papers, Box 40, CSUS.
57. For a list of pamphlets and books published by pro-EAM committees in the United States, see the relevant section of the bibliography.
58. Demetrius Christophoridis, "Government-in-Exile regarded as not Representative of the Country," *The New York Times*, 8 May 1944, 18.
59. "Protest for False Reports," *Bulletin of the Greek American Committee for National Unity*, 1 November 1944, 1.

60. "Greek-American Mass Meeting," 2 December 1944, in Vlanton, Issue 2, "Documents," 100–102.
61. Earl Browder, "Teheran: History's Greatest Turning Point," *The Communist*, January 1944, 3–8.
62. Communist Political Association, *The Path to Peace, Progress and Prosperity.*
63. Allen, *Classical Spies*, 242.
64. "Prologos," John Poulos and Constantine Poulos Papers, TAM 114, Box 1, Tamiment Library.
65. Allen, *Classical Spies*, 242.
66. Iatrides, *Revolt in Athens*, 211.
67. Travel Order, ELAS, 7th Infantry Regiment, 7 October 1944, John Poulos and Constantine Poulos Papers, TAM 114, Box 1, Tamiment Library; "Reports on Greece by Constantine Poulos, ONA War Correspondence," John Poulos and Constantine Poulos Papers, TAM 114, Box 1, Tamiment Library.
68. "Civil War Breaks Out in Greece," *Life Magazine*, 25 December 1944, 20.
69. Byford-Jones, *The Greek Trilogy*, 141.
70. Stephen Barber, "Battle Breaks Out in Athens," *Washington Post*, 4 December 1944, 1.
71. "What the Germans did to Greece," *Life Magazine*, 27 November 1944, 21–27.
72. Department of State, "Memorandum for the President" (12.30.1944), Franklin D. Roosevelt, Papers as President: The President's Secretary File (PSF), 1933–1945, Departmental Correspondence, Box 75, State-Stettinius, Edward R., December 1944, 000243.
73. "The British and the Civil Strife in Greece," *Philhellene*, January–March 1945, 1–10.
74. Frank Gervasi, "Russia vs. Britain in the Mediterranean," *Collier's*, 10 February 1945, 11–12.
75. "Leland Stowe on Greek Tragedy," *New York Post*, 14 February 1945.
76. "Greece: Workers' Meeting," 8 December 1944, Earl Browder Papers, Box 66, Syracuse University Libraries, Special Collections Research Center.
77. Basil Vlavianos to F. D. Roosevelt, 14 October 1944, Basil J. Vlavianos Papers, Box 59, California State University, Sacramento, Special Collections and University Archives.
78. "Greeks in the US File Protest in Capital," *The New York Times*, 12 December 1944, 6.
79. Saloutos, *The Greeks in the United States*, 358–59.
80. Churchill, *The Second World War*, 311.
81. Department of State, "Memorandum for the President" (12.30.1944), Franklin D. Roosevelt, Papers as President: The President's Secretary File (PSF), 1933–1945, Departmental Correspondence, Box 75, State-Stettinius, Edward R., December 1944, 000243.
82. To Lincoln McVeagh, Ambassador of the United States in Athens, 5 January 1945, John Poulos and Constantine Poulos Papers, TAM 114, Box 3, Tamiment Library.
83. Capell, *Simiomata*. 121, 142.
84. Wittner, *American Intervention in Greece*, 34.
85. *Greek Liberation*, Greek American Committee for National Unity, 1944.
86. "Reports on Greece by Constantine Poulos, ONA War Correspondence," 24 November 1944, 25–26, John Poulos and Constantine Poulos Papers, TAM 114, Box 1, Tamiment Library.
87. McNeill, *The Greek Dilemma*, 142.
88. "Civil War Breaks Out in Greece," *Life Magazine*, 25 December 1944, 21.
89. *Treis Mēnes tou Kōsta Karagiōrgē stēn Amerikē*, Greek-American Tribune Publishing Department, 1945.
90. "Greek Leader Says: Peace Will Depend on US and Russia," *Chicago Daily Tribune*, 23 June 1945, 9; *Rizospastēs*, 6 May 1945, 2; *Rizospastēs*, 18 June 1945, 4.
91. Kostas Karagiorgis, "Tory Terror in Greece," *The New Masses*, 24 July 1945, 5–6.
92. *Rizospastēs*, 1 August 1945, 1.
93. *Eleutheros Typos*, 5 May 1945, 2.
94. Letters to Ethnikos Kēryx, 5 February 1945 and 16 August 1945, Basil J. Vlavianos Papers, Box 14, CSUS.
95. Duclos, "On the Dissolution of the Communist Party of the United States," 21–35.

CHAPTER 6

Cold War Nation

The Great Transition

"The American Communist Party's disintegration," Joseph Starobin wrote in the mid-1970s, "had the quality of an inexorable process independent of the will of the actors involved."[1] Starobin was not a professional historian; he had been, though, a professional revolutionary. He had served as deputy editor of the *Daily Worker*, had left the United States in 1951 to escape the suffocating anti-communist environment, and had moved to Southeast Asia to study the rise of national liberation movements. Having devoted his life to the communist cause, he was the one to chronicle its crisis, combining his insider knowledge with a deep understanding of the change of atmosphere that took place after the end of World War II. By the time Starobin published his book, American communism was a thing of the past. There was nothing left that recalled the dynamic social and political constellation during the years of the Popular Front and anti-fascist unity. A series of internal crises—culminating in Khrushchev's "secret speech"—had turned the CPUSA into a minuscule group with minimal impact.

This was the result of developments that took place between 1945 and 1956. Ironically, these were also the years that the CPUSA had been in the public eye more than any other time. But this was not a reiteration of the Great Depression era or of the wartime successes of the anti-fascist alliance. Rather, it was the exact opposite: the postwar transition signaled the criminalization of the communist movement and the expulsion of communists from government agencies, public administration, educational institutions, labor unions, and the entertainment industry. The House Un-American Activities Committee (HUAC) was where the link between communism and un-Americanism was forged and then deployed, in order to unfold later in a dense network of practices designed to persecute and criminalize any activity even remotely connected with communism.[2]

The anti-communist campaign led to the ideological demonization and systematic persecution of US communism. What is more, it challenged the movement's main success: the association of national ideology with a class-driven analysis under the auspices of a radical reinterpretation of Americanism. This ideological concept went hand in hand with the social dynamics of the movement. The communist was identified more and more with the "man next door." Teachers, white-collar workers, and housewives had enlarged the social basis of the movement and up to a point had modified the equation between communism and industrial labor. When it came to the immigrant communities, the Americanization process meant the overall transformation of immigrant identity in the United States. The veterans from the era of "Language Federations" were joined by second-generation radicals for whom their ethnic background was an important but not the foundational dimension in their lives. These changes, along with the successes during the Popular Front years and the wartime effort, had led the communists to believe that they had left behind the time when they needed to prove that they were Americans.

Identifying the Communist Party with Soviet interests and emphasizing the role of the "foreign born" in its development, postwar anti-communism targeted the Americanism of the movement. Discrimination and surveillance eroded the movement's social fabric. For many members who were of immigrant descent and had fought hard to climb out of poverty, the prospect of a new round of complications proved terrifying. Some retreated to a sui generis hermeticism that equaled silence. Others, a minority, went on with their lives faithful to their party affiliation, reading the *Daily Worker* and attending a handful of social and political gatherings. Obviously, there was no blueprint to follow; people made choices and each one included the predictable and unpredictable variations and contradictions that mark the passage of people through history. At the same time, though, there was not a single person involved in any capacity in the communist movement whose life was not altered fundamentally during the years of anti-communist persecutions.

The consolidation of anti-communism in the United States intertwined with the transition to the Cold War era. On 12 March 1947, Harry Truman sought congressional approval for an ambitious financial and military program that would halt communist advancement in Greece and Turkey.[3] The Truman Doctrine marked the US intervention on a global level against the Soviet Union and the various movements that were associated with its strategic aims. At the same time, it paved the way for internal policies that targeted US communism. Ten days after his appearance in Congress, the president signed Executive Order 9835, which sanctioned the FBI to conduct loyalty screenings of two million federal employees in order to root out those who were associated with "subversive organizations."[4] In order to facilitate the process, the Attorney General's office compiled a list of subversive organizations; in 1947, there were fewer than 30, in 1950 there were close to 200, and by the mid-1950s there were 254.

The timing of the Truman Doctrine and Executive Order 9835 reflects the interplay between Cold War fronts both inside and outside the United States. As far as domestic threats were concerned, the anti-communist campaign came as a reaction to recent wartime experiences and to the dynamics of the communist movement dating back to the Depression years. The publication of the *Vital Center* by Arthur Schlesinger Jr., in 1949, was the culmination of the rift that had opened between the liberals and the communist Left.[5] One of the book's main arguments concerned the responsibilities of liberal intellectuals, who had ceded to the communists the tasks of defending the working class and fighting fascism. According to Schlesinger, the roots of the problem could be traced back to the Great Depression, when liberal thinkers had seen the financial crisis as their own failure and had thus tolerated, or even accepted, the communists' dynamic presence in the public sphere. Now, after World War II and the disclosure of the Soviet Union's true aims, the liberal progressive intellectuals were called upon to throw off the guilt complex of the past. They had a duty to defend American democracy, which was the main countermeasure against the two totalitarian systems and the sole alternative that could guarantee social stability and financial growth, both in the United States and in Europe.

Postwar anti-communism involved a revision of recent history and more particularly of the experiences of the joint anti-fascist war effort between the United States and the Soviet Union. According to this rationale, the liberal, tolerant environment of the United States and President Roosevelt's policies had fostered an increase in communist influence—and now the country was paying the cost of its indecisive stance against the "Red threat." Therefore, the main aim of militant anti-communist campaigns, such as the one orchestrated by Senator Joseph McCarthy, was the dismantling of the political and social ecosystem that had formed inside and to the left of the New Deal. McCarthy's efforts did not appear in a vacuum. They were based on an ideological premise that perceived the idea of class antagonism as a priori foreign to the USA, and associated class war's arrival with the destructive impact of immigration. Thus, anti-communism constituted on the one hand the modern expression of historical antiradicalism, but on the other it expressed something bigger: a systematic effort to roll back domestic policies introduced by the New Deal, policies that had allowed the Communist Left to grow. 1948, the year when Harry Truman won the presidency, was, as Michael Harrington wrote, "the last year of the politics of the Thirties."[6]

McCarthyism became the chief example of the rapid implementation of a state of emergency.[7] Its stated goal was to combat the spread of communism; its unstated one was to demonize liberal progressive experiments and the possibility of cooperation with the Soviet Union, as well as to denounce in retrospective the climate responsible for the communist movement's momentum. "Most Americans," according to William M. McGovern in his generous foreword to a book by Senator McCarthy, were living until quite recently "in a fool's paradise."[8] In a way, this was correct. In 1942, according to an opinion poll, one in four Americans held a favorable opinion of "socialism," while 35 percent of those asked responded that they were favorably disposed toward socialist ideas. The postwar persecutions soon drove down these numbers. In 1949, the "socialists" were down to 15 percent, and the opponents of socialism had skyrocketed to 61 percent. By the mid-1950s there was no point in even asking the question.[9]

The transition to the Cold War had a profound impact on the Greek American Left. By the mid-1950s the world of Greek American radicalism was in crisis, following the wider developments in the communist movement. The result was the demise of a political and social tradition that, despite having been through many instances of crisis and discontinuity, had remained resilient since the early twentieth century. Now, it was the end of an era. The last issue of *Ellēnoamerikanikon Vēma*, in 1957, terminated forty years of uninterrupted publication of newspapers related to the Greek American communist movement. When it shut down, the newspaper was a ghost of its former self, a mimeographed bulletin with minimal impact. The marginalization of the Left had significant consequences on the Greek American communities' political geography, leading to the imposition of a conservative hegemony.

This outcome represented the exact opposite of the conviction of Greek American communists, leftists, and liberals, in the mid-1940s, that the winds of history were blowing in their favor. They had envisioned progressive developments, both in the United States and Greece, based on anti-fascist values, and their efforts connected the Greek national liberation movement with the social platform of the New Deal. After the war, these connections were gradually dismantled. It did not happen overnight. It was a complex process that combined the decline of the wartime anti-fascist alliance, domestic developments in the USA, American intervention in Greece, and the Greek Civil War. Up to December 1944 the winds of history seemed to confirm the Greek American communists' expectations, but everything that came after led to what Starobin summarized as "disintegration."

Liberals in Crisis

Postwar developments in Europe, and news from Athens in particular, had a strong effect on liberal and non-communist intellectuals. When the fighting in Athens between the communist and the British forces came to an end, revelations about brutal purges of Trotskyites and photos of mass graves filled with "victims of communism" were broadly circulated by the Greek embassy in the United States. A report by British trade unionists who had visited Athens in the aftermath of the bloody incidents confirmed the fears of those who had been skeptical about Stalin's sincerity, since it recorded atrocities committed by the communist-dominated EAM (Ethniko Apelephtherōtiko Metōpo-National Liberation Front).[10] For Max Eastman, events in Greece verified that Moscow had dictated the overthrow of a legitimate government with the aim to impose a totalitarian regime.[11] Even those who disagreed with him, like Dwight Macdonald, recognized that "the role of Communists in the European resistance movements poses very difficult problems to all who oppose Stalinism from a progressive point of view."[12] Macdonald was trying to retain some optimism. His review, *Politics*, ran much of the correspondence from Athens sent by Connie Poulos, who, writing under a pseudonym, felt at greater liberty to report on the contradictions within EAM and the unclear intentions of the Communist Party.[13] Despite their disillusionment, both men were in essence arguing that the social momentum of the resistance experience would outweigh foreign intervention and would restrain communist aspirations for a takeover of power.

This scenario, though, became increasingly unlikely. Greece soon experienced a protracted Civil War that resulted in a hardening of the stance of all sides, and at the end minimized the emancipatory dynamics of the wartime resistance movement. Trapped between news of far-right persecution against the resistance legacy, on the one hand, and the hardening of the communist's stance, on the other, New York's progressive intellectuals became increasingly disgruntled with the EAM. The consolidation of socialist governments across the Balkans enhanced the visibility of Greece and led to a gradual underestimation of the systematic civil rights transgressions perpetrated by the Greek government. This conundrum was further complicated by the intensifying of anti-communism in the United States. The supporters of resistance movements, which now had been proved to be, as the developments in Europe showed, nothing but fronts for the Soviet Union's power aspirations, were judged retrospectively as, at best, naive fellow travelers. In the ideological transformations taking place in certain circles of the liberal and anti-Stalinist Left, Greece became a point of reference because it exemplified the need to combat communism. Writing on the cusp of the Cold War, James Burnham argued that the Third World War had begun back in 1943, when Greek anti-fascists in Egypt had mutinied against the Greek government-in-exile.[14]

This was not an unforeseen development. As World War II was coming to an end, ideological differences were coming to the fore. Up to that point, diverse ideological and political platforms had coexisted or remained in dialogue under the anti-fascist banner. The end of the war and questions about the postwar transition led to the dismantling of this shared space of action and expression. What is of interest in this process is the intersection of Greek and American developments. For instance, in the case of Dean Alfange, the split between communists and socialists in the American Labor Party led him to follow the latter in a newfound Liberal Party.[15] At the same time, after the Battle of Athens, Alfange distanced himself from the Greek American Council and was never to participate again in its activities. By 1948, Alfange was close to President Truman; when they met in the White House in July 1948, in order to discuss the Liberal Party's stance in the upcoming elections, Alfange expressed his support for the president who "had done more to create an awareness of the Communist danger and had done more to stop it than perhaps any man in our times."[16]

The distancing of liberals and progressives who had cooperated with the communist Left is exemplified in the case of the owner and editor in chief of *Ethnikos Kēryx*. From the summer of 1945, Basil Vlavianos appeared critical of "extremists" on both sides and argued for a coalition government in Greece between the moderate conservatives and the non-communist left.[17] This signaled his realignment with the old political order in Greece. Vlavianos was named the Greek government's legal counsel to the Greek delegation at the UN founding congress in San Francisco. He participated in deliberations concerning the restoration of the prewar political "Center" while arguing for the same cause in *Ethnikos Kēryx*.[18] "We are losing the battle," wrote an anxious Nikolaos Cheronis, president of the Greek American Council in Chicago, trying to bring him back to the aims of EAM.[19] Indifferent to such efforts, Vlavianos made a brief trip to Greece for the first time in many years. There he met with politicians and intellectuals who had distanced themselves from EAM, and he heard stories of communist atrocities during the December 1944 events.

In September 1945, Basil Vlavianos resigned from the Greek American Council. This was the end of the Greek American alliance between communists and liberals. Writing for the *Nation*, Vlavianos now blamed the Greek communists for taking advantage of EAM in order to pursue their own revolutionary aims.[20] At the same time, Vlavianos pointed out inconsistencies in US foreign policy; speaking on a CBS radio show a few days before the announcement of the Truman Doctrine, Vlavianos exposed the fault of supporting right-wing governments in Greece, as they were undemocratic and could not safeguard financial growth in the country. In essence, his criticism echoed a liberal skepticism concerning any military intervention that would not resolve the underlying social causes of the civil strife in Greece, and could also potentially turn a peripheral conflict into a general one, with unforeseen results.[21]

As is often the case in conditions of polarization, such criticism left many unsatisfied on both sides of the debate. The archive of *Ethnikos Kēryx* reflects the dissatisfaction of readers with the politics of Vlavianos. Their letters were hastily scrawled, often punctuated by insults, and above all linked the events in Greece with concurrent developments in the United States. "I don't like you one bit, you poor man," wrote a worker who signed the CIO's initials under his name, because "on the one hand you bash those inbred little tyrants [that is the royal family in Greece], and on the other you are in complete agreement with . . . those craven bastards in Wall Street."[22] Vlavianos's only comment in the margins of the letter was "Commun[ist]." It was not a marvel of clairvoyance, since the letter writer mentioned that his "favorite newspaper" was *Ellēnoamerikanikon Vēma*. The Greek American communist newspaper accused Vlavianos for siding with the reactionaries and reminded its readers—somewhat belatedly given the preexisting alliance with him—of Vlavianos's class origins and his links with the bourgeois establishment.[23]

On the other end of the political spectrum, Vlavianos's anti-communist opponents were also dissatisfied. *Atlantis* and *Eleutheros Typos* demanded from him a statement of social convictions, while he stubbornly defended his wartime choices by differentiating the EAM movement of that time from what it had evolved into since December 1944. The atmosphere inside *Ethnikos Kēryx* was steadily worsening, as journalists and commentators, one after the other, expressed their dissatisfaction. In March 1947, the month when the Truman Doctrine was announced, Vlavianos sold the newspaper to Babis Marketos and stepped down from the position of editor in chief. Marketos was supported by entrepreneurs such as Vasilios Helis, the candidate who had been favored by the Metaxas regime for the supreme presidency of AHEPA ten years earlier. The change in ownership signaled a return to normality. *Ethnikos Kēryx* stopped criticizing US foreign policy in Greece and denounced the experiments of the previous period, thus aligning itself with the dominant anti-communist trends of the period.

"These days, all good Greeks support America," wrote Demetrios Kallimachos in January 1948.[24] The fiercely anti-communist columnist had every reason to sound smug. In 1943 he had been forced to leave *Ethnikos Kēryx* when he disagreed with its leftist turn. Events since the end of the war confirmed what he had been saying since the 1930s: the battle for the future of the world was between civilized nations and communism's global threat of social unrest. The newspaper that had been his life's work had returned to familiar ideological paths, and it now presented the Greek Civil War as the product of a shadowy Slavic and communist conspiracy. The return of Kallimachos to the paper's roster confirmed the triumphant restoration of interwar social and political conservatism. This was not merely a historical restoration of the late 1930s. In these new circumstances, anti-communism was defined by the joint goals of the Greek and US governments and the latter's commitment to the protection of the former.

The change of ownership of *Ethnikos Kēryx* coincided with a consolidation of direct and indirect censorship methods and practices concerning the Greek Civil War and the role of the United States in it. The first one to feel this change was Connie Poulos. In June 1947, the Greek American journalist arrived in Vienna in order to pursue his mission and reach Allied-occupied Berlin. But a surprise awaited him in Vienna: the city's US military command informed him that his request to enter Berlin had been denied. This, however, was the least of his concerns. It seems he was now forced to return to the United States, following a decision by the War Department, which was responsible for war correspondents in "former enemy territory." The rationale for the decision, which was not communicated to him, was that while he was in Greece, Poulos "had met with and openly supported leftist and communist groups and organizations. . . . He had intercepted and publicized classified documents from the US military HQ. . . . He had expressed, in private and in public, critical views of the work and operations of the American Mission on the Greek plebiscite . . . and had violated the orders of the Mission Chief . . . to keep his distance from all political organizations and political activities for the duration of his stay in Greece."[25]

This was the end of the journey that had begun in the summer of 1944, when Poulos had left Izmir to cross the Aegean Sea and join the partisans in Greece. His travels included a Balkan and central European itinerary (during which he became skeptical of the Soviet Union's policies vis-à-vis provisional governments) and a brief stint in the Middle East (during which he criticized the British support for Arabs against the Jewish aims for an independent state).[26] All these years he had been traveling using temporary documents issued from rebel units or provisional accreditations from military authorities, which demonstrated the fleeting and hybrid nature of the postwar transition. The fact that he had been recalled to the United States emphasized a new development: freedom of movement was now linked to ideological obedience according to the respective dividing lines of the Cold War. Poulos did not have much choice. Despite strong objections by his employers and journalists' associations, he was forced to return to the USA without having full knowledge of the chain of events that had led up to the decision.

In part, the solution to the mystery could be traced to the dismissal of Madeline Karr, the White House correspondent of *Ethnikos Kēryx*, on

30 July 1947. Poulos was personally acquainted with Madeline Karr and her husband, David Karr, with whom he had worked in the Office of War Information (OWI). Poulos and David Karr had many things in common: they were second-generation immigrants (Greek and Russian-Jewish respectively), they had joined the Left in the 1930s, and they both resigned from the OWI (Karr after he was named as a communist by Martin Dies, chairman of HUAC). After handing in his resignation, Karr had joined the staff of star journalist Drew Pearson and soon became his closest associate while also maintaining close ties with the communist movement and Henry Wallace.[27] In early 1944, his wife, Madeline Karr, joined *Ethnikos Kēryx* and was issued a White House press pass. In a letter to Vlavianos, Madeline Karr mentioned Poulos, and in December 1944, Poulos's scoop about a telegram from Churchill ordering the bombing of Athens was taken up by Pearson, who from that point on regularly ran the Greek American journalist's correspondence and systematically attacked British foreign policy. Pearson, in turn, was a close friend of George C. Vournas (president of AHEPA), a friend of Vlavianos, and a supporter of EAM in the United States. These networks were defined by personal relationships and were reinforced by a shared political mission in support of the New Deal and the resistance movements in Europe.

Poulos, Pearson, and Karr had one more thing in common: they opposed an anti-communist network that extended from Truman's entourage all the way to Athens. Chief among the members of this network was Harry Vaughan, a military adviser in the White House and a close friend of the president from the time they had fought side by side in the trenches of World War I. Their friendship was tested after a cascade of revelations, most of them by Drew Pearson, concerning shady backroom deals by Vaughan, who was taking advantage of his connections to get all sorts of supply contracts. The dispute between them came to a head during a press conference, when the two men nearly came to blows. Among other charges brought against Vaughan, Pearson claimed that he was colluding with John Maragon, an enigmatic Greek American entrepreneur.

Maragon was also active in White House circles. "He looks like a foreigner and could easily pass for a Prohibition-era gangster," was how Eben A. Ayers, assistant White House press secretary at the time, described him in April 1945.[28] The information that Truman's staff had gathered on Maragon further increased their misgivings. He had indeed been implicated in illegal activities, had briefly cooperated with the FBI on undisclosed terms, and in 1926 had been accused of the murder of a policeman, whose fiancée Maragon later married.[29] Maragon's meteoric rise (among other impressive feats, he had managed to board FDR's funeral train) vexed Truman's staff. In April 1946, the president's close associates believed that, for the time being, they were free of his presence. "I pray to God that this is the last we see of Maragon," Charlie Ross, Truman's press secretary, said when he heard that Maragon had joined the American observation mission on the Greek plebiscite in March 1946, even though Truman had explicitly forbidden it.[30]

Poulos was the one who broke the news that Maragon was in Athens. Poulos also accused him of pressuring foreign press correspondents by invoking his close relations with the White House. According to associates of President Truman, as well as a later article in the *Nation*, the correspondence by Poulos was instrumental in Maragon being hastily recalled back to Washington, DC.[31] Among other things, Poulos revealed that Maragon had been in contact with the Greek government, promoting vague business plans connected with future American investments. Pearson made use of this correspondence, and in March 1947, he attacked Vaughan and Maragon— for their illegal business dealings and for the latter's activities in Greece.[32] Pearson's timing, one year after Maragon's visit to Greece, could be related to the announcement of the Truman Doctrine and the looming government media control concerning developments in Greece.

When Poulos came back to the United States in the summer of 1947, he was informed that his travel documents had been revoked because of his activities in Greece.[33] The fact that Poulos had been critical of the KKE's (Kommounistiko Komma Elladas-Communist Party of Greece) tactics and of the Soviet Union's foreign policy seems to have had no effect whatsoever. His articles were at odds with US foreign policy goals in the region, and so the verdict was inevitable: he was a communist fellow traveler, as Maragon had accused him of being right from the start. At the same time, encouraged by the change of ownership of *Ethnikos Kēryx*, Vaughan and Maragon dealt their final strike. Vaughan knew the new owner, Vasilios Helis, and asked him to fire Madeline Karr, since he believed—correctly—that she was supplying Pearson with information on his activities.[34] The conclusion of this episode has a distinctly Cold War flavor to it. Madeline Karr was accused of being a member of an espionage network and these accusations reached even Basil Vlavianos, who was her employer at the time.[35]

The dismantling of the network that connected Poulos, the Karrs, Pearson, and Vournas reveals the connections that led to the formation of a new media conformity designed to legitimize the Truman Doctrine. This was no half-baked plan. Quite the contrary. In July 1947, when Karr was laid off and Poulos was forced to return from Europe to the States, James Forrestal, the secretary of defense, proposed that newspaper owners should be informed about "left-wing or fellow-traveler writers serving the American press in Greece" and encouraged to "suggest . . . changes."[36] In this new era there was no room for fine distinctions; the correspondents would have to conform to the interests of the anti-communist campaign. Anti-communist persecution was based on the retrospective criminalization of political activities, a criminalization that was linked with a comprehensive revision of the recent history of the USA. From the moment that the attorney general included the Greek American Committee for National Unity in the index of subversive organizations, those who had participated in it in any way were retrospectively accused of being accomplices to a communist organization.[37] Vlavianos and Poulos, despite the fact that they had never been communists, defended their choices to the last and highlighted the inconsistencies of retrospective anti-communism.

"At that time," Vlavianos wrote in a memorandum to the FBI, trying to explain his participation in the Greek American Committee for National Unity, "we were still allies with the Soviets, the communists were accepted everywhere[,] and the mere fact of participating in such an organization cannot be possibly be held as a subversive activity.[38] Vlavianos submitted this memo because immigration authorities refused to renew his visa in 1952. Vlavianos, for reasons that may have had something to do with his ambition to play some kind of role in Greek politics, had not taken American citizenship. His complaints led to a reexamination of his case and a temporary settlement. When Vlavianos was able to access his personal FBI file in the 1980s, he found out that he had been under surveillance as early as the beginning of World War II. And as is often the case in such matters, the eager informers were people in his close professional or social circle.[39] Vlavianos had attempted the impossible: to separate the expectations that EAM had created from the postwar realities of the Greek Civil War. Along with Poulos, Vlavianos was the main representative of the postwar transition's defeated liberals. They had invested in a plan that never came to fruition, and they were now exposed both to anti-communist persecution and to the denouncements of the communist Left. Vlavianos was more fortunate; he was a man of independent means and, after a brief period far from the public eye, he turned to new ventures. He taught history and politics at New York University, and he founded a bookshop and press in Manhattan called Golden Griffin, specializing in modern art. Poulos, however, became a ghost of his former self. He could not go back to Europe, and he soon found himself trapped in a downward spiral of resignation, which afflicted many of those who had found themselves on the wrong side of the postwar transition.

Under Surveillance

On 4 June 1946, an attendee at a gala organized by the American Relief for Greek Democracy (ARGD) left early from the sumptuous hall of the

Commodore Hotel, in midtown Manhattan. Two days later he submitted a detailed report of what he had seen and heard. The document is signed "T-1" and concludes as follows: "Entertainment was provided by Norman Rosten, Stalinist poet, who read his own creation in praise of the Greek resistance movement, and a female singer whose name I did not get. Each diner received a folder issued by the Synergic Association which sells "Hygeia-Min Multiple Vitamin Tablets" at cost for relief of Greeks. A copy is attached."[40]

The ARGD was formed in early 1946 as a response to an appeal by Ethnikē Allēlengyi (EA-National Solidarity), the EAM welfare and mutual-aid organization. Ethnikē Allēlengyi, meaning "national solidarity," had called on all "immigrants around the world" and "philhellenes" to send material support to the victims of political persecution in Greece.[41] The EA refrained from naming the parties responsible for this predicament and presented the victims of political persecution in vague terms, as people who had fought the Nazis and were now confronted with oppressive measures and material hardship. The call reflected the EA's immediate priorities: the establishment of an international network of solidarity and support.

The United States held a unique place in the EA's plans. This followed an inherent logic of Greek politics, which reached out to the diaspora in times of crisis, and reflected the arrival of American humanitarian organizations in war-torn Greece. In this context, two leading figures of EAM, Georgios Georgalas, a professor of mineralogy and the president of the United Panhellenic Organization of Youth (Eniaia Panelladikē Organōsē Neōn-EPON), and Nikos Karvounis, a journalist, arrived in New York to provide a firsthand account of recent developments and coordinate the delivery of goods to Greece. T-1's notes from the American Relief for Greek Democracy's fundraising dinner provide a detailed summary of their speeches: the two EAM representatives—along with Leland Stowe, a journalist who had been in Athens in December 1944, and Kostas Kouvaras, who had cooperated with the Greek People's Liberation Army (Ellēnikos Laikos Apelephtherotikos Stratos-ELAS) as a member of the US Military Mission—condemned British foreign policy in Greece, pointed out the USA's responsibilities, and praised EAM's contributions to the Allied war effort.[42]

The links between EA and ARGD represented an alternative narrative to the emerging official relationship between the United States and Greece. For the communist movement, the American commitment to the idea of postwar economic intervention in Europe was turning into a political question on the allocation of American aid. Geography intertwined with politics, since material support was a necessary precondition for the stabilization of governments that had to face the accumulated consequences of the catastrophic war. In this climate, the communist Left attempted to establish autonomous humanitarian aid organizations to help the Greek resistance movement and the newly established governments in eastern Europe. This was a tactic that concealed the ambition to implement a parallel, unofficial foreign policy, which would incorporate the traditions of material support to social and political movements around the world.

The initial momentum of American Relief for Greek Democracy left room for optimism on both sides of the Atlantic. In the beginning of 1947, the organization had ten full-time employees, an extensive network of local committees, and a legal status stipulated by the relevant statutes of the state of New York. Its carefully worded rhetoric allowed it to tread a fine line, linking its activities with the emerging postwar ecosystem of aid and reconstruction organizations. The organization's publications and advertisements employed the methods that the American Left had developed during the Spanish Civil War. They routinely included photographs that revealed the scale of destruction in Greece and never failed to remind the citizens of the United States of their moral obligation to contribute to the relief of those who had fought against the Nazi occupation. The texts were brief and contained statistical data and quotes from prominent figures in both countries. Children of the war played a central role in the campaign. Photos showing wounded, crying, or exhausted children carried captions such as "It could have been your child," "For me the war hasn't ended," "His father was a Resistance fighter," and "This is Maria and there are 4,999 Marias like her in Greece."[43] The new generation functioned as a metonym for the future—a recurrent pattern in humanitarian rhetoric. At the same time, the frequent use of children permitted the organization to avoid direct references to the political circumstances in Greece.

The absence of any reference to the communist movement, and emphasis on the humanitarian aspect of the project painted a picture that was clear to those in the know but was also vague enough to allow collaborations with religious or nonpolitical organizations and communities.[44] One of the main goals was to attract leading figures who would add prestige to the whole endeavor. The organization succeeded admirably in this goal. "Mrs. Eleanor Roosevelt speaks for Greek orphans," was the poignant title of the half-page ad that the ARGD took out in major daily newspapers in December 1946.[45] The former first lady had indeed agreed to participate in a Christmas campaign that would raise funds for five thousand orphans supported by the EA. Robert St. John, a famous journalist, had been the one to approach her, and had informed her during their meeting that US aid in Greece was being used for political ends. "I'm stunned," was her response, and she immediately accepted the invitation to lead the campaign. Her willingness led St. John himself to wonder, years later, whether she had agreed out of naivete.[46] Most probably not. In January 1947, Eleanor Roosevelt gave the following response to Harry Boardman: "I have always felt that women and children should be helped regardless of political ideas, and food and medical supplies should not be used as a political weapon. Hence I have been willing to help any organization obtaining these two things for any portion of the population of the country involved. I do see, however, that there are a rather large number of fairly well-known communists[,] but I do not know that I feel for that reason that I should resign from a relief organization."[47]

Taking advantage of frequent complaints by American aid organizations about Greek government intervention in their work, the ARGD presented itself as having an advantage: the aid it sent would support a grassroots social and political movement that was independent from the Greek state. The organization's typewritten bulletin routinely published enthusiastic responses by readers who supported its work and pledged to contribute. As is usual in these matters, promises outnumbered actual monetary contributions. But even so, inside of a few months, in mid-1946, the ARGD announced that the organization's warehouses contained supplies in the amount of eight thousand dollars, while ten thousand more in cash had been raised toward the financial support of EA.[48]

The difficulty, at that point, lay not in raising the money and supplies but in sending them to Greece safely, as conditions on the ground were getting harder by the day in the lead-up to the Civil War.[49] The ARGD initially contacted the Cooperative for American Remittances to Europe (CARE), which coordinated the distribution of donated supplies across Europe in the form of individual packages that contained food and basic necessities. This proved to be a fruitful cooperation, and so in August 1946, one and a half metric tons of supplies (in CARE packages), along with five hundred dollars, were successfully delivered to EA.[50] The symbolic value of this operation was much more important that its actual one. In the EA magazine's last issue, as it proved to be, a full-page photograph shows the organization's president receiving CARE packages from a truck stenciled with the Greek and American flags.[51] It was a major victory for the Greek Communist Left, as the arrival of "US aid" was projected as proof of EAM's international appeal. Members of the American Military Mission, who were sympathetic to EAM, were instrumental in the success of this endeavor. Taking advantage of the chaos that reigned in Athens, one of them, Jim Charakas, a Greek American, led the trucks loaded with CARE packages to the EA offices, despite efforts by the British and Greek authorities to stop him.[52]

Civil strife and the Truman Doctrine put an end to such initiatives. Once more, the plans of the American Left were thwarted by developments in Greece and the United States, feeding back into and fueling each other. From the beginning of 1947, the US presence in Greece took on distinct political characteristics, aiming to secure the Greek state and support anti-communist governments. This was combined with the concurrent marginalization of the Left's alternative aid networks. In Greece the EA was outlawed, along with KKE and its coalition organizations. Across the Atlantic, the ARGD was steadily losing supporters after it came under the scrutiny of US law enforcement authorities.

In March 1947, just as Truman was preparing to appear before Congress, the ARGD organized a big fundraiser event with the slogan "The stars shine for Greece." "You and our stars will bring hope and life to the prisoners, the exiled, and the persecuted antifascists of Greece," announced the event's poster, which featured photographs of actors, singers, and radio producers next to the promethean image of a half-naked male figure helping a bedridden young woman. However, on 28 March, some of the "stars" that had been announced did not appear on the stage of Carnegie Hall because they felt that they had been deceived in a "Red Front Rally."[53] Two weeks after the announcement of the Truman Doctrine, J. Edgar Hoover, director of the FBI, requested the establishment of a body of intelligence on ARGD, noting also that Eleanor Roosevelt contributed to it.[54] His staff knew whom to ask about this. American Business Consultants was a peculiar company that gathered intelligence and compiled reports on all manner of subversive activities.[55] The file that the company had on the ARGD included the reports by the informer T-1, along with many of the organization's leaflets, publications, and letters. This body of evidence was transferred to the FBI, where it formed a new self-contained file.[56] The next step was to include the organization in the attorney general's index of subversive organizations. In this way, the ARGD would soon cease to exist.

Anti-Communist International

By the end of 1947, Greek American communists were in retreat. Their liberal allies had distanced themselves from the pro-EAM committees, the Civil War in Greece cut off their links to the country, and the shifting political atmosphere in the United States curtailed the social and political momentum of the Left. US intervention in Greece was the straw that broke the camel's back. Now, they were not just dissenters. Their actions were considered to be a threat against their country—a threat against the United States of America. Analogies between the Spanish and Greek Civil Wars played an important role in this development. According to postwar anti-communist revisionism, the Spanish Civil War had revealed Moscow's true intentions for global dominance and the American government ought to be cautious about repeating the same mistakes. On 21 July 1947, Walter S. Steele, editor in chief of the *National Republic* (with the telling subtitle "a monthly magazine of fundamental Americanism"), brought to the attention of HUAC

information that the Abraham Lincoln Brigade still maintained its oper-
ational capacity and acted as "a division of a global communist army"
in the service of the Soviet Union.[57] Along with this outrageous claim he
hinted that communists were forming a new International Brigade, this time
to assist the communist-backed Democratic Army of Greece. A few days
before Steele's testimony, George Marshall, the secretary of state, made a
similar statement on the prospects of a foreign intervention in Greece, citing
the International Brigade from the Spanish Civil War.[58]

Such statements resulted in law enforcement authorities taking an
increased interest in the activities of the American Relief for Greek Democracy and the American Council for a Democratic Greece. Both organizations were described as "Red fronts" opposing the legitimate government
of Greece and materially supporting an insurgent military force that was
waging war against American interests in the region.[59] In this context,
HUAC scrutinized the solidarity campaigns of the American Left. "They
are doing an excellent job at raising money for the Greek rebels," was how
the ex-communist Karolos Solounias (Charles Solon) accused the Fur and
Leather Workers' Union for its material support to the Greek people.[60] A
congressman from Texas asked the union's treasurer if a thousand dollars
donated to the ARGD ended up in the coffers of the communist army.[61] This
line of inquiry could be summarized in the rhetorical question by the president of a conservative organization: "Are we going to leave the back door
wide open for Communists and fellow travelers to spread their poisonous
work inside our own country?"[62]

The response was a return to the long tradition of conflating subversive
ideas with the presence of dangerous aliens inside the United States. In
earlier years, this conflation had served to fuel the persecution of radicals
and curtail immigration, as immigrants were perceived as carriers of social
unrest from the Old World to the New. In the era of mass immigration such
concerns had resulted in methods such as questioning newcomers whether
they were "anarchists." After the October Revolution it had contributed
to the introduction of quotas on immigrant entries and the deportation of
hundreds of radicals with an immigrant background. In the Cold War era
it was reflected in the question "Are you or have you ever been a member
of the Communist Party?"—a questions that was found for decades on visa
applications. "My bill," argued Senator Pat McCarran, the architect of
postwar immigration legislation and an ardent anti-communist, "is designed
to sever the international lifeline which is feeding the Communist conspiracy
in this country."[63]

However, there was a crucial difference. The prosecutions of the past had
been based on a doctrine of national security that argued for insulation from
the disastrous repercussions of Old World affairs. In the new globalized

realities of the Cold War, protecting the USA from dangerous aliens was linked to the active presence and interference of the United States in various parts of the world. Therefore, McCarran's "international lifeline" on the one hand referred to the introduction of anti-American ideas into the US, and on the other it targeted the moral and material support that immigrant communities provided to movements and regimes that challenged the USA's new global role.

Deportations became the most visible expression of the new national security doctrine. According to FBI records, more than ten thousand immigrants and political refugees who were not naturalized American citizens faced deportation because of their association with one or more subversive organizations on the attorney general's index. At the end, the actual deportations proved to be much fewer. Between 1946 and 1966, some 250 were classified as exclusively political (while an unknown number involves cases that were listed as violations of immigration law but whose motive was to persecute political activity). Basically, the main repressive measure was not deportation per se but fear of deportation. This resulted in the marginalization of those who were targeted as potential deportees. In some cases it was the community or family that turned against (and turned in) the potential suspect. Giannis Baharas had left Greece just before the outbreak of the civil war and was living with relatives in the Midwest. He had participated in the Greek resistance, so he started writing for *Ellēnoamerikanikon Vēma* and became politically active in Chicago circles. According to his own account, his terrified and conservative relatives were the ones who informed the immigration authorities that the newcomer was involved in subversive activities. Despite his efforts—including the popular practice of an expedited wedding with an American citizen—Baharas was deported.[64]

In January 1947, Carol King, a lawyer representing the American Committee for the Protection of Foreign Born (ACPFB), referred to a hundred individuals who were facing immediate deportation for their association with organizations listed in the attorney general's index.[65] King made a special mention of the case of Petros Harisiades. The Greek American communist had been sent to Ellis Island awaiting deportation on the grounds of an arrest warrant that had been issued in 1930. The ACPFB launched a protracted campaign in support of Harisiades based on the debate over US communism—that is, whether it was a product of social conditions in the United States or the result of its forced introduction by dangerous aliens. "American by choice" was the campaign's main slogan, insisting that Harisiades was a true American: he had never left the United States, and he had married an American citizen, with whom he had two children. In short, Harisiades "is as American as you and your next-door neighbor."[66] The ACPFB additionally argued that if Harisiades was deported to Greece he would face persecution not for something that he had done, but for his personal beliefs. In late 1951 the Supreme Court agreed to review his case. [67]

The Supreme Court's ruling echoed the understanding of communism as an imported evil. The United States was under siege, and deportation was internationally recognized as "a weapon of defense and reprisal," given the leading role that foreigners had played in the development of the communist movement in the United States. [68] Consequently, there was no room for doubt. The deportation was upheld, and on 12 November 1952, Petros Harisiades, accompanied by his family, boarded the Norwegian ocean liner "Oslofjord." [69] He was not the only one. By the mid-1950s around seventy to eighty Greek Americans and Greek citizens were deported or were forced to leave the United States for political reasons.

Greek authorities were in favor of this development. One of the main functions of Greek diplomatic services at the time was the surveillance of communist activities abroad. Similarities with the period of the Metaxas regime are evident, but there was a crucial difference: concern about communism in Greece was directly linked with the emergence of a global anti-communist front that included the government of the United States. In November 1948 the Greek embassy in Washington, DC, compiled a comprehensive list of three hundred "Greek nationals and immigrants who are forbidden to be issued or renew a passport." [70] At the same time, Greece sought to strip Greek citizenship from persons living abroad who had been actively supporting the communist army during the Greek Civil War. When the bill was brought to the Greek Parliament in 1947, the conversation involved explicit mention of activities by the Left's diasporic organizations, and especially the "wanton anti-Hellenic propaganda" in the States. [71] However, the Greek authorities did not proceed with depriving those three hundred people on the list of Greek citizenship. The reasons were purely practical. The Greek diplomats had requested the postponement of the "the proposed loss of Greek citizenship" in order to make it easier for US authorities to prosecute the suspects. [72] If the Greek state stripped them of their citizenship, the defendants could invoke loss of citizenship and seek asylum in the USA.

Deportations had a severe impact on the Greek American Left. Those who left (under any circumstances) were usually prominent members of the communist movement. Union organizers who had been named in the HUAC hearings were either deported or—like Giannis Vafeiadis, a fur worker—left the country in a hurry to avoid imprisonment. [73] Facing the gradual restriction of their freedoms in New York and the prospect of a court martial in Athens, a small group of maritime workers used forged papers to board "Batory," a Polish merchant ship, in May 1949. Traveling with them, also with forged papers, was Gerhart Eisler, a legendary figure in the communist movement. "They thought they could find work in Poland," was the disarming response that the representative of the Polish shipping company gave to the outraged members of HUAC when they asked him why they hired Greek sailors to head to the Port of Gdynia.[74]

Unwanted in the United States and facing prosecution in Greece, those who were deported or escaped chose a safe alternative: the emerging People's Republics in the Eastern bloc. Their choice is symbolic on multiple levels. For most of them Greece was a distant memory (and, it goes without saying, possibly a threat), and their second Atlantic crossing led them to regions unknown, in a choice based on ideological affinities. Poland became the destination of choice. It was there that the newcomers from the United States met their—much more numerous—comrades who had been defeated in the Greek Civil War and were now political refugees. It was a meeting like the one that had taken place in Spain in 1937, but the terms were now completely different. Back then the meeting was the result of anti-fascist enthusiasm, whereas now it was merely an extension of the communist movement's defeat.

Back in the States, the response of the CPUSA intensified the movement's isolation. Acting like a fortress under siege that had to protect itself from enemies both outside and inside the walls, the party retreated into disciplinary measures. "In this frightful cold war," wrote Mary Vardoulakis on 8 May 1950, "the truth is that Communists can also be victims."[75] Vardoulakis had worked for the Balkan Bureau of the Office of Strategic Services during the war, and had become a minor literary celebrity for a novel, *Gold in the Streets*, about Cretan immigrant workers in New England textile mills. The Wellesley College alumna was a leftist and had traveled to Crete in 1946 to record incidents of state terrorism against EAM. Upon her return, she appeared at numerous events organized by the American Council for Democratic Greece.[76]

When Vardoulakis referred to communists as "victims" she did not have the anti-communist persecutions in mind. She addressed her letter to the CPUSA's National Review Committee, asking for the reasons that led to her expulsion in February 1950. "I repeat, I am innocent of any acts or words or thoughts demonstrating disloyalty to the Party," she wrote, clearly upset, begging for just one hearing so that she could convince the Committee that "these words are the SOLEMN TRUTH." The letter has many things in common with others of its kind—initially Vardoulakis was certain that the party would realize there was a mistake or a misunderstanding of some sort; then she realized this was not going to happen; finally, she begged the party apparatus for a second chance to redeem herself. Vardoulakis's demand was not satisfied. She had probably been expelled—as she implies fleetingly in her letter—because she violated the rules of "increased vigilance" (according to the internal memos' lingo at the time), which defined the CPUSA's postwar course.[77] In such cases, the person expelled was truly and finally alone: a victim of the Cold War.

Greek American Anti-Communism

Developments in Greece and in the United States fueled the rise of anti-communism within Greek American communities. In the context of the Cold War, the concentrated efforts of the Greek state to revive its ties with immigrant communities was ideologically in accordance with US priorities and interests. The difference with the late 1930s is clear. Back then the Metaxas regime's efforts were perceived as potentially destabilizing activities that promoted an authoritarian government's aspirations and thus were under surveillance. After the war, things changed. The strategic alliance between the two countries in their common struggle against communism empowered conservative and anti-communist organizations within the Greek American community.

"The eradication of Communism in Macedonia" was one of the basic tenets of the Pan-Macedonian Association (PMA), which was established in 1947 in order to express the spirit of the new anti-communist diaspora.[78] In the organization's vocabulary, "national interests" meant both the US foreign policy in the Balkans and the Greek government's objectives in the Macedonian region. The PMA enjoyed the support of right-wing Greek governments and rose to become the main vehicle of Greek American anti-communism. Around that time, George C. Vournas was forced to resign from his position as the supreme president of AHEPA. His resignation followed intense and systematic efforts by conservative circles who had been annoyed by AHEPA's stance during the Battle of Athens back in December 1944. Vournas was labeled a communist fellow traveler. His successor, Harris J. Bouras, expressed the alignment of AHEPA with the emerging anti-communist dogma. In the 1947 congress, AHEPA enacted, in accordance with anti-communist legislation, the screening of new members for possible participation in subversive activities.[79]

Anti-communism became the lingua franca of Greek American organizations. Presenting themselves as representatives of a nation that had suffered from both totalitarian systems, they became pivotal in promoting the official Greek state's rhetoric on the catastrophic consequences of the civil war. The Greek government's campaign against the communist-orchestrated evacuation of children to the People's Republics became a cause célèbre in the United States. The annual celebrations of the Greek Day of Independence included floats commemorating the plight of those families whose children had been snatched and taken behind the Iron Curtain, and demanded their return.[80] Thanking the US government for its contribution to the fight against "the enemies of civilization and liberty" had become a typical introduction to any column concerning the relations between Greek Americans and their two countries. Appearing before a congressional committee hearing during the revision of immigrant legislation, the AHEPA leadership emphasized the disproportionately heavy price that the Greek people had paid at the hands of the "Reds," and they presented immigration as an escape from the country's accumulated plights. In these efforts, AHEPA could count on the help of an eminent supporter. President Truman disagreed with the McCarran-Walter Immigration and Nationality Act, stating that Greeks "struggling to assist the victims of a Communist civil war" deserved more than the 308 legal immigration spots provided for by the quotas of the new legislation.[81] These interventions bore fruit: from the end of the civil war up to 1960, almost fifty thousand Greeks were accepted into the United States. They created a new immigrant body—a priori anticommunist, since they had to sign certificates of social convictions in Greece and the USA—that gave new life to the aging immigrant communities.

Greek American anti-communism reflected the rise of ethnic anti-communism that became prevalent among immigrants hailing from central and eastern Europe.[82] The main difference lies in the exceptional position of Greece in the European political map. A country geographically belonging to the East, Greece had been transformed into the front line of the political "West" against communism. This allowed Greek American groups and individuals to intervene directly in Greek affairs. Greek Americans proved valuable assistants and protagonists in the US reconstruction program in Greece; they undertook the building of schools, hospitals, and infrastructure; they appeared in the CIA apparatus stationed in Athens; and they operated as a constant reminder of the new era of Greek American formal and diplomatic relations.

This went hand in hand with the decline of ideas that associated Americanism with a postwar anticolonial reconstruction project, one that would cooperate with the national resistance movements in Europe. On the map of the Cold War, the links between the USA and Greece were defined by the final defeat of this project and its replacement with a joint anti-communist campaign in which the imbalance of power was more than evident. At the end of 1953, King Paul of Greece made an official visit to the USA. In his speech, addressed to "Americans of Greek descent," King Paul repeated the stereotypical understanding of Greek American success as the natural outcome of a confluence of Greek virtues and American ideals; he emphasized the strong ties of immigrants with their country of origin; and he mentioned his audience's devotion "to the great country that you are privileged to be citizens of."[83]

These generalities were combined with specific references to recent deliveries of US humanitarian aid, as well as the strategic cooperation between the two countries on "the joint mission of Freedom." If his speech was not exceptionally original, his words revealed that Greece was ready to accept that the Greeks of the USA were now "Americans of Greek descent." Latent in this admission was an acknowledgment of the new global balance of power, and more specifically the inclusion of Greece in the American imperial project. "The great American Family" was how King Paul described the organic integration of yesterday's immigrants in the American present; at the same time, though, this "great American Family" was functioning as a metonym for the Free World. [84] Greece belonged in this family, and it was clear that the only ones who did not were the communists.

The Last Page

In November 1947 the last page of the *Voice of Hellenic American Youth*, the bulletin of the Greek American communist youth group, carried an announcement of an upcoming Thanksgiving Day dance organized by a charter of the International Workers Order.[85] The Greek American "young pioneers" were entirely at ease with this quintessentially American celebration (the more recent radical criticism of Thanksgiving would probably have sounded strange to them). They were giving political significance to the occasion, not by rejecting it, but by infusing it with the social values of the American Left. A comrade would make a speech on the urgent matters of the period, they would play songs by Pete Seeger and Paul Robeson, they would discuss the future activities of their group, and they would take note of newcomers and would make sure to retain contact with them. At the end of the day, they would do what the occasion called for—enjoy a stuffed turkey.

The dance included a raffle, whose prize proved in the most emphatic way that the young communists were people of their times. "A TELEVISION" was what the lucky winner would take home. "Yes, you heard right, a TELEVISION," declared the last-page announcement in the *Voice of Hellenic American Youth*. This minor detail of the Thanksgiving dance encapsulates the biggest challenge that the American Left was facing. Capitalism, now reborn, could guarantee access to a wondrous and constantly expanding world of services and consumer products, and it could provide this access to more people than ever before in history. The economic and social system that in 1929 gave the impression that it was on the brink of collapse had been reborn victorious from the ruins of World War II. Perhaps this was not yet clearly visible in 1947, but it would soon become more than obvious and inaugurate a momentous social, cultural, and political transformation.

The beginnings of this change could be traced back to the wartime economy. Central planning, state investment, and the increased needs of the war effort reversed the financial stagnation at the end of the 1930s. The central question of the time was whether the transition to postwar normality would lead to a new period of prolonged recession. History disproved those who predicted the worst. The golden era of American capitalism was built on the new global role of the USA and on a new social contract between capital and labor. At its core lay the power of consumerism: job stability and higher wages would permit wage earners to enjoy buying power, fueling the American economy, which in turn would guarantee stability and higher wages. This "consumers' republic"—to use the term that Lizabeth Cohen coined to describe the new social contract—was a nation that believed in the power of commerce and consumerism in order to consolidate equality and freedom, both inside and outside its borders.[86]

The results were soon evident. By 1950, US per capita income was the highest in the world, exceeding by one third the country in second place. Unemployment rates were down to 4 percent, and sales of consumer goods (clothes, jewelry, furniture, home appliances, etc.) had soared from 300 percent to 500 percent compared to 1939.[87] And this was only part of the larger picture. The new era soon witnessed a momentous transformation in the residential sector through large housing projects (construction and sales of new homes went up by 300 percent), the smooth reintegration and social mobility of veterans through the GI Bill, and a deluge of new and affordable consumer goods that took advantage of the defense industry's technological advances.

In the context of the country's financial transformation, the labor unions were upgraded to an institutional social partner, with the sole aim to guarantee the standard of living for their members. At the end of World War II, the unions were at the peak of their organizational power. On the eve of Pearl Harbor, the organized workers had numbered close to 10 million; by 1945, the number had surpassed the 14 million mark.[88] This upward trend demonstrated the wartime economy's transformational power, and especially the widespread adoption of collective bargaining. Bolstered by this, the CIO attempted in 1945 to secure the workplace victories won by labor during the war. Labor unrest took hold and started to spread.[89] However, the government responded promptly. Using the emergency wartime legislation, it resorted to civil conscription and succeeded in shutting down the labor movement. The year 1945, as Harry Truman wrote in his memoirs, was "the year of decisions"—and one of the most important was the decision to clash with the labor unions, which only a year earlier had mobilized to reelect his predecessor, Franklin Roosevelt, into the White House.[90]

The next step took place in 1947, signaled by a revision in labor legislation (the Taft-Hartley Act) and by a major compromise by the CIO. The new legislation utilized the legacy of the New Deal but criminalized "unfair labor practices," reinstating employer rights that had been challenged in the New Deal years. The CIO's leadership, defeated in 1945 and internally divided on the issue of anti-communist persecutions, sought an agreement that would protect the interests of its members and its role in collective agreements. As a consequence, the labor unions accepted the Truman Doctrine as beneficial to US workers and supported the president in the 1948 elections. The European Recovery Program, better known as the Marshall Plan, sustained the defense industry and tapped new global markets, thereby providing millions of workers in the USA with stable employment and high wages. In this context, the labor union members felt they had more to lose from a potential upheaval. The "conservative turn of the American working class" had just begun.[91]

Their participation in the Truman Doctrine global campaign turned the unions into participants of Cold War foreign policy. This development coincides with the introduction of certificates of social convictions. Nine national labor unions that were controlled by the Left were expelled from the CIO.[92] By the mid-1950s, the CIO had become a gigantic bureaucracy that defended a social contract that combined the financial security of the wage earners and the absence of ideological dissent. George Lipsitz has named this new era of social consensus "liberal corporatism"—it was a consensus based on public investment in heavy industry, uninterrupted production, and making the labor unions an institutional social partner, free from the radical tendencies of the past.[93] On 2 November 1948, the Progressive Party, which at the start of the election campaign had seemed like a noteworthy opponent to the Democrats, garnered 2.4 percent of the vote. Progressive Party nominee Henry Wallace's alternative program had managed to convince only 10 percent of CIO members.[94] The result emphasized the triumph of stability, which Truman expressed, over instability.

Immigrant and ethnic communities were among the winners of the postwar era. Higher wages, the entry of women into the workforce, job stability, and veterans benefits all affected millions of Americans belonging to the first, and especially to the second, immigrant generation. Large housing developments and social mobility meant that many of them could move from the old working-class neighborhoods to the suburbs, which was a definite step toward social acceptability, equality with nonimmigrant Americans, and fulfilling the American Dream. The wartime sacrifices resulted in significant changes in political equality and signaled the emergent American ideology, which held that the American nation was multiethnic, that its superiority was founded on the political rights it guaranteed for each of its inhabitants, and that ethnic diversity was to be respected. There was, though, an exception: the association of ethnic identity with anti-American ideologies, specifically communism. In this case, the immigrants would not fit into the multicultural mosaic that had replaced the older symbol of a Melting Pot producing a uniform American identity.

As Gary Gerstle has written, anti-communism reinforced national unity in an ever-changing political climate, which was dominated by the cultural acceptance of ethnic descent and the financial security of the old immigrant communities.[95] In this context, the ethnic communities proudly exhibited their anti-communist sentiments in order to enter "the era of respectability."[96] The Greek American communities provide an example of the way that developments in their country of origin went hand in hand with dominant American values. A number of demographic and social shifts were transforming these communities. A house in the suburbs and a new car functioned as the culmination of a "whitening" process, which carried with it significant ideological and social connotations.[97] Upward mobility, second- and third-generation immigrants going to college, and a constant comparison with conditions in Greece made Greek Americans the successful example of a reborn American Dream.

The American communists watched with unease the unfolding of this new reality. During the last few years, all their efforts had gone to improving the standard of living of wage earners and consigning the Great Depression to the past. During the war, they had abandoned their revolutionary vision to promote a plan for a postwar transition that would provide job stability and high wages for those who had fought against fascism, both in the front lines and in the wartime factories. The communist movement had focused on wages, unemployment rates, job stability. In its political vocabulary these issues were inextricably linked with the prospect of postwar cooperation between the USA and the Soviet Union. Put simply, the communists believed that an improvement of the American working class's everyday life necessitated a progressive social contract, which would be based on the New Deal and the wartime anti-fascist coalition.

The postwar economic miracle proved that history moves in mysterious ways. The communists' demands had been satisfied. After a brief period of unrest right after the end of World War II, all economic indicators shot upward, while the decline in unemployment rates, the steady increase in wages, and the recognition of labor unions finally satisfied long-standing demands of the working-class movement. The American working class seemed to be the undisputed winner of the new social contract. In the center of all these changes was World War II. Despite its significant successes, the 1930s New Deal had managed, at best, first to stabilize the economy and then to improve it slightly. When the United States entered the war, industrial production skyrocketed and unemployment rates reversed their upward course. The Great Depression ended just as it had begun; no one came out to announce one day that it had ended, but gradually everybody felt that it had run its course. The generous rewards given to veterans, the recognition of labor unions, and the new possibilities for social mobility functioned as retrospective compensation for those who had suffered during the years of the Great Depression and had been at the forefront of the fight against fascism.

At the same time, the war economy along with the reborn American Dream had proved something more: capitalism could work. The crisis of the interwar years had given rise to widespread doubts about the survival possibilities of a capitalist economy. The facts now offered a convincing answer. State intervention and the regulation of relations between capital and labor could guarantee the long life of the system. For many, this was the answer they needed. The American labor movement, as early as the beginning of the 1930s, had reined in its anti-capitalist views, embracing instead a radical shift in collective agreements and labor rights, in the present rather than in some distant future. The communists had played a decisive role in this realignment, certain that they were working toward a Popular Front in the USA. Now, they were facing a social contract that included their labor demands and at the same time was turning against them.

Notes

1. Starobin, *American Communism in Crisis*, 224.
2. Schrecker, *Many Are the Crimes*, xviiii.
3. United States President, "Address of the President of the United States . . . Recommending Assistance to Greece and Turkey."
4. Goldstein, *American Blacklist*, 62.
5. Schlesinger, *The Vital Center*.
6. Michael Harrington, "Mystical Militants," *The New Republic*, 19 February 1966, 20.
7. Morgan, *Reds*; Caute, *The Great Fear*; Schrecker, *Many Are the Crimes*.
8. McGovern, "Forward," vii.
9. Gerstle, *American Crucible*, 245–46.
10. "Citrine Labor Mission Reports Chaotic Conditions," *The New York Times*, 9 February 1945, 6.
11. Eastman, "A Cerebral Revolution Busts Loose," *The New Leader*, 13 January 1945.
12. Macdonald, "Eastmania," *Politics*, February 1945, 58–60.
13. "The Greek Tragedy," *Politics*, February 1945, 38–42.
14. Burnham, *The Struggle for the World*, 1.
15. "New Liberal Party Formed Officially," *The New York Times*, 20 May 1944, 9.
16. "Memorandum of Conference with President Truman at the White House, Thursday, July 8, 1948," Dean Alfange Papers, Series 1, "Correspondence 1929–1988," Manuscripts and Archives Division, New York Public Library.
17. "Exclusive interviews: Basil J. Vlavianos, leading Greek Liberal, Writer and Publisher," Basil J. Vlavianos Papers, Box 17, CSUS.

18. Richardson, "The Basil John Vlavianos Papers," 97.
19. Nicholas Cheronis to Basil Vlavianos, 23 October 1945, Basil J. Vlavianos Papers, Box 154, CSUS.
20. Basil Vlavianos, "Greece and Its Allies," *The Nation*, 28 June 1946, 342.
21. McAuliffe, *Crisis on the Left*, 23.
22. George Orfanson to Basil Vlavianos, 17 July 1946, Basil J. Vlavianos Papers, Box 154, CSUS.
23. "Excerpts from the Greek American Tribune of New York, August 23, 1946," Basil J. Vlavianos Papers, Box 153, CSUS.
24. Demetrios Callimachos to Syngelakis, 30 January 1948, Greek American Collection, Immigration History Research Center, University of Minnesota.
25. F. L. Parks to Herbert Bayard Swope, 23 July 1947, John Poulos and Constantine Poulos Papers, Box 2, Tamiment Library.
26. Basil Vlavianos, "Greece and its Allies," *The Nation*, 23 June 1945, 696.
27. Klehr and Haynes, *Venona*, 245.
28. Ferrell, *Truman in the White House*, 12.
29. Klara, *FDR's Funeral Train*, 141.
30. Hechler, *Working with Truman*, 55.
31. For instance, see Connie Poulos, "Maragon in Greece," *The Nation*, 17 September 1949, 266.
32. Drew Pearson, "Harry Truman has Good Intentions, but Bad Friends," The Washington Merry-Go-Round, 18 March 1947; Drew Pearson, "John Maragon Protests at White House," The Washington Merry-Go-Round, 1 April 1947; Drew Pearson, "Senator McCarthy Learning Greek," The Washington Merry-Go-Round, 11 April 1947. The Washington-Merry-Go-Round was Pearson's syndicated column from 1932 to 1969. Pearson continued his attacks against Vaughan in the 1950s. All references (and a complete collection of typescripts): American University Digital Research Archive.
33. "Grady Memorandum on Poulos," John Poulos and Constantine Poulos Papers, Box 3, Tamiment Library.
34. Ferrell, *Truman in the White House*, 189.
35. Westbrook Pegler, "Peculiar Career of a Peculiar Capital Scribe," *Evening Independent*, 28 July 1949, 6.
36. Wittner, *American Intervention in Greece*, 157.
37. United States Congress, Committee on Un-American Activities, *Guide to Subversive Organizations and Publications*, 42.
38. Basil J. Vlavianos to Federal Bureau of Investigation, 29 May 1952, Basil J. Vlavianos Papers, Box 153, CSUS.
39. Federal Bureau of Investigation, Basil Vlavianos File, Internal Security-G, 26 December 1941, Basil J. Vlavianos Papers, Box 245, CSUS.
40. "Memorandum," Greek American Council-American Relief for Greek Democracy, Church League of America Collection of the Research Files of Counterattack, the Wackenhut Corporation and Karl Baarslag, Counterattack Research Files, Box 13, 12-10, Tamiment Library.
41. Ethnikē Allēlengyi Ellados, *Gia tous Ellēnes kai philellēnes tou exoterikou*, 4–5; "Ē EA sto exoteriko," *Ethnikē Allēlengyi*, 10 May 1946, 6.
42. "Memorandum," Greek American Council-American Relief for Greek Democracy, Church League of America Collection of the Research Files of Counterattack, the Wackenhut Corporation and Karl Baarslag, Counterattack Research Files, Box 13, 12-10, Tamiment Library.
43. Greek American Council-American Relief for Greek Democracy, Church League of America Collection of the Research Files of Counterattack, the Wackenhut Corporation and Karl Baarslag, Counterattack Research Files, Box 13, 12-10, Tamiment Library.
44. American Relief for Greek Democracy, "Elias Barzalai, Chief Rabbi of Athens: Appeal to the Jews of America," Greek American Council-American Relief for Greek Democracy, Church League of America Collection of the Research Files of Counterattack, the

Wackenhut Corporation and Karl Baarslag, Counterattack Research Files, Box 13, 12-10, Tamiment Library.

45. For example: "Mrs. Eleanor Roosevelt Speaks for Greek Orphans," *The New York Times*, 24 December 1946, 11.

46. Horowitz, *Merchant of Words*, 149–50.

47. Black, *The Eleanor Roosevelt Papers*, 468.

48. "Financial Report for American Relief for Greek Democracy, June 30, 1946," Basil J. Vlavianos Papers, Box 142, CSUS.

49. Saloutos, *The Greeks in the United States*, 363.

50. "CARE Packages Reach National Mutual Aid in Greece," *American Relief for Greek Democracy*, 4 August 1946, 1; "Greek Group Joins CARE," *The New York Times*, 3 August 1946, 6.

51. *Ethnikē Allēlengyi*, 25 December 1946.

52. Nikos Cheronis to Basil Vlavianos, 20 August 1945, Basil J. Vlavianos Papers, Box 134, CSUS.

53. "Greek-American Red Front Fights Truman Program," *New York World-Telegram*, 1 April 1947; "Stars Shine for Greece," Greek American Council-American Relief for Greek Democracy, Church League of America Collection of the Research Files of Counterattack, the Wackenhut Corporation and Karl Baarslag, Counterattack Research Files, Box 13, 12-10, Tamiment Library.

54. John Edgar Hoover, "Memorandum," 27 March 1947, Federal Bureau of Investigations, FBI File on Eleanor Roosevelt, 0998-1274, Internal Security: American Relief for Greek Democracy.

55. Filardo, "The Counterattack Research Files on American Communism," 189–91.

56. John Edgar Hoover, "Memorandum," 27 March 1947, Federal Bureau of Investigations, FBI File on Eleanor Roosevelt, 0998-1274, Internal Security: American Relief for Greek Democracy.

57. United States Congress, *Testimony of Walter S. Steele Regarding Communist*, 23–24.

58. Wittner, *American Intervention in Greece*, 257.

59. "2 Red Fronts Plug Party Line on Greece," *New York World-Telegram*, 13 March 1947, 1.

60. United States Congress, *Investigation of Communist Infiltration into the Fur Industry*, 200.

61. United States Congress, *Investigation of Communist Infiltration into the Fur Industry*, 238.

62. United States Congress, *Investigation of Un-American Propaganda Activities in the United States*, 269.

63. United States Congress, *Communist Activities Among Aliens and National Groups*, A1.

64. Giannis Baharas, interview, footage for the documentary *Taxisyneidēsia: Ē agnōstē istoria tou ellēnoamerikanikou rizospastismou* (director: Kostas Vakkas, script: Kostis Karpozilos, production: Non-profit organization "Apostolis Berdebes," 2013).

65. "Deportation of Present and Ex-Members of Communist Party to Be Fought in Test," *The New York Times*, 22 January 1947, 15.

66. "Peter Harisiades: American by Choice," National Conference against Deportation Hysteria (1949), American Committee for Protection of Foreign Born Papers, Box 1, Tamiment Library; King and Englander, *Memorandum for Peter Harisiades*.

67. For an overview of the case, see Smith, *Torch of Liberty*, 292-98.

68. Murphy and Smith, *Liberty and Justice*, 551–52.

69. "Communist is Deported," *The New York Times*, 13 November 1952, 12.

70. Index, November 1948 and Index, November 1949, YDIA/MFA, 1950/20/3.

71. Kostopoulos, "Afaireseis ithageneias," 56–57.

72. Vasileios Dendramis to the Ministry of Foreign Affairs, 28 June 1949, YDIA/MFA, 1950/20/3.

73. For Vafeiadis, see United States Congress, *Investigation of Communist Infiltration into the Fur Industry*, 195–96.

74. United States Congress, *Communist Activities Among Aliens and National Groups*, 739.
75. Mary Vardoulakis to National Review Committee, Communist Party USA, 8 May 1950, File C, Central Control Commission Records, MN# 5507, Tamiment Library.
76. "Speaker to Review Conditions in Greece," *Reading Eagle*, 28 February 1947, 25.
77. State Review Commission, "Regarding the need for increased vigilance in combatting the attacks of the FBI," Central Control Commission Records, MN 5507, Tamiment Library.
78. Minutes of the first Pan-Macedonian convention held in Plaza Hotel, New York City, 19–21 September 1947, Pan-Macedonian Association Records, 1.6 Minutes, Annual Conventions 1947–1953, MSS 106, The Balch Institute for Ethnic Studies, Historical Society of Pennsylvania.
79. Zervakis, "The Greek Lobby and the Reemergence of Anti-Communism," 312, 334.
80. Greek Independence New York City Parade, Press Release, 1951, Nicholas Vagionis Papers, 1923–1973, MSS 33, Box 10, The Balch Institute for Ethnic Studies, Historical Society of Pennsylvania.
81. Saloutos, *Greeks in the United States*, 378.
82. Zake, "Preface," ix.
83. *Logoi ekfonēthentes ypo tēs AM tou Vasileōs Paulou.*
84. *Logoi ekfonēthentes ypo tēs AM tou Vasileōs Paulou.*
85. *Voice of the Hellenic American Youth*, November 1947.
86. Cohen, *A Consumers' Republic.*
87. Patterson, *Grand Expectations*, 61–71.
88. United States Department of Commerce, *Historical Statistics of the US, 1789–1945*, 72.
89. Ginger and Christiano, *The Cold War Against Labor*, 200–13; Zieger, *The CIO*, 212–41.
90. Truman, *1945. Year of Decisions*, 431ff.
91. Cowie, "Introduction: The Conservative Turn in Postwar United States Working-Class History," 70–75.
92. Rosswurm, *The CIO's Left-Led Unions.*
93. Lipsitz, *Rainbow at Midnight.*
94. Zieger, *The CIO*, 276.
95. Gerstle, *American Crucible*, 240.
96. Saloutos, *The Greeks in the United States*, 362.
97. Roediger, *Working Toward Whiteness*, 199ff.

Conclusion

The concept of a radical political project in the immigrant communities was based on the prospect of transcending ethnic cohesion for the benefit of a unified American working class, regardless of racial or ethnic descent. In this sense, the immigrant Left functioned as an intermediate step in the greater project of radical Americanization, sharing the core belief of Americanization's dominant narrative: the inescapable gradual decline of ethnic cohesion. However, this conviction (and prediction) proved to be wrong. Ethnic descent remained (and became) a point of reference for millions of first- and second-generation immigrants. When the communists realized this, they attempted a radical reorientation. They tried to associate class with ethnic descent under the umbrella of the Popular Front. In the favorable circumstances of the New Deal and the wartime anti-fascist unity, the results were more than encouraging. The communists' organizational boost, the labor movement's gathering momentum, and the diasporic initiatives of the immigrant Left seemed to resolve the tension between ethnicity and class.

The end of World War II revealed the limitations of this model. The immigrant Left was addressing an audience that identified itself less and less with the traditional working class and more and more enjoyed the opportunities for upward social mobility. At the same time, the communist political vocabulary that identified patriotism with anti-fascism was completely at odds with the global emergence of anti-communism and a renewed understanding of Americanism. In the Cold War years, ethnicity and immigrant descent were no longer a problem in the dominant American setting. Quite the contrary—they functioned as proof of the liberal and dynamic nature of the American Republic. There was only one crucial requirement: to renounce subversive ideas, and more specifically "Red totalitarianism." The vast majority of immigrants had no trouble whatsoever in adjusting to the new reality; fear, personal considerations, and conformism each played their part, along with the new anti-communist dimension of patriotism, both in Greece and the USA.

For many of those who had joined the Left, the experience of their polit-icization was based on openness, participation in labor struggles, and faith that History (always with a capital H) was moving, regardless of various setbacks, ultimately forward. In the new circumstances, optimism was a luxury they could not afford. Being a communist in the United States was fast becoming an increasingly difficult proposition, caught between political persecution, the party's stagnation, and the appeal of American capitalism.

The success of the communist movement during the Popular Front years was based on its ability to claim an alternative version of Americanism. The slogan "Communism is the Americanism of the 20th Century" carried with it a set of revolutionary traditions expressing the belief that the USA would witness a radical social transformation. In this context, the decision of the CPUSA to self-dissolve, in early 1944, demonstrated the lengths that American communists were willing to go in order to convince the public of their intentions, and at the same time to shake off accusations of Moscow's influence. This attempt was not some nefarious plot, as many critics of every political persuasion claimed at the time. Rather, it was part of wider social dynamics, and especially the formation of working-class Americanism during the New Deal era. For many first- and second-generation immi-grants, being a communist was one of the ways to be an American. In the new postwar circumstance, this was no longer an option. In order to be an American, one had to be an anti-communist.

BIBLIOGRAPHY

Archival Sources

Special Collections and University Archives, California State University, Sacramento (CSUS).
Oral History Collection, Special Collections, Columbia University.
Diplomatic and Historical Archives of the Hellenic Ministry of Foreign Affairs (YDIA/MFA).
Federal Bureau of Investigations (FBI).
Immigration History Research Center, University of Minnesota.
Hellenic Literary and Historical Archive Society (ELIA).
Historical Society of Pennsylvania (HSP).
National Archives and Records Administration (NARA).
Department of Rare Books and Special Collections, Princeton University Library.
Russian State Archive of Social and Political History (RGASPI).
Manuscripts and Archives Division, The New York Public Library (NYPL).
The Tamiment Library and Robert F. Wagner Labor Archives, New York University (Tamiment).

Newspapers, Bulletins, and Reviews

American Relief for Greek Democracy (1946)
Atlantis (1909, 1925–26, 1934–35)
Bulletin of the Greek American Committee for National Unity (1944–46)
Christian Science Monitor (1912)
Ē Phonē tou Ergatou [Voice of the worker] (1917, 1919, 1922–23)
Ellēnoamerikanon Vēma [Greek American tribune] (1942, 1944–46)
Empros [Forward] (1925–27, 1931, 1937–38)
Ereuna [Inquiry] (1910–12)
Ethnikē Allēlengyi [National solidarity] (1941–46)
Ethnikos Kēryx [National herald] (1925–26, 1926–36)
Evening Independent (1949)
Fortune (1936)
Free World (1941–46)
Industrial Pioneer (1921–23)
Labor Defender (1926–40)
New Europe (1944–45)
New Masses (1940)
O Dēmokrates [The democrat] (1937)
Organōsis [Organization] (1922–24)
Philhellene (1945)
Politics (1945)

Prōtoporos [Pioneer] (1935–37)
Reading Eagle (1947)
Revolutionary Age (1929–32)
Rizospastēs [Radical] (1921-36, 1945)
Saloniki-Greek Press (1934)
The AHEPAN (1942)
The Communist (1919–21)
The International Socialist Review (1907–14)
The Militant (1933)
The New Leader (1945)
The New Republic (1946)
The New York Times (1912–14, 1930–47)
The Party Organizer (1927–39)
The Woman Rebel (1914)
Voice of Hellenic American Youth (1947)

Greek American Radical Books and Pamphlets

Baby, Jean. *Tria mathēmata koinōniologias: taxeis, isotēs, kratos* [*Three courses on sociology: classes, equality, and state*]. New York: Workers' Press, 1928.
Brown, William Montgomery. *Kommounismos kai Christianismos: Analysē kai antiparavolē tous apo tēn apopsē tou Marx kai tou Darvinou* [*Communism and Christianism: Analyzed and Contrasted from the Marxian and Darwinian Points of View*]. Ohio: Greek Federation of Workers' Party of America, 1925.
Christophorides, Demetrius. *A New American Problem in the Light of Nazi Aggression.* New York: n.p., 1939.
Croubaugh, Clyde. *O proletarios dia mesou ton aionon* [*The Proletarian through the Ages*]. Cincinnati: Organosis, 1918.
De Leon, Daniel. *Metarrythmisis ē epanastasis;* [*Reform or Revolution?*]. Cincinnati: Organosis, 1917.
———. *Ti simainei aftē ē apergia;* [*What Means This Strike?*]. Cincinnati: Organosis, 1917.
———. *Sosialistikē anoikodomēsis tēs koinōnias* [*Socialist Reconstruction of Society*]. New York: Organosis, 1920.
———. *Viomēchanikē enotēs* [*Industrial Unionism*]. New York: Organosis, 1920.
———. *To flegon zētēma tēs epaggelmatikēs enotētos* [*The Burning Question of Trade Unionism*]. New York: n.p., 1928.
Drakoulis, Plato. *Ē koinōnia tou mellontos* [The future society]. New York: Divry Press, 1916.
EAM: White Book. New York: Greek American Council, 1945.
Genar, Giannis. *Gia to psōmi kai tē leuteria* [For bread and freedom]. Chicago: Greek Workers' Press, 1926.
Georgiou, Vasos. *Ē exathliōsē tou laou kai o ploutos tēs chōras* [The pauperization of the people and the country's wealth]. New York: Greek American Tribune, 1946.
Gervasi, Frank, Leland Stowe and Panos Morphopoulos. *Greek Liberation.* New York: Greek American Committee for National Unity, 1944.
Greek Workers' Educational Club, Spartakus. *Ellēnes ethelontai eis tēn Ispanian: anamnēstikon leukōma* [Greek volunteers in Spain: commemorative photobook]. New York: n.p., 1938.
In our Fight for Freedom: The Cause of the United Nations Demands Greek Independence! New York: Greek American Committee for National Unity, 1944.
Johnson, Hewlett. *Ē sovietikē dynamis* [*The Soviet Power*]. New York: Greek American Tribune, 1943.

Katastatikon tou Ergatikou Kommatos tēs Amerikēs kai esōterikoi kanonismoi tis Ellinikēs Omospondias [Statutes of the workers party of America and internal rules of the Greek Federation]. New York: n.p., 1924.

Katsiolis, Georgios. *Ta egklēmata tou politismou* [The crimes of civilization]. Chicago: Saloniki Printing and Publishing, 1922.

Kazavis, Iakovos. *O Sosialismos erchetai* [Socialism is coming]. New York: n.p., 1924.

Kollontai, Alexandra. *Ē oikogeneia kai to kommounistiko politevma* [*Communism and the Family*]. New York: Greek Socialist Union, 1920.

Leondopoulos, Steve. *Greece Fights for Freedom*. New York: Greek American Labor Committee, 1944.

Lenin, Nikolai. *Kratos kai Epanastasis* [*The State and Revolution*]. New York: Greek Federation of Workers Party of America, 1924.

Lozovsky, Alexander. *O Lenin: o megas stratēgos tou polemou tōn taxeōn* [*Lenin: the Great Strategist of the Class War*]. Chicago: Greek Workers' Press, 1925.

Marcy, Mary. *Oikonomologikes Kouventes* [*Shop Talks on Economics*]. New York: Greek Socialist Association of America, 1921.

Marx, Karl. *Ē kritikē tou programmatos tou Gotha* [*Critique of the Gotha Program*]. Chicago: Greek Workers' Press, 1927.

Paroritis, Kostas. *Oi dyo dromoi* [The two roads]. Chicago: Greek Workers' Press, 1927.

Pistolakis, Stelios. *The Truth about Greece*. New York: Greek American Committee for National Unity, 1944.

Roussos, Petros. *Perissotero phōs ston ethnikoapeleutherōtiko agōna tou ellēnikou laou* [More light on the fight for liberation of the Greek people]. New York: n.p., 1947.

Stowe, Leland, and Constantine Poulos. *Challenge to Freedom: The Story of what Happened in Greece*. New York: Greek American Council, 1945.

Sue, Eugène. *O Argyrous Stavros* [*The Silver Cross*]. New York: Organosis, 1923.

Terror in Greece! Bloody Act of Fake Elections. New York: Greek-American Council, 1946.

The Youth of Greece is Fighting for Freedom, Independence and Democracy. New York: American Youth for the Youth of Greece, 1948.

Ti einai to IWW [*What is the IWW?*]. Chicago: n.p., 1920.

Treis mēnes tou Kōsta Karagiōrgē stēn Amerikē [Three months of Kostas Karagiorgis in America]. New York: Greek American Tribune Publishing Department, 1945.

Trotsky, Leon. *O polemos kai oi mpolsevikoi* [The war and the Bolsheviks]. New York: n.p., 1918.

Tyranny and Terror, the Betrayal of Greece. New York: Greek-American Council, 1946.

Zachariadēs, Nikos. *O Alēthinos Palamas* [The true Palamas]. New York: Ellēnoamerikanikon Vēma, 1945.

Secondary Sources

Abraham, Joseph. "State Regulation of Foreign Banks." *Fordham Law Review* 9 (1940): 343–61.

Allen, Susan Heuck. *Classical Spies: American Archaeologists with the OSS in World War II Greece*. Ann Arbor, MI: University of Michigan Press, 2011.

Andersen, Kristi. *The Creation of a Democratic Majority, 1928–1936*. Chicago: University of Chicago Press, 1979.

Anderson, Perry. "Communist Party History." In *People's History and Socialist Theory*, edited by Raphael Samuel, 145–56. Milton Park: Routledge 1981.

Antoniou, Mary. "Welfare Activities Among the Greek People in Los Angeles." Ph.D. dissertation. Los Angeles: University of Southern California, 1939.

Baker, Jean H. *Margaret Sanger: A Life of Passion*. New York: Hill and Wang, 2012.

Barrett, James. "Americanization from the Bottom Up: Immigration and the Remaking of the Working Class in the United States, 1880–1930." *The Journal of American History* 79, no. 3 (1992): 996–1020.

Bell, Daniel. *Marxian Socialism in the United States*. Princeton, NJ: Princeton University Press 1967.

Bencivenni, Marcella. *Italian Immigrant Radical Culture: The Idealism of the Sovversivi in the United States, 1890–1940*. New York: New York University Press, 2011.

Bernstein, Irving. *The Lean Years: A History of the American Worker, 1920–1933*. Boston: Houghton Mifflin, 1960.

Black, Allida, ed. *The Eleanor Roosevelt Papers: The Human Rights Years, 1945–1948*. Volume 1. Detroit: Thompson Gale, 2007.

Browder, Earl. *What is Communism?* New York: The Vanguard Press, 1936.

Brown, Francis, and Joseph S. Roucek, eds. *Our Racial and National Minorities: Their History, Contribution and Present Problems*. New York: Prentice Hall, 1937.

Burgess, Thomas. *Greeks in America: An Account of their Coming, Progress, Customs, Living and Aspirations with an Historical Introduction and the Stories of Some Famous American-Greeks*. Boston: Sherman French, 1913.

Burnham, James. *The Struggle for the World*. New York: John Day, 1947.

Byford-Jones, Wilfred. *The Greek Trilogy: Resistance, Liberation, Revolution*. London: Hutchinson, 1945.

Capell, Richard. *Simiomata: A Greek Note Book, 1944–1945*. London: Macdonald, 1946.

Carr, E. H. *Twilight of the Comintern, 1930–1935*. New York: Pantheon Books, 1982.

Carroll, Peter. *The Odyssey of the Abraham Lincoln Brigade: Americans in the Spanish Civil War*. Stanford, CA: Stanford University Press, 1994.

Caute, David. *The Great Fear: The Anti-Communist Purge Under Truman and Eisenhower*. London: Martin Secker & Warburg, 1978.

Churchill, Winston. *The Second World War: Triumph and Tragedy*. Volume 6. Boston: Houghton Mifflin, 1953.

Cohen, Lizabeth. *Making a New Deal: Industrial Workers in Chicago, 1919–1939*. Cambridge: Cambridge University Press, 1990.

———. *A Consumers' Republic: The Politics of Mass Consumption in Postwar America*. New York: Knopf Doubleday, 2008.

Committee for Industrial Organization. *Industrial Unionism, the Vital Problem of Organized Labor*. Washington, DC: CIO, 1935.

Commonwealth of Massachusetts, The Director of the Bureau of Statistics, *Forty-Third Annual Report on the Statistics of Labor for the Year 1912*. Boston: Wright & Potter Printing, 1913.

Communist Party of the United States of America. *Thesis and Resolutions for the Seventh National Convention of the Communist Party of the United States of America by Central Committee Plenum, March 31–April 4 1930*. New York: Workers Library Publishers, 1930.

Communist Party of the United States of America. *Stalin's Speeches on the American Communist Party*. New York: n.p., 1931.

Communist Political Association. *The Path to Peace, Progress and Prosperity: Proceedings of the Constitutional Convention of the Communist Political Association*. New York: Communist Political Association, 1944.

Cononelos, Louis. *In Search of Gold Paved Streets: Greek Immigrant Labor in the Far West, 1900–1920*. New York: AMS Press, 1989.

Constant, Constance. *Austin Lunch: Greek-American Recollections*. River Vale, NJ: Cosmos Publishing, 2004.

Cowie, Jefferson. "Introduction: The Conservative Turn in Postwar United States Working-Class History." *International Labor and Working-Class History* 74 (2008): 70–75.

Crowther, Don. "Analysis of Strikes in 1937." *Labor Information Bulletin* 5, no. 5 (1938): 11–13.

De Caux, Len. *Labor Radical: From the Wobblies to CIO, A Personal History*. Boston: Beacon Press, 1970.

Degras, Jane, ed. *The Communist International, 1919–1943*. Volume 3, *1929–1943*. London: Frank Cass, 1971.

Dimitrov, Georgi. *The Fascist Offensive and the Tasks of the Communist International in the Struggle of the Working Class against Fascism*. New York: Workers Library Press, 1935.

Draper, Theodore. *The Roots of American Communism*. New York: The Viking Press, 1957.

———. *American Communism and Soviet Russia: The Formative Period*. New York: The Viking Press, 1963.

Dreyfus, Philip. "The IWW and the Limits of Inter-Ethnic Organizing: Reds, Whites, and Greeks in Grays Harbor, Washington, 1912." *Labor History* 38, no. 4 (1997): 450–70.

Dubofsky, Melvyn. *Industrialism and the American Worker, 1865–1920*. Arlington Heights, IL: H. Davidson, 1985.

Duclos, Jacques. "On the Dissolution of the Communist Party of the United States." In *Marxism-Leninism vs. Revisionism*, edited by William Z. Foster, 21–35. New York: New Century Publishers, 1946.

Eley, Geoff. *Forging Democracy: The History of the Left in Europe, 1850–2000*. Oxford: Oxford University Press, 2002.

Eliel, Paul. *The Waterfront and General Strikes, San Francisco, 1934: A Brief History*. San Francisco: Hooper Print, 1934.

Ethnikē Allēlengyi Ellados. *Gia tous Ellēnes kai philellēnes tou exoterikou* [For the Greeks and philhellenes abroad]. Athens: n.p., 1946.

Fairchild, Henry Pratt. *Greek Immigration to the United States*. New Haven, CT: Yale University Press, 1911.

Ferrell, Robert, ed. *Truman in the White House: The Diary of Eben A. Ayers*. Columbia, MO: University of Missouri Press, 1991.

Filardo, Peter. "The Counterattack Research Files on American Communism, Tamiment Institute Library, New York University." *Labor History* 39, no. 2 (1998): 189–91.

Fine, Sidney. *Sitdown: The General Motors Strike of 1936–1937*. Ann Arbor, MI: University of Michigan Press, 1969.

Firsov, Fridrikh Igorevich, Harvey Klehr, and John Earl Haynes, eds. *Secret Cables of the Comintern, 1933–1943*. New Haven, CT: Yale University Press, 2014.

Foner, Philip Sheldon. *The Fur and Leather Workers Union: A Story of Dramatic Struggles and Achievements*. Newark, NJ: Nordan Press, 1950.

Foreign Nationalities Branch. *Foreign National Groups in the United States: A Handbook Prepared in the Foreign Nationalities Branch for Use in the Office of Strategic Services*. Washington, DC: n.p., 1943.

Foster, William. *Toward Soviet America*. New York: Coward-McCann, 1932.

Fowler, Josephine. *Japanese and Chinese Immigrant Activists: Organizing in American and International Communist Movements, 1919–1933*. New Brunswick, NJ: Rutgers University Press, 2007.

Fried, Albert, ed. *Communism in America: A History in Documents*. New York: Columbia University Press, 1997.

Geia sou periphanē kai athanatē ergatia: mia diadromē sto ergatiko-koinōniko tragoudi [Long live proud and immortal working class: a journey in the labor-social song]. Athens: Archeio Istorias Syndikatōn, Genikē Synomospondia Ergatōn Elladas, 2000.

Georgakas, Dan. "Constantine Yavis: Propaganda in the Greek-American Community (21.4.1944)," *Journal of the Hellenic Diaspora* 14, nos. 1–2 (1987): 105–30.

———. "Demosthenes Nikas: Labor Radical." In *New Directions in Greek American Studies*, edited by Dan Georgakas and Charles S. Moskos, 95–110. New York: Pella Publishing Company, 1991.

———. "Greek-American Radicalism: The Twentieth Century." In *The Immigrant Left in the United States*, edited by Paul Buhle and Dan Georgakas, 207–32. Albany, NY: State University of New York Press, 1996.

Gerstle, Gary. *American Crucible: Race and Nation in the Twentieth Century*. Princeton, NJ: Princeton University Press, 2001.

Ginger, Ann Fagan, and David Christiano, eds. *The Cold War Against Labor*. Volume 1. Berkeley: Meiklejohn Civil Liberties Institute, 1987.

Gitlow, Benjamin. *I Confess: The Truth about American Communism*. New York: E. P. Dutton, 1940.

Gold, Ben. *Memoirs*. New York: William Howard Publishers, 1984.

Goldstein, Robert Justin. *American Blacklist: The Attorney General's List of Subversive Organizations*. Lawrence, KS: University Press of Kansas, 2008.

Gosnell, Harold, and Norman N. Gill. "An Analysis of the 1932 Presidential Vote in Chicago." *American Political Science Review* 29, no. 6 (1935): 967–84.

Guglielmo, Jennifer. *Living the Revolution: Italian Women's Resistance and Radicalism in New York City, 1880–1945*. Chapel Hill, NC: The University of North Carolina Press, 2010.

Havel, Hippolyte, ed. *The Revolutionary Almanac 1914*. New York: The Rabelais Press, 1913.

Hechler, Ken. *Working with Truman: A Personal Memoir of the White House Years*. Columbia, MO: University of Missouri Press, 1982.

Hennen, John. "E. T. Weir, Employee Representation and the Dimensions of Social Control: Weirton Steel, 1933–1937." *Labor Studies Journal* 26, no 3 (2001): 25–49.

Hoffman, Matthew and Henry Srebrnik, eds. *A Vanished Ideology: Essays on the Jewish Communist Movement in the English-Speaking World in the Twentieth Century*. Albany, NY: State University of New York Press, 2016.

Horowitz, Terry. *Merchant of Words: The Life of Robert St. John*. Lanham: Rowman and Littlefield, 2014.

Howe, Irving, and Lewis Coser. *The American Communist Party: A Critical History*. New York: Frederic A. Praeger, 1962.

Iatrides, John. *Revolt in Athens: The Greek Communist "Second Round," 1944–1945*. Princeton, NJ: Princeton University Press, 1972.

Jones, Thai. *More Powerful Than Dynamite: Radicals, Plutocrats, Progressives and New York's Year of Anarchy*. New York: Walker and Co., 2012.

Josephson, Matthew. *Union House, Union Bar: The History of the Hotel and Restaurant Employees and Bartenders International Union, AFL-CIO*. New York: Random House, 1956.

Kamp, Joseph Peter. *Join the CIO and Help Build a Soviet America: A Factual Narrative*. New Haven: Constitutional Educational League, 1937.

Karpozilos, Kostis. "Apopeires sygkrotēsēs tou ellēnikou Laikou Metōpou: ē Dēmokratiki Enōsē Ellēnōn Gallias" [Trying to forge the Greek Popular Front: the Greek Democratic Union of France]. *Archeiotaxio* 10 (2008): 37–53.

Karvonides-Nkosi, Joanna. "Greek Immigrants in the Fur Manufacturing Industry in New York City, 1887 to 1943: Class and Ethnicity at the Workplace." Ph.D. Dissertation. New York: City University of New York, 1991.

Katznelson, Ira. *Fear Itself: The New Deal and the Origins of Our Time*. New York: Liveright Publishing Corporation, 2013.

Kautsky, Karl. *The Class Struggle*. Chicago: Charles H. Kerr, 1910.

Kazin, Michael. *The Populist Persuasion: An American History*. Ithaca, NY: Cornell University Press, 1998.

Keeran, Roger. "The International Workers Order and the origins of the CIO." *Labor History* 30, no. 3 (1989): 385–408.

———. "National Groups and the Popular Front: The Case of the International Workers Order." *Journal of American Ethnic History* 14, no. 3 (1995): 23–29.

Kerr, Charles. *Socialist Songs with Music*. Chicago: Charles H. Kerr and Company, 1902.

King, Carol, and Isidore Englander. *Memorandum for Peter Harisiades*. New York: American Committee for the Protection of Foreign Born, 1947.

Kitroeff, Alexandros. "Ē Yperatlantiki Metanastefsē" [Transatlantic immigration]. In *Istoria tēs Ellados tou 20ou aiōna, 1900–1922* [History of 20th-century Greece, 1900–1922], edited by Christos Chatziosif, 122–71. Athens: Vivliorama, 1999.

Kivisto, Peter. *Immigrant Socialists in the United States: The Case of Finns and the Left*. Madison, NJ: Fairleigh Dickinson University Press, 1984.

Klara, Robert. *FDR's Funeral Train: A Betrayed Widow, a Soviet Spy and a Presidency in the Balance*. New York: Palgrave, 2010.

Klehr, Harvey. *The Heyday of American Communism: The Depression Decade*. New York: Basic Books, 1984.

———. *The Communist Experience in America: A Political and Social History*. New Jersey: Transaction Publishers, 2010.

Klehr, Harvey, and John E. Haynes. *Venona: Decoding Soviet Espionage in America*. New Haven, CT: Yale University Press, 1999.

Kornbluh, Joyce L. *Rebel Voices: An IWW Anthology*. Ann Arbor, MI: University of Michigan Press 1964.

Kostopoulos, Tasos. "Afaireseis ithageneias: Ē skoteinē pleura tēs neoellēnikēs istorias (1926–2003)" [Stripping citizenship: the dark side of modern Greek history (1926–2003)]. *Synchrona Themata* 83 (2003): 53–76.

Kovel, Joel. *Red Hunting in the Promised Land: Anticommunism and the Making of America*. New York: Basic Books, 1994.

Kraditor, Aileen. *The Radical Persuasion, 1890–1917: Aspects of the Intellectual History and the Historiography of Three American Radical Organizations*. Baton Rouge, LA: Louisiana State University Press, 1981.

Laliotou, Ioanna. *Transatlantic Subjects: Acts of Migration and Cultures of Transnationalism between Greece and America*. Chicago: University of Chicago Press, 2004.

Leber, George. *The History of the Order of AHEPA, 1922–1972*. Washington, DC: The Order of AHEPA, 1972.

Lees, Lorraine. "National Security and Ethnicity: Contrasting Views During World War II." *Diplomatic History* 11, no. 2 (1987): 113–25.

———. *Yugoslav-Americans and National Security during World War II*. Urbana-Champaign, IL: University of Illinois Press, 2007.

Lenin, Vladimir. "Capitalism and Workers' Immigration (October 29, 1913)." In *Lenin Collected Works*, Vol. 19, 454–57. Moscow: Progress Publishers, 1963.

Leuchtenburg, William. *Franklin D. Roosevelt and the New Deal, 1932–1940*. New York: Harper Torchbooks, 1963.

Levinson, Edward. *Labor on the March*. New York: ILR Press, 1995.

Lipset, Seymour Martin, and Gary Marks. *It Didn't Happen Here. Why Socialism Failed in the United States*. New York: W.W. Norton & Company, 2000.

Lipsitz, George. *Rainbow at Midnight: Labor and Culture in the 40s*. Chicago: University of Illinois Press, 1994.

———. *American Studies in a Moment of Danger*. Minneapolis: University of Minnesota Press, 2001.

Logoi ekfonēthentes ypo tēs AM tou Vasileōs Paulou kata tēn episēmon episkepsin eis Ēnom. Politeias tēs Amerikēs, 28 Oct.–3 Dec. 1953 [Speeches by HM King Paul during his official visit to the United States, 28 October–3 December 1953]. Athens: Genikē Dieythinsis Typou, 1954.

Longa, Ernesto. *Anarchist Periodicals in English Published in the United States (1833–1955). An Annotated Guide*. Lanham: Scarecrow Press, 2010.

Luhan, Mabel Dodge. *Movers and Shakers: Volume Three of Intimate Memories*. New York: Harcourt, Brace and Company, 1936.

Magil, A. B., and Joseph North, *Steve Katovis: Life and Death of a Worker*. New York: International Pamphlets, 1930.

Malafouris, Mpampis. *Ellēnes tēs Amerikēs, 1528–1948* [The Greeks of America, 1528–1948]. New York: n.p., 1948.

McAuliffe, Mary Sperling. *Crisis on the Left: Cold War Politics and American Liberals, 1947–1954*. Amherst, MA: University of Massachusetts Press, 1978.

McCarthy, Joseph. *McCarthyism, the Fight for America: Documented Answers to Questions Asked by Friend and Foe*. New York: Devin-Adair, 1952.

McElvaine, Robert. *The Great Depression: America, 1929–1941*. New York: Times Books, 1993.

McGill, Nettie Pauline, and Ellen Nathalie Matthews. *The Youth of New York City*. New York: Macmillan, 1940.

McNeill, William Hardy. *The Greek Dilemma: War and Aftermath*. London: V. Gollancz, 1947.

Meyer, Gerald. "Italian Americans and the American Communist Party." In *The Lost World of Italian American Radicalism*, edited by Philip Cannistraro and Gerald Meyer, 205–28. Westport: Praeger Publishers, 2003.

Michels, Tony. *A Fire in Their Hearts: Yiddish Socialists in New York*. Cambridge, MA: Harvard University Press, 2009.

Miller, Sally, ed. *Race, Ethnicity, and Gender in Early Twentieth-Century American Socialism*. New York City: Garland Press, 1996.

Morawska, Ewa. *For Bread with Butter: The Life-Worlds of East Central Europeans in Johnstown, Pennsylvania, 1890–1940*. Cambridge: Cambridge University Press, 1985.

Morgan, Ted. *Reds: McCarthyism in Twentieth-Century America*. New York: Random House, 2003.

Murphy, Paul, and James Morton Smith, eds. *Liberty and Justice: A Historical Record of American Constitutional Development*. New York: Alfred A. Knopf, 1958.

Myer, Stephen. *The Five Dollar Day: Labor Management and Social Control in the Ford Motor Company, 1908–1921*. Albany, NY: State University of New York Press, 1981.

National Labor Relations Board. "In the Matter of Republic Steel Corporation and Steel Workers Organizing Committee. Case No. C-184. Decided October 18, 1938." *National Labor Relations Board's Decisions and Orders*. Volume 29, 1939.

National Labor Relations Board. "In the matter of Republic Steel Corporation and Steel Workers Organizing Committee, Local Unions No. 1033 and No. 1303 (Formerly Amalgamated Association of Iron, Steel & Tin Workers of North America, Lodges No. 1033 and No. 1303, through Steel Workers Organizing Committee), affiliated with the Congress of Industrial Organizations. Case No. C-1883. Decided August 12, 1941." *National Labor Relations Board's Decisions and Orders*. Volume 32, 1942.

National Labor Relations Board, "In the Matter of Weirton Steel Company and Steel Workers Organizing Committee. Cases Nos. C-1184 and R-1229. Decided June 25, 1941." *National Labor Relations Board's Decisions and Orders*. Volume 32, 1942.

Nelson, Steve, James Barrett, and Rob Ruck. *Steve Nelson: American Radical*. Pittsburgh, PA: University of Pittsburgh Press, 1981.

Ngai, Mae. *Impossible Subjects: Illegal Aliens and the Making of Modern America*. Princeton, NJ: Princeton University Press, 2004.

Olney, Martha. "Avoiding Default: The Role of Credit in the Consumption Collapse of 1930." *The Quarterly Journal of Economics* 114, no. 1 (1999): 319–35.

Ottanelli, Fraser. "If Fascism Comes to America, We Will Push It Back into the Ocean." In *Italian Workers of the World: Labor Migration and the Formation of Multiethnic States*, edited by Donna R. Gabaccia and Fraser M. Ottanelli, 178–95. Urbana-Champaign, IL: University of Illinois Press, 2001.

Papadopoulos, Giannis. *Ē metanasteusē apo tin Othōmanikē Autokratoria stēn Amerikē (19os aionas-1923): Oi ellēnikes koinotētes tēs Amerikēs kai ē alytrōtiki politikē tou ellēnikou kratous* [Immigration from the Ottoman Empire to America (19th century–1923): the Greek communities in America and the irridentist politics of the Greek state]. Ph.D. dissertation. Athens: Panteio University, 2008.

Papaioannou, George. *The Odyssey of Hellenism in America*. Thessaloniki: Patriarchal Institute for Patristic Studies, 1985.

Papanikolas, Helen. "The Great Bingham Strike of 1912." *Utah Historical Quarterly* 38 (1968): 121–33.

Papanikolas, Zeese. *Buried Unsung: Louis Tikas and the Ludlow Massacre*. Salt Lake City, UT: University of Utah Press, 1982.

Papoulias, Aggelos. *Anamnēseis apo ti zōe tou ellēnismou tēs Kalifornias* [Recollections of Greek life in California]. San Francisco: n.p., 1960.

Patrikiou, Alexandra. *Apeikoniseis tēs Gēraias Ēpeirou: o "dialogos" gia tēn Eurōpē stēn Ellada, 1941–1946* [Reflections of the old continent: the "dialogue" on Europe in Greece, 1941–1946]. Ph.D. Dissertation. Athens: Panteio University, 2012.

Patterson, James. *Grand Expectations: The United States, 1945–1974*. Oxford: Oxford University Press, 1996.

Peck, Gunther. *Reinventing Free Labor: Padrones and Immigrant Workers in the North American West, 1880–1930*. Cambridge: Cambridge University Press, 2000.

Post, Louis Freeland. *The Deportation Delirium of Nineteen-Twenty: A Personal Narrative of an Historic Official Experience*. Chicago: C.H. Kerr, 1923.

Rand School of Social Science. *The American Labor Yearbook: 1926*. New York: Rand Book Store, 1927.

———. *The American Labor Yearbook: 1927*. New York: Rand Book Store, 1928.

———. *The American Labor Yearbook: 1931*. New York: Rand School of Social Science, 1932.

Reesman, Jeanne Campbell. *Jack London's Racial Lives: A Critical Biography*. Athens, GA: University Georgia Press, 2009.

Richardson, Aaron. "The Basil John Vlavianos Papers (1890–1994)." *Journal of the Hellenic Diaspora* 35, no. 1 (2009): 91–110.

Rocha, Edward. "The Lowell Shoe Strike in 1933." In *Surviving Hard Times: The Working People of Lowell*, edited by Mary H. Blewett, 115–25. Lowell, MA: Lowell Museum, 1982.

Roediger, David. *Working Toward Whiteness: How America's Immigrants Became White*. New York: Basic Books, 2005.

Rompapas, John. *The Book of My Life*. New York: The Rabelais Press, 1914.

Rose, Jonathan. *The Intellectual Life of the British Working Classes*. New Haven, CT: Yale University Press, 2001.

Rosenman, Samuel. *The Public Papers of Franklin D. Roosevelt: The Year of Crisis, 1933*. New York: Random House, 1938.

Rosswurm, Steve. *The CIO's Left-Led Unions*. New Brunswick, NJ: Rutgers University Press 1992.

Sakmyster, Thomas. *Red Conspirator: J. Peters and the American Communist Underground*. Urbana-Champaign, IL: University of Illinois Press, 2011.

Saloutos, Theodore. *The Greeks in the United States*. Cambridge, MA: Harvard University Press, 1964.

Sanger, Margaret. *What Every Mother Should Know; or, How Six Little Children Were Taught the Truth*. New York: The Rabelais Press, 1914.

Schlesinger, Arthur M., Jr. *The Vital Center. Our Purposes and Perils on the Tightrope of American Liberalism*. Boston: Houghton Mifflin, 1949.

———. *The Crisis of the Old Order, 1919–1933*. Boston: Houghton Mifflin, 2002.

———. *The Coming of the New Deal, 1933–1935*. Boston: Houghton Mifflin, 2003.

Schneider, David. *The Workers (Communist) Party and American Trade Unions*. Baltimore, MD: John Hopkins Press, 1928.

Schrecker, Hellen. *Many Are the Crimes: McCarthyism in America*. Princeton, NJ: Princeton University Press, 1998.

Shannon, David. *The Socialist Party of America: AHistory*. Chicago: Quadrangle Paperbacks, 1967.

Shiffman, Dan. *Rooting Multiculturalism: The Work of Louis Adamic*. Madison, NJ: Farleigh Dickinson Press, 2003.

Smith, Louise Pettibone. *Torch of Liberty: Twenty-Five Years in the Life of the Foreign Born in the USA*. New York: Dwight-King Publishers, 1959.

Sombart, Werner. *Why Is There No Socialism in the United States?* New York: Routledge, 2019.

Song, Jingyi. *Shaping and Reshaping Chinese American Identity: New York's Chinese during the Depression and World War II*. Lanham, MD: Lexington Books, 2010.

Stalin, Joseph. "The Foundations of Leninism." In *Stalin: Works*, Vol. 6, 71–196. Moscow: Foreign Languages Publishing House, 1953.

Starobin, Joseph. *American Communism in Crisis, 1943–1957*. Berkeley, CA: University of California Press, 1975.

Stein, Rose. "The National Relations Board in the USA." *The Economic Journal* 48, no. 192 (1938): 685–94.

Stinas, Agis. *Anamnēseis: Evdomēnta chronia katō apo tē sēmaia tēs sosialistikēs epanastasēs* [Memoir: seventy years under the banner of the socialist revolution]. Athens: Ypsilon, 1985.

Storch, Randi. *Red Chicago: American Communism at its Grassroots*. Chicago: University of Illinois Press, 2007.

Tessara chronia diakyvernēseōs I. Metaxa [Four years of government under I. Metaxas]. Vol. 4. Athens: Yfypourgeion Typou kai Tourismou, 1940.

Thompson, E. P. *The Making of the English Working Class*. New York: Vintage Books, 1966.

To ergon tēs kyvernēseōs Venizelou kata tēn tetraetian 1928–1932 [The work of the Venizelos government, 1928–1932]. Athens: Pyrsos, 1932.

Truman, Harry. *1945: Year of Decisions*. London: Hodder and Stoughton, 1955.

Tzouliadis, Tim. *The Forsaken: An American Tragedy in Stalin's Russia*. New York: Penguin, 2008.

United States Congress, House Committee on Rules. *The Strike at Lawrence, Mass. Hearings Before the Committee on Rules of the House of Representatives on House Resolutions 409 and 433*, March 2–7, 1912. Washington, DC: Government Printing Office, 1912.

United States Congress. *Investigation of Un-American Propaganda Activities in the United States: Hearings Before the Committee on Un-American Activities, House of Representatives, Eightieth Congress, First Session on H.R. 1884 and H.R 2122 Bills to Curb or Outlaw the Communist Party in the United States, March 24, 25, 26, 27, 28, 1947*. Washington, DC: United States Government Printing Office, 1947.

United States Congress. *Testimony of Walter S. Steele Regarding Communist Activities in the United States: Hearings Before the Committee on Un-American Activities, House of Representatives, Eightieth Congress, First Session on HR 1884 and HR 2122 Bills to Curb or Outlaw the Communist Party in the United States, July 21, 1947*. Washington, DC: United States Government Printing Office, 1947

United States Congress. *Investigation of Communist Infiltration into the Fur Industry: Hearings Before a Special Subcommittee of the Committee on Education and Labor, House of Representatives, Eightieth Congress, Second Session Pursuant to H. Res 111, Hearings Held at Washington D.C. September 8, 9, 10, 13, 14, 15 and 16, 1948*. Washington, DC: United States Government Printing Office, 1948.

United States Congress. *Communist Activities Among Aliens and National Groups: Hearings Before the Subcommittee on Immigration and Naturalization of the Committee on the Judiciary, United States Senate, Eighty-First Congress, First Session on S. 1832, a Bill to Amend the Immigration Act of October 16, 1918, as Amended, Part 3, Appendixes I to VIII*. Washington, DC: United States Government Printing Office, 1950.

United States Congress, Committee on Un-American Activities. *Guide to Subversive Organizations and Publications (and Appendix), revised, 14.5.1951*. Washington, DC: Committee on Un-American Activities, US House of Representatives, 1951.

United States Department of Commerce. *Historical Statistics of the US, 1789–1945. A Supplement to the Statistical Abstracts of the United States*. Washington, DC: Department of Commerce, 1949.

United States Department of Commerce. *Statistical Abstract of the United States 1951*. Washington, DC: Bureau of the Census, 1951.

United States President, *Address of the President of the United States Delivered Before a Joint Session of the Senate and the House of Representatives Recommending Assistance to Greece and Turkey*, 80th Congress, House of Representatives, Document No. 171.

Valaoras, Vassilios. *O ellēnismos tōn Ēnomenon Politeiōn* [Greeks of the United States]. Athens: n.p., 1937.

Varano, Charles. *Forced Choices: Class, Community, and Worker Ownership*. Albany, NY: State University of New York Press, 1999.

Vardoulakis, Mary. *Gold in the Streets*. New York: Dodd, Mead and Company, 1945.

Vials, Chris. *Haunted by Hitler: Liberals, the Left and the Fight against Fascism in the United States*. Amherst, MA: University of Massachusetts Press, 2014.

Vlanton, Elias. "Documents: The OSS and Greek-Americans." *Journal of Hellenic Diaspora* 9, no. 1 (1982): 31–84.

Vlanton, Elias. "Documents: The OSS and Greek-Americans." *Journal of Hellenic Diaspora* 9, no. 2 (1982): 36–104.

Wecter, Dixon. *The Age of the Great Depression*. New York: Macmillan, 1948.

Weitz, Eric. *Creating German Communism, 1890–1990: From Popular Protests to Socialist State*. Princeton, NJ: Princeton University Press 1997.

Wittner, Lawrence. *American Intervention in Greece, 1943–1949*. New York: Columbia University Press, 1982.

Workers (Communist) Party of America. *The Fourth National Convention of the Workers (Communist) Party of America: Report of the Central Executive Committee to the 4th National Convention held in Chicago, Illinois, August 21st to 30th, 1925*. Chicago: Daily Worker Publishing Company, 1925.

Zake, Ieva, ed. *Anti-Communist Minorities in the US: Political Activism of Ethnic Refugees*. London: Palgrave MacMillan, 2009.

Zangwill, Israel. *The Melting Pot*. New York: Macmillan, 1909.

Zervakis, Peter. "The Greek Lobby and the Reemergence of Anti-Communism in the United States After World War II." In *Enemy Images in American History*, edited by Ragnhild Fiebig-von Hase and Ursula Lehmkuhl, 301–38. Providence, RI: Berghahn Books, 1997.

Zieger, Robert. *The CIO, 1935–1955*. Chapel Hill, NC: University of North Carolina Press, 1995.

Zumoff, Jacob. "The African Blood Brotherhood: From Caribbean Nationalism to Communism." *The Journal of Caribbean History* 41, nos. 1–2 (2007): 200–26.

———. *The Communist International and US Communism, 1919-1929*. Chicago: Haymarket Books, 2015.

INDEX